JULIA MARLOWE BOYES
MEMORIAL
DRAMA COLLECTION
MAYFIELD

THE THEATRE
AND DRAMATIC THEORY

The Development of the Theatre
World Drama
British Drama
A History of English Drama, 1660–1900
(Cambridge University Press)
The Elizabethans
(Cambridge University Press)

The Theatre
and
Dramatic Theory

by

ALLARDYCE NICOLL

GREENWOOD PRESS, PUBLISHERS
WESTPORT, CONNECTICUT

Library of Congress Cataloging in Publication Data

Nicoll, Allardyce, 1894–
    The theatre and dramatic theory.

    Reprint of the ed. published by G. G. Harrap,
London.
    Includes bibliographical references and index.
    1. Drama.   2. Theater.   I. Title.
[PN1631.N42 1978]   792'.09   78-5609
ISBN 0-313-20433-0

Originally published in 1962 by George G. Harrap & Co. Ltd.

Copyright Allardyce Nicoll 1962

Reprinted with the permission of George G. Harrap and Company Limited

Reprinted in 1978 by Greenwood Press
A division of Congressional Information Service, Inc.
88 Post Road West, Westport, Connecticut 06881

Printed in the United States of America

10 9 8 7 6 5 4 3 2

Preface

To a certain extent this book may be thought of as originating from a basic question. Since the time of the eighteenth-century sentimentalists, the drama has proceeded in a series of successively new waves, all of them impelled by a current which moved counter to that which gave force to the drama of earlier years. Naturally we take pride in the achievements inspired by this fresh and 'modern' approach to the stage, yet at the same time we are troubled by the thought that, despite the vast increase in population, the play-going public has markedly declined. The question which arises is simply this: is the theoretical approach which ultimately stems from the sentimental movement of two centuries ago and which still remains dominant really giving to the general public what subconsciously it seeks for in the theatre? Perhaps, too, the question might be put in another way: is the theatre, because of its essential nature, capable of dealing satisfactorily with such material as, for example, so effectively can be provided for individual readers in the novel?

In the search for an answer to this question (or questions), it has been necessary to start with a tentative examination of a much-neglected and difficult subject—the characteristics, the potential virtues, and the limitations of the average audience, so that this study might almost have been called "The Theatre Audience and the Drama." It has also been necessary to proceed from examination of the audience to a discussion, first, of some general trends in earlier dramatic theory and, secondly, of the prevailing forms assumed by the drama in preceding epochs. Obviously it would be foolish to suggest that imitation of these by-gone forms could prove fruitful in the present, but there does seem to be an imperative need in these our days to pause for a moment to consider basic principles. Thus, although no attempt has been made here to survey dramatic theory in general or to deal with more than a selected few aspects of earlier dramatic writing, this study has had perforce to direct itself outwards from the specific question, fundamentally concerned with the present-day stage, to the broader theme indicated by its title, *The Theatre and Dramatic Theory*. I can only hope that the particular may give focus to a consideration of the general, and that the general may provide a practically useful background for a consideration of the particular.

I wish to thank the following for permission to quote from plays and critical works: Messrs Bowes and Bowes, Ltd, for extracts from Erich Heller's *The Disinherited Mind*; Messrs Brandt and Brandt for an extract from Maxwell Anderson's *Wingless Victory* (Copyright 1936 by Maxwell Anderson. Reprinted by arrangement with Anderson House, Hinsdale, N.Y. and Harold Freedman, Brandt and Brandt Dramatic Department, Inc., New York, N.Y.); Columbia University Press for extracts from F. Sarcey's *A Theory of the Theatre*; the Syndics of the Cambridge University Press for extracts from J. L. Styan's *The Elements of Drama*; Messrs Faber and Faber, Ltd, for extracts from T. S. Eliot's *Selected Essays, Murder in the Cathedral, The Cocktail Party*, and *The Confidential Clerk*; Messrs Harcourt, Brace and World, Inc., for extracts from Eric Bentley's *The Playwright as Thinker*, J. E. Spingarn's *Creative Criticism*, and D. Fitts' and R. Fitzgerald's translation *The Antigone of Sophocles*; Harvard University Press for an extract from N. Holland's *The First Modern Comedies*; Messrs William Heinemann, Ltd, for an extract from J. B. Priestley's *Literature and the Modern Man*; Mr W. Somerset Maugham, Messrs William Heinemann, Ltd, and Doubleday and Company, Inc., for extracts from W. Somerset Maugham's *The Summing Up*; Oxford University Press for extracts from Christopher Fry's *The Lady's Not for Burning*, and *Curtmantle*; Mr Henry Ten Eyck Perry for extracts from his *The Comic Spirit in Restoration Drama*; Messrs Max Reinhardt, Ltd, for extracts from Walter Kerr's *How not to write a Play*; Mrs W. B. Yeats, Messrs Macmillan and Co., Ltd (London) and The Macmillan Company (New York), for extracts from W. B. Yeats' *Plays and Controversies, Essays*, and *Plays in Prose and Verse* (copyright 1923, 1924, and 1922); Messrs George Braziller, Inc., for an extract from J. W. Krutch's *The American Drama since 1918*; and Alfred A. Knopf, Inc., for an extract from Harold Clurman's *The Fervent Years*.

A.N.

Contents

I

The Theatre

In 1883 Henry Irving wrote a short preface for an English translation of Talma's essay on the actor's art. "Few things," he declared,

> can be said about the stage at any time which will not excite controversy; but I think one of the few is that the influence of the drama to-day is wider than it ever was. There is a vast increase of playgoers; the intellectual interest in the stage is steadily growing; and there is a general conviction that the actor is placed in a position of trust which he cannot worthily fill without a strong sense of responsibility.[1]

Three-quarters of a century has passed by since the penning of these words, and for a modern contrast we may turn to the Arts Council's report for the year 1958–59.[2] Rather ominously, this is entitled *The Struggle for Survival.* "In the West End of London," it states, "one of the playgrounds of the world, the theatre continues to attract substantial audiences," but "takings have fallen in most of the provincial theatres, and on the average they are now not more than half full." Most serious of all, "the people who are staying away from them in increasing number are the 'steadies': the ones who could formerly be counted upon to visit every new production. The hard core of support is diminishing." And consequently the question is asked:

> Must all this mean that, outside London, we are bound to accept the dissolution of the professional theatre within the next few years?

The contrast between these two pronouncements of 1883 and 1959 requires no stressing. Nor can we gloss over the sombre note in the latter. Many other similar comments have been made during recent years, and the comments have not been confined to a single country. The old American stock companies, which once brought the theatre close to communities east and west, north and south, have vanished, and Broadway, like London's West End, now stands without the support of the far-flung theatrical empire amid which it once had its being. In many European countries a similar story is being told. Italy, for example, the land of Goldoni and Pirandello, seems fast to be losing its interest in the stage; playhouses which once were open through most of the year are being abandoned; the flocking spectators of the past have vanished. Thousands of people who, had they lived before our time, would have been regular attenders at the playhouses, "are staying away from them in increasing numbers." "The hard core of support is diminishing."

This means that at no moment in the theatre's history for the past four centuries has there ever been so imperative a need for an assessment both of what the stage has characteristically to offer and of its relationship to the public. Particularly important is it to inquire whether the decline in attendance has been due to the presence of other attractions unknown in the past or whether the fault lies within. In order to answer such a question two things are essential: a search for fundamentals and the avoidance of a merely enthusiastic, emotional approach.

By nature the theatre shows itself prone to sentimentalisms. Unquestionably it can exert a peculiar fascination of its own, and many of those who eagerly apply themselves to its fortunes remain bound within that fascination's appeal. We still use the term 'stage-struck' for a young man or girl who seeks to go on the boards, almost as though magic were in the air, and, while we never would consider referring to avid readers of prose-fiction as 'novel-lovers,' 'theatre-lovers' is a phrase in common parlance. Thus those active in the playhouse only too often are subject to one or another hastily conceived sentimental approach. Eager experiments are tried out, but because of the sentimentality there is vagueness and confusion of mind, so that many among the experiments, instead of aiding the stage, result in still greater estrangement between it and the public.

What seems to be demanded now is an attempt to escape from immersion in facile and often irrational emotionalisms and to apply ourselves as critically and exactly as we may to a consideration of the basic qualities which have given the theatre its true strength. This will involve our taking into account some at least of the more significant critical pronouncements of the past and we shall probably find it useful, as a kind of 'control,' to bear in mind the conditions operative in some period, let us say the Elizabethan, when the theatre was at its most flourishing. Any endeavour to impose on one age the forms of another must, of course, end in disaster, but the consideration of past forms may provide us with much material of service and may lead us towards the winnowing of inessentials from basic principles.

The Theatre's Range

At the very start a confusion has to be noted in our familiar use of the terms 'theatre' (or 'stage') and 'drama' (or 'play'). Again and again we hear these employed as though they were identical. For an example we need go no farther than the passage already cited from Sir Henry Irving's preface: "Few things," he remarks, "can be said about *the stage* at any time which will not excite controversy; but I think one of the few is that the influence of *the drama* to-day is wider than it ever was." Now, anyone who knows anything at all about the drama in 1883 will realize that Irving was not, in fact, thinking of drama at all; what he had in mind was the then flourishing condition of the theatres and the new, distinguished position which the actor had won in society. When we find a great performer thus employing the two words in a single sentence without making any distinction between them, and when we are forced to admit that this is precisely what we all do, we need not doubt that it is high time to stop at the very beginning and consider exactly what we mean.

The best plan will be to start with a couple of working definitions. Leaving aside its significance as applied to a building, we may say that the word 'theatre' implies 'a performance given by one group of persons (who may be called "the actors") before an assembled audience.' If, for the moment, this be accepted as a working definition, what is the significance of the words 'drama' and 'play'? Basically these may be taken as synonyms conveying the idea of 'a literary work written, by an author or by several authors in collaboration, in a form suitable for stage presentation.'

Just as soon as these working definitions have been formulated, two things become apparent; (1) 'theatre' and 'drama' are by no means the same, and (2) even if they stand in close relationship to each other, they have each their own boundaries. The 'theatre' extends considerably beyond the frontiers of the 'drama,' while the 'drama' similarly extends as far on the other side beyond the frontiers of the 'theatre.' Any refusal to admit this, or any careless use of the two words in an identical sense, can result only in confusion.

Let us take the theatre first. We are bound to agree that a very considerable area of theatrical endeavour has absolutely nothing to do with dramatic literature. The entire field of opera has no concern with drama. Although we have here a narrative plot expressed in words, although at its inception in Renaissance Italy the *melodramma* was designed to reproduce the main features of ancient Greek tragedy, and although in the eighteenth century Metastasio gave a rich lyrical quality to the form, it is obvious that in opera music assumes predominant importance and that the words, even when they are heard, receive little attention. Wagner dreamed of opera as a vast art-work, wherein poetry and music might combine with related spectacle to create one tremendous whole, but the facts remain that Wagner's fame rests on his musical compositions and that when we refer to any opera it is of the composer we think; in all probability we do not know even the librettist's name. We find it impossible to conceive of the successful performance of a play in which a single actor speaks one language and his companions another; yet, despite Addison's satirical comments in *The Spectator*, such practice in opera has been frequent, and freely accepted. No one even now seriously objects to an operatic production where the star sings in Russian and the cast answer him in English, French, or Italian; the music subsumes all verbal difference.

Opera brings ballet to mind, and here words disappear entirely, even if narrative of a kind usually provides a framework for the dancers' movements. An author hovers uneasily behind the wings of opera, but in a ballet production he has absolutely no place at all. With the ballet, too, may be associated the wordless mime, not so common a form, yet at times of some significance. The ancient Roman pantomimes were of this sort, and not so many decades ago every one was talking about *The Miracle*, a work which, however effective theatrically, lay well outside of the range of drama.

Nor can we bring within the range of our working definition of 'drama' the *commedia dell' arte*, so popular a theatrical display for well over two centuries, wherein the actors created their lines within the course of performance on the basis of a scenario, or plot. Spoken dialogue occurs here, but a moment's thought will convince us that the difference between the display of actors who have memorized an author's lines and that of comedians inventing dialogue on the spur of the moment must produce two entirely different impressions, and that, as a result, these two performances must be regarded as wholly distinct in kind.

The theatre, then, embraces far more than the production of plays.

Opera, ballet, *commedia dell' arte*, mime—all these, and more, extend its territory and carry us far away from the boundaries of drama, especially during modern times. For the Elizabethans the only kind of theatre known was that in which groups of actors interpreted the texts provided for them by their poets. Dramatists and actors, accordingly, were the only persons concerned with the performances, and these performances were specifically limited to interpretations of plays. In effect there was thus little prime distinction between 'theatrical' and 'dramatic' objectives; the poets wrote for the stage, and the stage depended upon the comedies and the tragedies provided for them.

During recent years, however, a new concept has entered in. Because the Elizabethan playhouse had more or less established companies of actors familiar with each other's skill, because this playhouse had no scenery or lighting, and because the age possessed a characteristic style of its own, the theatre needed no producer or director. During the period of the Renaissance we have only two glimpses of a functionary of this kind; both occur in Italy and the appearance of both can easily be explained. The first is associated with performances at ducal courts, performances given not by professionals but by amateurs, in playhouses wherein the pictorial artists of the time amused themselves with scenic experiments. Some one obviously had to take control, and hence we need feel no surprise at finding a Leone di Somi at Mantua actively engaged in what we now call 'production' and even writing a treatise on the subject.[3] The second glimpse we get of a director comes from the *commedia dell' arte*. The actors here were professional, but, since all they had was a brief scenario, a *concertatore*, or *guida*, usually the most experienced performer in the troupe, had to conduct rehearsals and give advice on the conduct of the various scenes. Neither of these two kinds of Italian theatrical activity, however, approximates the professional Elizabethan in scope or style; consequently, in Shakespeare's playhouse there was no demand for any single person to take command of the stage.

Nor was there any demand so long as the stock company tradition persisted and so long as the stage remained relatively simple in its appointments. We hear of the actor Thomas Betterton, in his old age, being paid for taking rehearsals, but there is no sign of anything approaching the office of producer until a completely new set of theatrical conditions came into being about the middle of the nineteenth century. At that time the stock companies disintegrated and groups of actors were engaged for particular performances; scenic effects became more elaborate; the introduction of gas and electric lighting brought something fresh to the stage; and, beyond all of this, there no longer existed that definite sense of a characteristic style which had been present in Elizabethan days. The result was that harmony could be secured only by making one man responsible for co-ordinating all the diverse elements within this complex framework.

As we know, the passage of years tended to give the director more and more authority, and at times his function began to change. Ideally, he has the responsibility of interpreting the play chosen for performance and of controlling the work of all those concerned with the production, but in practice, as Eric Bentley has well emphasized,[4] his ever extending activities have led to exaltation of what has come to be called the 'theatre arts.' In an extreme form this trend may be found expressed in the concepts of Gordon Craig, who reaches the conclusion that it would be well to dismiss both drama and actors from the stage. "I believe in the time," he says, "when we shall be able to create works of art in the Theatre without the use of the written play, without the use of actors." "We have to banish from our mind all thought of the use of a human form as the instrument which we are to use to translate what we call *Movement*":[5]

> The actor must go, and in his place comes the inanimate figure—the Über-marionette we may call him, until he has won for himself a better name.[6]

To Craig's desire to banish the drama from his ideal performances we can have no valid objection, since, as has been seen, the theatre's range embraces far more than the presentation of plays. But when he proposes the banishing of living performers we are bound to pause. If this were done the theatre would no longer be theatre; it would become something wholly different in kind. Maybe Craig's concept, if carried out, could produce things memorable, but for these things another name than 'theatre' would have to be found. Thus an ironical paradox emerges: in its extreme forms the cult of 'theatre arts' leads us outside of the playhouse.

Not many, of course, are likely to pursue the extreme forms to their logical conclusion in the way Craig has done, and consequently the sort of performance he envisages need not be more fully discussed. More important are the consequences of these aims when applied to the production of plays. Quite clearly, one dominating motive which led Craig to dream of his actorless theatre was the thought that actors, being human, could not be trusted to perform with the absolute precision of a mechanically contrived object; and numerous stage directors, also intent on these 'theatre arts,' have shown an inclination to devote inordinate care to the material side of the stage, precisely because these material things can be brought entirely under their control. The result of this has been the development of 'theatricality,' in the less admirable sense of that term, and a lack of balance in the presentation of plays. Of this trend Eric Bentley chooses Max Reinhardt as a symbol, and his remarks well outline the dangers involved:

> It was not the greatness of a style that Reinhardt stood for, nor, after a few years, was it zeal for any particular plays or playwrights. It was the greatness of the stage itself. As Mr Vladimir Horowitz seems to love the piano more than music, so Reinhardt seemed to love the stage more than drama. Not that there is anything unique in this. It is true of most directors.... Reinhardt was a great man. But his theatricalism made him more and more a great showman and less and less a great servant of the drama.[7]

The wider implications of this development of 'theatrical' as opposed to 'dramatic' objectives must be put aside for later discussion, since our immediate concern here is with the theatre in general and not solely with that particular form of stage activity which consists in the performance of plays; but it is essential, before we proceed further, to recognize several things—that 'theatre' and 'drama' are separate entities, that in our own times peculiar confusion is arising because of the exaltation of 'theatre arts,' and that, if we are to seek for fundamentals, it may be necessary to go back beyond the confusion of the modern stage to periods, such as the Elizabethan, when conditions were simpler.

The Audience in the Theatre

Gordon Craig has suggested that we should abandon both play and players, but neither he nor anyone else has proposed that the audience be done away with. Our working definition of the basic concept of 'theatre' was 'a performance given by one group of persons (the actors) before an assembled "audience," a group of spectators'—and it is the presence of these spectators which provides the first prime characteristic of theatrical endeavour. Nearly all other arts—poetry, painting, sculpture—make their appeal to individuals; indeed, the only art which approaches the theatre in this respect is music, and even music does not provide an exact parallel—a symphony orchestra may perform before a group of auditors, but the appreciation of many kinds of music asks for no mass perception. We can take delight in listening, without any companions, to a violinist's interpretation of some master's composition, but we cannot enjoy a theatrical performance in loneliness. A certain bygone king of Bavaria is said to have commanded his players to act before him as he sat alone in an empty auditorium; but this king was mad, and the command was part of his lunacy.

At first glance it may appear strange, in approaching the theatre, to select for primal consideration the recipients rather than the creators. After all, we would not expect a study of poetry to begin with the readers. The comparison with poetry, however, serves to emphasize an essential difference, occasioned by the presence of the audience, between the theatre and the other arts. In penning his verses a poet cannot have any clear image in his mind of the persons who will peruse them; he no doubt hopes his lines will be read, but precisely by whom he can have no way of conjecturing. Those concerned with any theatrical production, on the other hand, have had previous experience of audiences, and, since these audiences, although made up of many individuals, form palpable units, they can be felt as one, leaving on the consciousness a clear mental image. Furthermore, the performers must have this audience immediately before them. There have been numerous poets, writing in styles beyond those of their own ages, who have been content to dream of readers yet to be born—

> Singing hymns unbidden
> Till the world is wrought
> To sympathy with hopes and fears it heeded not.

In contradistinction, those concerned with the theatre are bound primarily by the immediate present; they could not find strength for their efforts without concentrating on the audiences of the time in which they live. There exists, therefore, an urgent immediacy in the playhouse lacking in all the other arts—and that immediacy derives ultimately from the presence of the assembled spectators.

Strangely, in view of this consideration, amid the multitudes of critical and historical writings on the stage, comparatively little attention has been devoted to this subject, and the meagre comment accorded to it has been concerned rather with the drama than with the theatre itself. Aristotle, it is true, introduced some remarks on the spectators when he was dealing with tragedy in his *Poetics*; occasionally in later criticism incidental comments were made on the subject; and from time to time practising dramatists, such as Lope de Vega, Molière, and Farquhar, emphasized that their works had been designed for "Pit, Box, and Galleries." Yet in essence none of these observations contributed anything save general platitudes; they merely offered confirmation of the obvious—that plays are presented before a public, and that, as Johnson put it,

The drama's laws the drama's patrons give.

We have had to wait until the middle of the twentieth century for an adequate assessment of the kinds of people, their numbers, and interests, who supported Shakespeare's Globe,[8] or who saw the first productions of Racine and Molière at the original Comédie Française.[9] We have still to wait for a complete historical survey, and, even although the significance of the audience is now coming to be recognized, we have also still to wait for a truly adequate psychological assessment of its fundamental qualities. Certainly, Francisque Sarcey, nearly a century ago in his *Essai d'une esthétique de théâtre* (1876), had stated emphatically that consideration of the audience "should form the first chapter of a treatise on the art of the theatre." Unfortunately, however, after this promising start he proceeded to confuse the issue by referring constantly to 'play' where he had in mind 'theatrical performance,' while he drew from his observation conclusions so trivial and superficial as to obscure the true significance of his basic concept. When Francis Fergusson declares:

> The great Sarcey said that the art of drama can only be understood as that of holding an audience in a theatre; beyond that it is merely a subjective matter of taste—[10]

he is at one and the same time offering a perfectly just summary of Sarcey's thesis and ignoring its potentialities. And the potentialities have in general been ignored, save for a very few attempts made during the last few years, notably by G. F. Reynolds[11] and by the dramatists W. Somerset Maugham and J. B. Priestley, to sketch a picture of audience tastes.

The composition of audiences, of course, obviously varies from age to age, yet perhaps there is justification for assuming that their

B

basic approach to theatrical performances remains relatively constant. It is true that an experienced modern author, W. A. Darlington, comes to the conclusion that the divergences between spectator-groups in successive periods are of prime significance. "As a dramatist," he says,

> who has had the experience of seeing his own play night after night before different audiences, I have been able to find out for myself what I had only half understood from hearsay, how much the tempo of actors' performances, and therefore the atmosphere of a whole play, can vary according as an audience is quick or slow, warm or cold. Gradually I have reached the conviction that what is true of day-to-day variations in the temper of audiences in the same period must be equally true of variations from one period to another, and that those variations are much more important.[12]

Yet, despite these arguments, there seems to be warrant for Somerset Maugham's assertion that

> in essentials audiences never change, but at different periods and in different countries at the same period they rise to different levels of sophistication.[13]

Perhaps, in the end, both are right. Without doubt audiences at different times summon forth plays of markedly different styles; one inspires *Hamlet*, another *The Conquest of Granada*, another *The London Merchant*, another *The Ticket-of-Leave Man*. If, however, we look below the surface, we can discern certain features which link together the spectators of 1600, 1670, 1740, and 1870; and these enduring features are also to be found among the audiences of to-day, in spite of the mighty alteration which separates the modern stage from the stages of the past. It seems, therefore, entirely justifiable, even while recognizing the gulfs that separate audience from audience in time and place, to distinguish certain elements which all share in common.

In seeking for these elements, help may be gained from the attempt to compare and contrast a theatre audience with a crowd. There are likenesses between them, yet the differences which separate the one from the other are of deeper significance than the features which make them akin.

Let us start with the crowd. Two detailed studies in particular have been devoted to its psychology, one by Gustave Le Bon and the other by E. D. Martin.[14] Although on some points these two studies vary from one another in their conclusions, the variations concern relatively unimportant aspects of crowd behaviour; on fundamentals Le Bon and Martin are in agreement, and the results of their investigations may be accepted as determining at least the salient qualities made manifest when an assemblage of men and women takes shape as a crowd or a mob. Such an assemblage may, of course, remain uncrowdlike, but it will do so only when an atmosphere of debate exists in its midst or when it remains almost entirely impassive. In using the words 'crowd' or 'mob' we have in mind an assemblage intent upon one object, swayed thereto either by an orator or by some common sense of purpose welling up from within the group itself. A definition of the term 'crowd,' then, as it is employed here might be 'a gathering of human beings engrossed in a single collective experience' —and the very fact that this definition might be extended to embrace a theatrical audience demonstrates how important it is to seek out and specify the elements which make the one distinct from the other.

Briefly, the main characteristics of the crowd may be summarized as follows:

1. In a crowd the individualities of the persons gathered together almost wholly vanish, submerged in the totality of the group as a whole. The educated and the ignorant, the timorous and the bold, the vulgar and the refined, all tend to be levelled. Thus, in Hitler-led Germany the identities of the members of the mob whom the Führer harangued were of no importance; he addressed himself to the mob as a unit and his diabolical and cynical skill in doing so was the basis of his success.

2. The resultant crowd-spirit is, in general, lower than and different from the sum total of its parts. Martin speaks of the mob as "a device for indulging ourselves in a kind of temporary insanity by all going crazy together."[15] This temporary insanity may at times produce an heroic quality, but more commonly it leads towards the brutal, the criminal, and the primitively absurd.

3. This crowd-spirit definitely is unintellectual. "We think as a crowd only in platitudes, propaganda, visual dogma, and symbol."[16] "The exercise of logic disappears and credulity reigns."[17]

4. At the same time, the passions are stimulated, and mob-orators know well that, while intellectual arguments are

not likely to make any appeal to their listeners, emotional clichés—patriotic, revolutionary, and the like—will stir the mob to frenzy. The more primitive the expression and application of such clichés, the deeper their hold on the crowd spirit; for crowds, although emotional, are only crudely so: they are "notoriously anaesthetic toward the finer values of art, music and poetry."[18]

5. In a mob there exists a special tendency towards confusing the imaginary and the real. "The unreal has almost as much influence on them as the real. They have an evident tendency not to distinguish between the two."[19] Thus the marvellous and the legendary make strong appeal.

6. Finally may be noted the obvious fact that, when a mob has become highly excited, it generally calls for direct or indirect action. On occasion it will sweep hysterically and confusedly towards a lynching, towards destruction of a hated object, or towards wanton havoc; when such immediate action is not possible, it will clamour for action from those who are in control. Every mob-orator knows how to shout out inflammatory questions which summon forth clamorous affirmative cries from his listeners.

Keeping these salient crowd features in mind, we may now turn to the theatre audience. Clearly the two are associated and yet they inhabit absolutely different realms. It is not so much that the audience shares some of the crowd's qualities and adds others of its own as that nearly all these qualities, while present, are so modified that they become something totally distinct.

First, there can be no doubt but that the audience, when it has been caught up by a theatrical performance, becomes a unit; the collective term 'audience' is, therefore, much more appropriate than the plural 'spectators.' The individuals, as in a crowd, tend to have their own personalities subsumed by the spirit of the group of which they form part, and, again as with a crowd, the very size of the group has a definite bearing on the extent to which the individual reacts, not according to his own nature, but according to the atmosphere around him. In a large packed house we may easily be impressed by something which, under other conditions, we might well be disposed to look upon with disfavour.

At the same time a vast chasm yawns between the crowd-spirit and the audience-spirit. At a theatrical performance the spectators normally remain, so to say, at least dimly conscious of themselves, and, perhaps even more important, of the assemblage in which they are incorporated. Thus we are confronted by a strange, paradoxical duality: while we, as individuals, delight in being portions of a large social unit and thus to a certain extent willingly surrender ourselves for the moment to a mass, we rarely permit this abandoning of ourselves to become total. Not only do we retain our own entities, we can also, if we so wish, shift our attention, withdraw ourselves momentarily from our companions, and contemplate the whole audience objectively, even although we know that, a few seconds later, we shall be prepared once more to let our own personalities slide back into the mass. This means that we can do two things simultaneously. We can, on the one hand, be involved in and become largely dependent upon the audience as a whole. At a comedy, only rarely does a single laugh sound in lonely isolation, and often we laugh simply because the general laughter is infectious; correspondingly, that intense expectant stillness which arises at crucial moments in a tragically emotional performance appears to be not simply the rapt attention of single spectators multiplied, but rather the expression of interest within an entire audience regarded as an *ens* in itself. Yet even on such occasions we may still remain aware of the other individuals around us—even of the lady in front whose hat is a hindrance, of the gentleman behind with the irritating cough, or the schoolgirl two seats along who cannot refrain from rustling her box of chocolates. In a real crowd the individuals become immersed in one vast primitive enveloping ocean; being part of an audience is a social experience. Had we been German Nazis, presumably we should never have thought of asking a particular friend to accompany us to a mass demonstration, or, if we did, we should not long have remained conscious of his or her presence; in going to the theatre our most usual procedure is to invite a companion to go with us or to arrange a small playhouse party. In the mob all intimate relationships between individual and individual vanish; in the theatre these intimate relationships are usually preserved within the audience's composite body.

The second thing to be observed is that the audience, like the crowd, displays an intellectual awareness of a definitely lowered kind. All who have tried honestly to analyse audience attitudes are agreed on this. In a theatre, declares Somerset Maugham, the "mental capacity" of the assembled spectators is markedly "less than that of its most intelligent members"; the audience "does not think with its brain, but with its solar plexus."[20] "I have a notion," he continues, "that when the intelligent look for thought in a playhouse, they show less intelligence than one would have expected of them. Thought is a private thing." And J. B. Priestley comes to precisely the same conclusion:

> Anybody in search of pure thought will be well advised not to sit in a building with a thousand other people, a large company of actors, and an orchestra; better find a quiet corner at home and read a few books.... Nobody in his senses goes to the theatre to be told what to think.[21]

With this unintellectual quality goes a strong emotional sensitivity; "an audience is affected by mass suggestion and mass suggestion is excited by emotion."[22] At the same time, there is evidenced a marked distinction between the "immensely suggestible" attitude of a theatre audience and the clamorous movement of the passions in a mob. The mob-spirit is entirely serious and absorbed, but as Somerset Maugham notes, an assemblage in the playhouse "instinctively resents having its emotions stirred" inadequately and "is always ready to escape with a giggle"[23]—and obviously this depends upon its basic duality. A giggle at a Nazi demonstration would be unthinkable. And, besides this, we are aware that we are concerned here not merely with emotional susceptibility, but also with emotional alertness. An audience may not be able to follow logical argument, but emotionally it is acute; and where a mob could appreciate or be moved by nothing save passions crass and blatant, an audience in the theatre can appreciate emotional subtleties.

The third thing to be noted depends upon the same duality of approach. We have seen that the mob constantly confuses the imaginary and the real. In the theatre we certainly want to be caught up in the imaginary world presented by the performers, but our ambivalent attitude permits us simultaneously to be gripped by the make-believe and to stand apart from it. No doubt it may be true that on rare occasions some untutored and naïve spectators have taken the performers' words and actions as real; yet very seldom indeed can anyone bring forward positively authenticated instances of such behaviour, while the fact that the majority of examples cited fall into marked patterns makes one wonder whether, instead of being records of actual occurrences, most of them are not simply fabricated stories.

The tale of the cowboy who took the frontier actor's "A horse, a horse, my kingdom for a horse!" at face value, offering him a steed for sale, thus takes the same form as Langfeld's similar instance cast in equally vague terms:

> A famous actor delighted to recount an incident while he was playing *The Middleman.* He was a poor inventor who had used up his last resources and could not obtain sufficient fuel to keep up the furnace fire in which the pottery was being hardened. Only a few moments more and his fortune would have been made. Moved by the excitement of the scene, a man in the gallery threw down fifty cents, shouting "Here, old man, buy wood with it."[24]

Chu Kwiang-Tsien refers, with corresponding vagueness, to an unspecified "Chinese actor" who took the part of a disloyal minister:

> He played so well that the scenes unfolded themselves in a life-like vividness. Just at the moment when he was planning to betray the emperor, a simple wood-cutter among the audience became indignant, took his axe, mounted the stage and killed the villain at one stroke![25]

This has every appearance of being an oriental variant of the tale told by Gustave Le Bon concerning the also unnamed "manager of a popular Theatre," who was compelled to provide a bodyguard for the actor who habitually assumed the villain's rôles, lest irate members of the audience might do him harm as he left the playhouse.[26]

There seems to be some justification for supposing that very occasionally a spectator may be so carried away as to call out a warning to hero or heroine regarding a danger of which they show themselves unaware; but, even if one or two genuine examples of such behaviour are to be found, the fact remains that, in general, the imaginary and the real are held distinct in the theatre. Occasionally we encounter some enthusiasts, usually young, who endeavour to deny this, asserting that when they attend a performance they are completely 'carried away,' or 'caught up,' or 'involved.' Even when we make all allowances for differing individual reactions, such declarations must be regarded as self-delusion, one of the theatre's numerous sentimentalisms. Were it true that there was complete involvement, then, for example, at those times when an actor loses his words and the prompter's voice is heard, there would be so severe a shock as to prohibit any further interest in the performance. In fact, of course, we take distractions of this kind in our stride: we may be annoyed at or sorry for the actor whose skill thus fails him, but the attention which has been drawn to the actor does not prevent us from reverting easily to an acceptance of the rôle he is interpreting. Here, Diderot's famous 'paradox of the actor' may with perfect propriety be applied to the spectators as the 'paradox of the audience.' Just as the player is and is not the person he pretends to be, so the members of the audience enter into the world of illusion without completely leaving their own world of actuality.

Perhaps, when we search down deeply enough, we find an audience's attitude closely akin to that of the child listening to a fairytale. "Men and women," remarks J. B. Priestley,

> who are completely removed from their childhood, who for one reason or another have had to take the child in them and wring its neck, generally dislike the theatre and are reluctant and unresponsive playgoers.[27]

In essence, what most appeals to audiences is the escape into a world of the imaginary, wherein the skill of those concerned with the production induces a momentary belief in the fiction, without, however, leading the spectators to confound that fiction with actual existence. This, no doubt, explains the widespread appeal of ballet and of similar theatrical forms. The performance is appreciated emotionally, not intellectually; the fantastic is invested, by the skill of the performers, with another reality of its own, separate from and not to be brought into association with common reality. In this sense, the theatre should be regarded as a form of escape, just as the fairy-story is an escape for the child, and we ought to recognize that our attitude to what is put upon the stage is often clearly allied to the child's attitude towards the story: we know what is going to happen but always we gain delight from listening to the familiar.

Finally, and once more based on the same ambivalent attitude, we come to the fundamental difference between the mob and the audience proper. With the former there is always the desire and call for action; with the latter there either is none, or ought to be none. The man caught up in the crowd confounds the imaginary and the real, and he clamours for action; an audience may experience dominant emotions akin to those experienced by a crowd, but, as Le Bon observes, "these emotions are not at once transformed into acts... because the most unconscious spectator cannot ignore that he is the victim of illusions, and that he has laughed or wept over imaginary adventures."[28]

This final distinction between the mob and the audience forms, or certainly ought to form, a great wall separating the two. Although that truth may appear so obvious as hardly to need any emphasis, it requires to be heavily underlined in these our days when some misguided enthusiasts deliberately seek to destroy the firm division marking off the one from the other and thus to translate the audience's characteristic attitude into the crowd's primitive and involved passions. Such, for example, happened when the New York Group Theatre in 1935 presented Clifford Odets' *Waiting for Lefty*. In effect, the actors endeavoured to suggest that the whole theatre was not a playhouse, but a militant trades-union meeting engaged in planning a strike. Harold Clurman describes the atmosphere at the première:

> The first scene of *Lefty* had not played two minutes when a shock of delighted recognition struck the audience like a tidal wave. Deep laughter, hot assent, a kind of joyous fervor seemed to sweep the audience toward the stage. The actors no longer performed; they were being carried along as if by an exultancy of communication such as I had never witnessed in the theatre before. Audience and actors had become one. Line after line brought applause, whistles, bravos, and heartfelt shouts of kinship.
>
> The taxi strike of February 1934 had been a minor incident in the labor crisis of this period. There were very few taxi-drivers in that first audience, I am sure; very few indeed who had ever been directly connected with such an event as the union meeting that provided the play its pivotal situation. When the audience at the end of the play responded to the militant question from the stage: "Well, what's the answer?" with a spontaneous roar of "Strike! Strike!" it was something more than a tribute to the play's effectiveness, more even than a testimony of the audience's hunger for constructive social action. It was the birth cry of the thirties. Our youth had found its voice. It was a call to join the good fight for a greater measure of life in a world free of economic fear, falsehood, and craven servitude to stupidity and greed. "Strike!" was *Lefty*'s lyric message, not alone for a few extra pennies of wages or for shorter hours of work, strike for greater dignity, strike for a bolder humanity, strike for the full stature of man.[29]

If Clurman had boldly declared that he and his fellows were animated by a purely political or social objective and that they were using the theatre as a means towards this end, we should have been forced to admit that all the arts have at times been subordinated to propagandist aims; but the members of the Group Theatre were

honestly interested in the good of the playhouse and Clurman's sentimentally ecstatic account of the performance well illustrates the way
in which during recent years well-meaning, although thoroughly
mistaken, efforts by enthusiasts have served to harm the theatre. The
truly significant phrase in Clurman's report is his statement that "the
actors no longer performed," suggesting that, at least for the moment,
both players and spectators were being swept into the mob's inability
to distinguish between the real and the imaginary—a mood which
spells death for the playhouse—and also into the mob's vociferous
demand for action. For some of these enthusiasts the occasion may
have been exciting, but the normal spectator does not go to the playhouse in order to become part of a trades-union gathering, and we
can easily see how this production and other inflammatory 'action-
productions' of the same period aided towards estranging the general
public from the stage. Here, indeed, is theatrical suicide.

An Art being shaped

The analysis of the typical audience has indicated that, in approaching the theatre, prime attention has to be concentrated upon the
collective body before which the performances are given, a body
quite distinct from individual readers of a literary work or viewers
of a painter's canvas. Fundamentally, this body of auditors and spectators (a) has a spirit of its own, (b) is dominated by emotion, (c)
wishes to accept the make-believe yet recognizes it as an illusion,
and (d) does not seek to make this make-believe a motive for action.
These qualities are basic.

What we must now do is to consider the relationship between this
assembled gathering and the stage-performance, and this must involve
us in an attempt to determine the precise nature of theatre art, the
essence which separates it from other arts. A painter's canvas is
worked upon, finished, varnished, and framed in a studio; then it is
hung on the wall of a gallery. When we go to the gallery, we look
upon this finished object; in no wise do we catch a glimpse of the
process of manufacture. In precisely the same way a poem or a novel,
written by an author seated at his desk, corrected and re-corrected,
comes to us as a thing immutably fashioned, a final completed art-
object. The theatrical performance clearly exists in a different world.
Here the spectators and auditors have the privilege, as it were, of
watching and hearing an art-object being shaped and moulded. The
performers, of course, have spent time and care on modelling and

polishing their respective skills, and a large part of an audience's enjoyment in the theatre derives from the exhibition of these skills, whether exemplified in a dancer's movements, a singer's notes, an actor's intonations, or an acrobat's agility. At the same time, all these performers are human; they are living organisms, not mechanical automata. The automaton will reproduce with absolute precision the same movements over and over again; this the human performer, no matter how perfected his skill may be, cannot do. He is subject to human frailties; a headache, a sudden indisposition, an emotional disturbance, and a thousand other distractions may modify what he has to present to us. Thus, no single performance is exactly the same as the one which preceded it, or the one which comes after.

Much more important than the possibly minute variations in the performers' display, consequent upon their states of mind or physical health, are the variations which result from the interactions between them and the spectators. A theatrical performance does not consist simply of an art-object being shaped; it is an art-object being shaped to a certain extent by the spectators themselves. Performances differ from performances not only because the players, being human, cannot repeat their actions and intonations with mechanical exactitude, but also because, being human, they are affected by the attitudes of their audiences. On one evening the spectators will be warm, on another cold; and the performers' displays will be conditioned by their awareness of the changed conditions. It is, of course, true that only very rarely are there violent deviations from set routine. Frederick Reynolds, for instance, records how, when one of his comedies was first brought before the public, its reception went far beyond what the players had anticipated. The principal actor, Lewis, had "disliked his part,"

but on the night the comedy was produced, he played with such skill, spirit and enthusiasm, that, when he rushed out of a china closet, in the fourth act, the roars of laughter were immense, and his triumph was complete. Delighted, but astonished, at his own success, and having fractured the trifling quantity of China-ware, that was prepared, (*trifling*, from his distrust of the situation) he knew not what to do either with himself or his hands. The roars still continuing, in the exhilaration of the moment, seizing Quick, who played *Lord Scratch*, with one hand, and his wig with the other, he threw it up to the ceiling; leaving his bald Lordship no alternative, but to quit the stage; which he did in grand dudgeon, amidst shouts of raillery, and approbation.[30]

There certainly are actors given to indulging in unrehearsed effects of a sort perhaps less extreme though similar in kind, and numerous productions have witnessed the sudden invention of 'business,' either because a warm house stimulated the performer or because a cold house seemed to demand special effort. At the same time, it is not these palpable aberrations that we think of when we consider the variations between performance and performance. Rather do we have in mind qualities so subtle as often to defy definitions—inflections, hardly perceptible movements, nuances arising from the interplay of performer and performer.

This give-and-take between those on the stage and those in the auditorium does not remain constant; it is, indeed, conditioned by three things—the shape of the theatre itself, the nature of the theatrical skill demanded of the performer, and the orientation of the production. These factors may be briefly considered.

1. Although modern theatre architects are inclined to worry most about the designing of that part of the playhouse structure which extends back from the 'curtain-line,' the essence of the theatre rests in the relationship between stage and public. When Shakespeare acted at the Globe in 1600 he found himself on a platform jutting out into the auditorium, closely surrounded by spectators, some even seated on the very edges of the stage; since this playhouse was open to the sky, he and his fellow-comedians stood in the same illumination as did the members of the audience; usually the costumes worn by the actors were not markedly different from the attire of those who watched them. In effect, the Elizabethan stage was *within* the auditorium, and thus was secured a peculiar intimacy between the performing group and the watching group. "The actor surrounded by his audience," declares a modern playwright,

> on a stage where he is not dwarfed and dimmed by the scene painter, is a solid compelling figure; and he and the dramatist, creating everything between them, can reach a far more imaginative and intimate relationship with the audience.[31]

Fortunate indeed were the Elizabethan actors in inheriting and in having the opportunity of improving upon the histrionic methods which had developed in the playing of sixteenth-century interludes, when actors and audience occupied the same level floor of some great hall, and when the former, instead of pretending that they had no spectators of their actions, deliberately brought these spectators within the framework of their performances.

When the Elizabethan type of playhouse disappeared and a new model was adopted for the theatre-buildings erected at the end of the seventeenth century, a step was taken towards the establishment of an entirely different audience-actor relationship, although for some considerable time the old conditions continued to endure. The stage, it is true, now had a proscenium arch and a curtain, but part of the acting area jutted out curvingly into the auditorium, the curtain was not put to much use, and stage-boxes set at the stage level brought some spectators close to the comedians. Above all, the whole house, stage and auditorium alike, remained for the most part evenly lit. Thus, when an eighteenth-century painter turned to depict a performance in action he showed spectators seated in as full illumination as the actors on the stage. As the playhouses gradually became larger and larger during the second half of this century, the separation of those performing from those watching tended to increase, but even so the two remained bound together in one general whole, and relics could still linger on of the original meaning of that French word, *assister*, applied to attending a performance; the spectators did not merely go to see a show, they assisted in its representation.

When, however, the new means of lighting, first gas and then electricity, came into common use, a sharp cleavage resulted between the whole of theatrical tradition from the Greek era onward, and a fresh actor-audience relationship was established. With these new means, light could be controlled in a way impossible during earlier times, and consequently it was easy to move into our familiar present-day convention, which presents a brightly lit stage while the spectators, cast into a discreet semi-darkness, look at, instead of sharing in, the performance. Resultant upon this arose a different fundamental attitude among those who went to the theatre. In the new theatrical world, the spectators—

and especially the comfortable class whose money paid for the extravagant stage production—no longer went to the play in the same spirit as their ancestors had done, innocently and widely receptive in mind and heart. They paid their money to be amused, to be 'taken out of themselves', not into themselves. And so what is now called 'show-business' was born.[32]

There is no need to underline the self-apparent fact that thus one principal element in the art of the theatre, that on which primarily its appeal had been soundly based through scores of generations, has in our own days deliberately been inhibited by the shape chosen for our playhouses.

2. The second factor determining the amount of give-and-take between performers and spectators is the nature of the skill demanded of the former. An actor in a play may introduce a new piece of business without disrupting a performance, but a new dance step could hardly be brought in, unrehearsed, by a ballerina, while in an acrobatic display an unexpected movement might well prove fatal. We must, then, recognize that, within the theatre's range, the amount of variation consequent upon the impact of audience on performers must depend upon the nature of these performers' media of expression. If we attend a score of performances of a play production and sit through them critically with notebooks in our hands, we shall be likely to record many deviations—a minutely longer pause here, a slightly changed gesture there, an alteration in pitch, a shift in emphasis. If we attend twenty performances of the same ballet, the same will not be true; provided that the dancers are highly trained, the tangible signs of emotional response to the spectators' reactions are likely to be exceedingly rare, or probably non-existent.

Nevertheless, ballet-dancers are as sensitive as dramatic actors are to the warm house and the cold; and those who are expert in this field can distinguish the temper of performances, not by observing palpable variations in movement, but by sensing the imaginative quality of the interpretation. And recognition of this fact serves to impress upon us the truth that, when we speak of variations observable in successive exhibitions of a play production, we do ill to fix our attention solely upon the tangible and physical; the imponderable variations are, in fact, of far greater significance.

3. Here, of course, a further consideration must enter in as we look upon the modern dramatic theatre. We may believe that in Shakespeare's playhouse the 'production' style shown in one drama did not differ a whit from the 'production' style in another. To-day, however, the range of styles is infinite. One director may encourage the actors to modify their performances from evening to evening. Another may insist on setting a fixed pattern and wrathfully condemn any deviations from it. At one extreme stands the model of the *commedia dell' arte*; at the other extreme stands that of Stanislavski's

Moscow Art Theatre, with its numerous pale replicas; in between
we encounter scores of different approaches, some of them dependent
upon no more than an individual director's feeling, many of them,
like Bertolt Brecht's recently much-publicized emphasis upon encouraging a "critical attitude on the part of the spectator," based on
more or less cloudy philosophizing.

This brief survey of some of the factors which condition the
element of give-and-take in the dramatic theatre perhaps may aid us
towards determining just how far 'audience participation' should
be stimulated and just what it contributes towards encouraging a
powerful theatrical impression. In general, it may be suggested that
the ideal rests in keeping a balance. Undoubtedly, when the attempt
is made to avoid imposing a set pattern on the actors there is an
ever-present danger that the entire performance may produce the
impression of a charade. Those directors who talk vaguely of the
commedia dell' arte usually tend to forget or to ignore the facts that
in the finer Italian performances the element of improvisation was
accompanied by a highly polished, traditional skill and that the
players did not have any written texts. Thus the presentation by such
actors of a co-ordinated exhibition of expert artistry based on a
scenario must remain worlds apart from, let us say, the presentation
of Jonson's *Every Man in his Humour* by actors necessarily lacking
such skill and with interpolated lines almost certain to clash with
the author's text. As one critic noted concerning such a production
in 1960, there was

> qualified success for the servants, who quip with passable verve, and
> total failure for their masters, who are saddled with the metrical
> burden of blank verse. Lines from *Othello* are tossed in to emphasise
> the inane jealousy of Kitely, the usurer; and at one point a poetaster
> declaims "Go, lovely rose", a phrase that was coined by Waller, who
> published nothing until eight years after Jonson's death.

As a result, the plot was "buried beneath these well-meaning improvements."[33] This kind of thing will not do.

A further danger emerges. Some forty years ago the Russian
director, Vladimir Meyerhold, made a number of experiments all
calculated to underline the 'theatricality' of the theatre, and in
various countries similar experiments, imitative of his, followed
during later decades. Some were motivated by genuinely artistic
aims, some were merely cheap vulgarizations. At first glance, it

would seem as though this kind of effort, even the most vulgar, ought to have had value in drawing actors and audiences together, but a recent comment by J. L. Styan well sums up its essential weakness. "Productions," he says,

> arranged so that we do not forget we are in a theatre, do not for that reason touch the nervous core of drama. On the contrary, actors who are not allowed to get under the skin of their parts, who mix with their audience, who use the auditorium as an acting area indiscriminately, have a strictly limited usefulness. These methods are more likely to exclude the spectator than to involve him, more likely to make him aware of the mechanics of the theatre at the expense of the theatre's own emotional persuasiveness.[34]

If this is true, it is also true, obviously because of diametrically opposed objectives, for the ideal enshrined in the Moscow Art Theatre. Every one knows about Stanislavski's aims, and many have had the opportunity of seeing these aims brought to realization. As given by the Russian actors trained in his spirit, *The Cherry Orchard* and *Uncle Vanya* are flawless in their exactitude. Not the slightest gesture, we feel, not the subtlest inflection, has been left to chance; the precision almost parallels the precision of the ballet. Ballet and play-production are, however, two distinct things; both belong to the theatre, but both have their own separate values and their own distinct methods. What happens with the Moscow Art Theatre's productions is that, despite their unfolding in time, they seem to become moving pictures, approaching the condition of a painter's canvas, unchanging and unchangeable.

Recently, in the United States particularly, Stanislavski's aims have become incorporated, somewhat too solemnly, in that 'Method' to which numerous young players refer with reverent and bated breath, but it may well be thought that these 'Methodists' are also tramping along a road away from the theatre's highway. Their map-reading is at fault. Without doubt the system itself can produce something of excellence; but in that excellence much that is proper to the dramatic theatre is being lost. After making all allowances, productions executed under familiar conditions, within a limited rehearsal period, are capable of arousing greater warmth in an audience precisely because of a lack of fixed forms, as opposed to the almost mathematically conceived accuracy of the other. Paradoxically, therefore, the more polished a performance becomes, the greater is the chance that the dramatic theatre's basic quality may be dissipated. If we think of theatrical art in terms of other arts, then the 'Methodists' are justified in their efforts; but if we try to seek out the inner qualities of which theatrical art is the sole possessor, we are forced to believe that such endeavours, although inspired by apparently worthy ideals, are inherently irreconcilable with the theatre's true being and consequently are capable ultimately of destroying it.

Film, Radio, and Television

The consideration of these qualities must also make us determine that film, radio, and television have nothing in common with the theatre. Actors may be seen or heard in all three; all three may take dramas from the stage and present them in their own ways; but any features they have in common with the playhouse are merely external.

These three modern forms exist in the world of the other arts. Here, as in painting, are shapes established beforehand and subject to no fluctuation. If we are asked to say wherein theatre and film differ, our first immediate answer will almost certainly be that the contrast between them arises from the three-dimensional nature of the former and the two-dimensional nature of the latter; yet far more important is the cleavage between the object-in-process-of-moulding and the object-already-moulded. On this depends the fundamental distinction between the impressions made by the one and the other. A great gulf thus yawns between them. The fact that actors nowadays move freely from film to stage, and from stage to television, should not allow us to become confused; the impact made by a theatrical performance of *Hamlet* and that made by a film version of the play are essentially at variance.

This distinction between them may be further exemplified by observing the differing audience reactions. Most of us have had the experience of attending a playhouse when the auditorium was but half or a quarter filled, and of visiting a picture-house at some off-peak hour when but a few scores of seats were occupied. In both instances we have been aware of the emptiness, but the consequences of this awareness were not by any means the same. The empty seats did not in any way affect our attention given to the film; indeed, after a moment or two, we ceased entirely to think of the absence of spectators around us; whereas in the theatre the empty seats remained to the end a disturbing element, always hovering on the

c

fringe of our consciousness. Partly, no doubt, this may be explained by assuming that, since actors are living beings dependent upon public support, we sympathized with the players in their meagre takings; partly we might attribute our feelings to regret that their efforts were being appreciated by such a small gathering of spectators. But the real inner core of our disturbance must be sought elsewhere. In the theatre we expect to be immersed in the social group; even although we do not think about it consciously, we know that our excitement and interest are stimulated by the shared experience, that our reception of a theatrical performance is deeply conditioned by the size of the audience and by our own relationship to it. We are not worried about the largeness or smallness of the audience at a film because we know that our reception of the film will not differ in any respect whether we see its projection in complete loneliness or whether we are seated in a crowded house. And, when we turn from the cinema to radio and television, we recognize that the very idea of an audience, which after all is basic to the theatre, has vanished.

Television, radio, and film have definite values, but their values belong to themselves alone, and it is exceedingly unfortunate that in our thoughts and practice they should so commonly be confused with theatrical values. When the film first became popular, and when those concerned with the fortunes of the playhouse saw their audiences drifting to the cinemas, mistaken attempts were made to copy the film's characteristic means of expression. Indeed, to a certain extent the lauded precision of a Moscow Art Theatre production may be regarded as one aspect of this endeavour. Two things, however, were forgotten. The first was that the film has diverse means of accomplishing its own ends, which can go far beyond the corresponding means possessed by the stage; its realism can be more exact, its attention to detail more effective, its spectacle vaster. The second was that the film, although possessing these powers, could not even vaguely approach the characteristic powers of the stage.

If the foregoing arguments have validity it follows that the theatre must, if it hopes for survival, capitalize upon its own peculiar source of strength. It must also recognize that its declining fortunes outside the metropolitan centres have not resulted merely from the attack of other entertainment forms unknown in the past; they have been conditioned by a series of no doubt well-meaning but nevertheless destructive movements within the theatre itself. Many of these movements have aimed at encouraging the stage to attempt what it is not fitted to do and thus at thwarting the natural expectations of the audience. And therefore we need not wonder that during the past few decades thousands of erstwhile theatre-goers, finding that the innate fascination and special quality of the playhouse was being lost, turned to-the easier delights of the cinema or elected to stay at home with their television sets, cheaply and in comfort.

It may be well, before turning from the theatre in general to a consideration of certain basic features of dramatic literature, summarily to review what has been discussed above. We may say, first of all, that audiences in the past have gone to the theatre for enjoyment of a particular kind. Without consciously thinking about æsthetic matters, they have sensed that in the playhouse there exists an art form with exclusive and special qualities of its own, which separate it from all other forms of artistic expression—no less from film, radio, and television than from painting, sculpture, and non-dramatic literature. They have been aware, too, that within itself the theatre embraces much more than simply the area of play-production, and yet that it is the dramatic stage which permits fullest scope to its potency. In this sphere the most ample opportunities are offered for the exploitation of the theatre's greatest asset, its ability to present to us, not a completely fashioned and unalterable art-object, but an art-object seen in process of formation. Technique is essential and careful preparation, but always, when the theatre is at its best, there remains the subtle interplay between the actors and the spectators. These spectators, accordingly, are not just an assemblage of men and women who have been willing to pay their money for the privilege of sitting passively in stalls or galleries; it is their subconscious wish to become an integral part of the force inherent in the playhouse, and if this wish or expectation is not satisfied their interest in the performance is bound to decline.

With these considerations held firmly in our minds, we may, then, turn now to examine the qualities of dramatic literature.

NOTES TO CHAPTER 1

1. *Talma on The Actor's Art, with preface by Henry Irving* (Samuel French; undated, but preface inscribed March 22, 1883).
2. *The Arts Council of Great Britain, Fourteenth Annual Report 1958–1959* pp. 5–10.

3. *The Development of the Theatre* (4th edition, 1958), pp. 237–262.

4. Eric Bentley, *The Playwright as Thinker* (1946), pp. 37–40. On the development and functions of the director Tyrone Guthrie has some interesting comments in *A Life in the Theatre* (1960), pp. 119–141.

5. E. Gordon Craig, *On the Art of the Theatre* (ed. 1924); "The Artists of the Theatre of the Future," pp. 50, 53.

6. "The Actor and the Über-marionette," p. 81.

7. Eric Bentley, *The Playwright as Thinker*, p. 39.

8. Alfred Harbage, *Shakespeare's Audience* (1941).

9. John Lough, *Paris Theatre Audiences in the Seventeenth and Eighteenth Centuries* (1957).

10. Francis Fergusson, *The Idea of a Theater* (1949), p. 66.

11. G. F. Reynolds, 'Literature for an Audience' (*Studies in Philology*, xxxviii, 1931, pp. 273–287) and *Plays as Literature for an Audience* (1953).

12. W. A. Darlington, *The Actor and his Audience* (1949), p. 7.

13. W. Somerset Maugham, *The Summing Up* (1938), p. 133.

14. Gustave Le Bon, *The Crowd* (1897); E. D. Martin, *The Behavior of Crowds* (1920).

15. E. D. Martin, *op. cit.*, p. 37.

16. E. D. Martin, *op. cit.*, p. 26.

17. G. Le Bon, *op. cit.*, pp. 14–33.

18. E. D. Martin, *op. cit.*, p. 12.

19. G. Le Bon, *op. cit.*, p. 58.

20. W. S. Maugham, *The Summing Up* (1938), pp. 131–132.

21. J. B. Priestley, *The Art of the Dramatist* (1957), p. 10.

22. W. S. Maugham, *op. cit.*, p. 135.

23. W. S. Maugham, *op. cit.*, p. 132.

24. H. S. Langfeld, *The Aesthetic Attitude* (1928), p. 61.

25. Chu Kwang-Tsien, *The Psychology of Tragedy* (1933), pp. 66–67.

26. G. Le Bon, *op. cit.*, pp. 57–58.

27. J. B. Priestley, *op. cit.*, pp. 35–36.

28. G. Le Bon, *op. cit.*, p. 57.

29. Harold Clurman, *The Fervent Years* (1945), pp. 147–148.

30. Frederick Reynolds, *Life and Times* (1827), ii, 32–33.

31. J. B. Priestley, *Literature and Western Man* (1960), p. 32.

32. J. B. Priestley, *op. cit.*, p. 275.

33. Kenneth Tynan in *The Observer*, July 10, 1960.

34. J. L. Styan, *The Elements of Drama* (1960), p. 231.

2

The Drama

Our attention must now proceed, past all the diverse forms of theatrical expression, past ballet and opera, past music-hall turn and wordless mime, to the drama, the play, which has already been defined as 'a literary work written, by an author or by several authors in collaboration, in a form suitable for stage presentation.'

What exactly does this mean and imply?

The Drama's Prime Objective

Several modern critics would be prepared to question the validity of the definition, or at least to cast doubt upon what seems to follow from its acceptance. Their arguments may be exemplified by the approach taken towards this problem by J. E. Spingarn. Following the critical lead of Benedetto Croce, he insists (*a*) that literature is an art of expression, (*b*) that each work of literature has to be considered in itself, hence (*c*) that the classification of literary 'kinds' is wholly false. "Shakespeare," he says,

> wrote *King Lear, Venus and Adonis* and a sequence of sonnets. What becomes of Shakespeare, the creative artist, when these three works are separated from one another by the historian of poetry; when they lose their connection with his single creative soul, and are classified with other works with which they have only a loose and vague relation?[1]

Thus "the tragic does not exist for Criticism, but only Aeschylus and Calderón, Shakespeare and Racine."[2]

Such a critical attitude has exercised considerable force in recent times, leading, for example, to the declaration of L. C. Knights that

> *Macbeth* has greater affinity with *The Waste Land* than with *The Doll's House.*[3]

Its fundamental assumption is that

> Poets do not really write epics, pastorals, lyrics, however much they
> may be deceived by these false abstractions; they express themselves,
> and this expression is their only form.[4]

Quite clearly the force of the assumption becomes peculiarly strong
when it is applied to the drama, for, as Spingarn remarks, if we
accept this theory of expression,

> we have done with the confusion between the drama and the theatre
> which has permeated dramatic criticism for over half a century.... As
> a matter of fact, the dramatic artist is to be judged by no other standard
> than that applied to any other creative artist: what has he tried to
> express, and how has he expressed it?[5]

It is not denied that a work of creative literature cast in a 'dramatic'
manner may, after it has been written, prove suitable for actors to
interpret, or that "the actor's art may in a sense vitalize the written
word and give it a new magic,"[6] or even that practising dramatists
have hoped for interpretation of their works in the theatre. What is
denied is that there exists any greater justification for assuming the
influence of theatrical considerations upon a poet-dramatist's creative
processes than there is for assuming the influence of printing considerations upon any author's creative processes. Both printing and
theatrical representation are after-results which do not concern the
composition of the poems themselves. "The changing conditions of
the theatre and the vicissitudes of taste on the part of theatrical
audiences" have no more connexion with drama as an art than the
circumstances of printing have with non-dramatic poetry.

That some truth is enshrined in these arguments may be admitted,
but it is a very partial truth. A poet decides to write a sonnet, and
inevitably the traditional sonnet-form conditions his expression. A
painter is commissioned to execute a design within a pre-determined
space, and the design itself, if it has quality, must adjust itself to the
space available. Continually, in the records of all the arts, we find
the creative artist accepting and even seeking for limitations of this
kind, and the greater the artist the more his creative spirit seems to
be inspired by the necessity of rising to the challenge. One cannot
dismiss so cavalierly the impress made upon the creative force by
pre-determined forms, nor can we permit the erroneous identification
of what are genuine after-results (such as the printed shape of a book)
with equally genuine impulses which are so much a part of the

creative process that they cannot be taken separately from the whole. While it is true that the later stage-history of *Hamlet* has nothing to do with the inception of that tragedy, *Hamlet* was wrought by Shakespeare in dramatic form, with thought of the theatre definitely and constantly in his mind.

There would seem to be no doubt that we must take the obvious as the truth, recognizing that an image of the theatre persists potently in the mind of the true dramatist, and that if his play, written for the stage, fails to appeal then somehow he has failed. It is true that John Osborne has recently declared that dramatists should be allowed "a complete artistic freedom, so that sometimes" they do not "have to please audiences or please critics or please anybody" but themselves;[7] but that has not been the view of dramatists who have contributed most to the stage. "A play that does not appeal to an audience," typically remarks Somerset Maugham, "may have merits, but it is no more a play than a mule is a horse";[8] "a dramatist," declares J. B. Priestley, "writes for the Theatre. A man who writes to be read and not to be performed is not a dramatist."[9] Although, as will be seen later, the question is not quite so simple as these statements suggest, we must accept as a fundamental principle that dramatic literature inevitably depends on conditions absent in the composition of non-dramatic poetry and prose.

Plays and Plays

The acceptance of such a principle of judgment leads inevitably to certain conclusions.

In the first place, it means, clearly, that, in discussing drama, poetic compositions such as Shelley's *Prometheus Unbound*, which, although making use of dialogue, are admittedly not conceived in a form suitable for the stage, are at once to be dismissed. Certain elements essential in the writing of drama have here been adopted, but the objective of the poet was not 'dramatic' in the strict sense of that term. Thus may we leave out of consideration scores of works, from Browning's 'Dramatic Lyrics' to Hardy's *The Dynasts*. This is simple and easy, but as soon as we move beyond into other spheres we are confronted by several awkward problems.

A play, we say, must have as its primal purpose suitability for the stage, and, if it has dramatic quality, it must appeal to an audience. So far, so good; but immediately we recognize that there are hundreds upon hundreds of plays, which, although they have satisfied these conditions, at least in their own times, are completely worthless except as historical documents. Nor can we argue that the difference between these ephemeral compositions and, say, *Hamlet* rests in the power of Shakespeare's tragedy to make an impact not only upon contemporary spectators but also upon spectators of later times. *Charley's Aunt*, regarded as a literary composition, merits hardly more than a moment's attention, yet it has held the stage since it first appeared in 1892; even in our own times an official committee, set up to determine which dramatic works might be regarded as 'educational' and worthy of being exempted from the operation of the entertainments tax, decided that this farce, because it had become a 'classic,' should be included in the select list.

The matter is still further complicated by the attitude of a number of authors, who, although perhaps aiming at something higher, are prepared to assume that it is their duty as dramatists to abandon literary pretensions. In the preface to his *Lucky Sam McCarver* (1926), Sidney Howard put this attitude trenchantly. "The actor," he averred,

> is the only theatrical element who matters. . . . Of all those concerned in the production of a play, only the actor utilizes his talents to their fullest. . . . The dramatist—what, after all, is he but a vicarious actor who happens to write well enough to be useful to real actors? . . . Very few men of literary genius have written plays. . . . The drama does not spring from a literary impulse but from a love of the brave, ephemeral, beautiful art of acting.

These sentimental words demand careful scrutiny, the more particularly since they offer support for the view recently expressed by some theatre-men, that, when all has been said, plays are merely the raw material for stage productions.

The plain truth is, of course, that Sidney Howard was talking nonsense, and that his remarks, at the opposite pole, are as far astray from the truth as were the critical pronouncements of Spingarn. If Æschylus, Sophocles, Euripides, and Aristophanes were not men of literary genius, it would be hard indeed to determine which writers possessed that quality; if Shakespeare, if Racine, if Schiller, if Chekhov were not impelled by a literary impulse, we should find it impossible to discover that impulse elsewhere. It was to a kind of Russian Sidney Howard that Chekhov wrote in 1888. "The theatre," he told him, "is a serpent that sucks your blood. Until the writer has conquered the playwright in you I shall harass you and curse your plays."

At this point we may well return to our initial definition. There, the drama was described as a 'literary work,' and as such it must be accepted. What causes difficulty is the fact that, while we all know what we mean when we refer to literature in general, we often do not know what we mean when we speak of dramatic literature. Technically, a short novelette in some *Girl's Own Paper* or some verses by an Ella Wheeler Wilcox are literature, yet we should not bother to give critical consideration to such writings, unless perhaps our objective were the exploration of popular taste or the study of social conditions. When we speak of 'literature,' we have in mind the greater achievements in the art of literary composition; and thus, for us, 'literature' means the more worthy writings in prose and verse. Without any effort we make a clear distinction between the novelette and *War and Peace*, between an ode by Keats and Ella Wheeler Wilcox' jingling, shallow rimes. Many lovers of the theatre, on the other hand, are inclined to lump together every kind of play written for the stage, and, in their anxiety to support the theatre, to accept everything within their emotionally motivated approval. 'The drama, good or bad' becomes their motto, and their minds make little distinction between a profound tragedy or a penetrating comedy and all those lesser pieces which skilled actors have made momentarily palatable.

The fact is, of course, that, just as the theatre extends its scope in breadth to embrace more than the performance of plays, so the drama's scope is extended in depth to embrace more than the immediately theatrical. While thousands of trivial pieces come within Sidney Howard's net, corresponding to the thousands of cheap novelettes and tinkling stanzas, the drama has had the power to produce some of the world's greatest literary masterpieces—and to ignore this truth, to dismiss these works because of a facile and simpering affection for "the brave, ephemeral, beautiful art of acting," savours of adolescent folly.

Plays and Performances

This whole subject demands further exploration, and the confusions attending upon it may well be illustrated by reference to two comments which are frequently to be heard when plays are being discussed.

The first occurs again and again during debates on particular dramas, taking the form of a statement: "You ought to see this piece on the stage before passing judgment on it." In books on the drama, this assertion finds constant repetition:

> the play as it is seen in any theatre, with its effect and the response in that theatre, is what really matters.[10]

The tacit assumptions here are (1) that theatre and drama are so deeply and intimately in accord that no division can be made between them, (2) that the performance is in effect the play, and (3) that a performance, any performance, will serve to reveal the true virtues of the text.

The second comment frequently heard bears a different emphasis. "Of course," we are told after some performance, "it isn't Shakespeare, but it's good theatre." Clearly, behind these words lies the thought that the drama, with its particular virtues, and the theatre, with its particular virtues, remain separate, and, indeed, inhabit dissociated realms. And this thought has a kind of double force.

In the first place, we are bound to admit that often a poor play can prove to be the basis for an exceedingly vivid and vital production. Usually there exists a certain element of dissatisfaction when witnessing a show of this kind, yet at times the sheer skill of the actors and the adroit employment of the theatrical means at their disposal almost persuade us to forget the inadequacy of the dramatic work they are presenting. A rough-and-tumble farce may not have the slightest value as a printed text, but in the theatre it may provide the basis for a hilarious evening's entertainment. And there is no need to restrict ourselves to such an extreme example. *Titus Andronicus* is assuredly no masterpiece, but a recent production of the play could legitimately be hailed as a triumph. On an occasion such as this it might be said with reason that the drama, even although it does possess some inherent interest, was little more than the raw material from which a prime example of theatrical art had been wrought. The actor, and the director, can often thus make the absurd seem credible, and the shoddy fine. "An actor like Marlon Brando," it has been said lately,

> can give a quotidian reality to any cardboard part. . . . Elia Kazan can transform any play into something far better than its text.[11]

We all know, from the many accounts which have come down to us, what Irving made of *The Bells*, a play now, and perhaps even then, almost unreadable; and more recent examples of trivial or pretentious plays made to seem masterpieces will come readily to mind.

If, however, we have these many examples of poor plays rendered attractive by theatrical means, only too often are we confronted by others wherein a great play has been so performed as, through the imposition upon it of an alien concept or through incompetence, to lose all its essential quality. Here, perhaps, a comment made by Charles Lamb on the actor, Frederick Cooke, may aid us in our inquiry. Cooke was a popular player and in certain parts effective, but, says Lamb,

> Cooke in *Richard III* is a perfect caricature. He gives you the *monster* Richard, but not the *man* Richard. Shakespeare's bloody character impresses you with awe and deep admiration of his witty parts, his consummate hypocrisy, and indefatigable prosecution of purpose. You despise, detest, and loathe the cunning, vulgar, low and fierce Richard, which Cooke substitutes in his place. He gives you no other idea than of a vulgar villain, rejoicing in his being able to overreach, and not possessing that joy in *silent* consciousness, but betraying it, like a *poor* villain, in sneers and distortions of the face, like a droll at a country fair: not to add that cunning so self-betraying and manner so vulgar could never have deceived the politic Buckingham nor the soft Lady Anne: *both* bred in courts, would have turned with disgust from such a fellow. Not but Cooke has *powers*; but not of discrimination. His manner is strong, coarse, and vigorous, and well adapted to some characters. But the lofty imagery and high sentiments and high passions of *Poetry* come black and prose-smoked from his prose lips.[12]

We can all think of similar instances; and we can think of many more wherein the director rather than the actor was responsible for transforming the values of some particular drama. When we find a dramatic critic saying of a production of *Julius Cæsar* in which the mob was treated with extreme realism:

> There is little trace of poetry; but that is a price worth paying in a production that restores vitality to the plot—

we realize fully how the theatre can at times utterly fail to express dramatic values. Recalling these instances, we must admit that the simple assertion about the necessity of seeing a play in performance in order to appreciate its worth demands severe qualifications.

Even so, however, we may fall back on another proposition. Poor plays made to seem good, we may argue, and good plays badly produced are not what we have in mind: we are thinking of an integrated fusion of drama and theatre, of the ideal production in which great actors interpret a great playwright's lines. Yet once

more we are forced to pause, and, in pausing, we may recall another
of Lamb's comments—this time not on a miscast actor, but upon two
brilliant players:

> It is difficult for a frequent play-goer to disembarrass the idea of
> Hamlet from the person and voice of Mr K[emble]. We speak of
> Lady Macbeth, while we are in reality thinking of Mrs S[iddons].
> Nor is this confusion incidental alone to unlettered persons, who, not
> possessing the advantage of reading, are necessarily dependent upon
> the stage-player for all the pleasure which they can receive from the
> drama, and to whom the very idea of *what an author is* cannot be
> made comprehensible without some pain and perplexity of mind: the
> error is one from which persons otherwise not meanly lettered, find it
> almost impossible to extricate themselves.
>
> Never let me be so ungrateful as to forget the very high degree of
> satisfaction which I received some years back from seeing for the first
> time a tragedy of Shakespeare performed, in which those two great
> performers sustained the principal parts. It seemed to embody and
> realise conceptions which had hitherto assumed no distinct shape. But
> dearly do we pay all our life after for this juvenile pleasure, this sense
> of distinctness. When the novelty is past, we find to our cost that
> instead of realising an idea, we have only materialised and brought
> down a fine vision to the standard of flesh and blood. We have let go
> a dream, in quest of an unattainable substance.

Hence Lamb arrives at his revolutionary conclusion:

> that the plays of Shakespeare are less calculated for performance on a
> stage, than those of almost any other dramatist whatever. Their dis-
> tinguishing excellence is a reason that they should be so. There is so
> much in them, which comes not under the province of acting, with
> which eye, and tone, and gesture, have nothing to do.[13]

Although Lamb's words at first may seem paradoxical, even
although they may appear unpalatable, careful consideration must
be given them. Basically, those who insist in declaring that only in
performance can a play's true worth be appreciated make two further
assumptions: (1) that the values of a great drama can be fully revealed in a theatrical production and (2) that it is possible to determine with fair accuracy what in fact a play's values are. Both these
assumptions will hardly stand up to close examination, precisely
because the drama, as we have seen, extends in depth beyond the
theatre's range. A tragedy such as *Hamlet* includes within itself so
much that no performance, however finely conceived and executed,

can give us the whole of its content. L. C. Knights was obviously thinking of this when he made his statement about *Macbeth* and *The Waste Land*. *Macbeth*, he pointed out, "is a statement of evil" and he added:

> It also happens to be poetry, which means that the apprehension of the whole can only be obtained from a lively attention to the parts—[14]

and this lively attention goes beyond what can be secured in watching a performance.

The "apprehension of the whole," moreover, apart from involving long and detailed scrutiny and contemplation of the text, is something which cannot be determined with absolute assurance. As Lamb observed, the greater plays are, the more they include within themselves, and therefore the less possibility is there of assessing their values and inherent spirit definitely and firmly. While it is true that the general run of drama consists of works—skilfully fashioned, mediocre, or poor—which offer opportunities only for certain specific judgments concerning their essential aims, numerous outstanding dramas bear within themselves diverse possibilities, sometimes markedly at variance with each other, of creating more than one single theatrical impression. Thus, to take a simple example, *The Merchant of Venice* might be presented with Antonio as the focal point of interest, and this would be justified by the fact that, after all, he gives his professional name to the title of the play; some of the lines offer justification for the treatment of Shylock as a villain to be despised; many other lines suggest sympathy for him and implied condemnation of the standards of Venetian life; the play's structure might seem to warrant either a realistic or a purely romantic approach to its story. Perhaps Shakespeare himself intended all these qualities to be inherent in his drama; perhaps, even at a time when he had become a master of his craft, he failed to consolidate all the various elements harmoniously together; but, whatever our judgment of the comedy, the plain fact is that the theatre, by the very nature of its being, possesses only limited power to exhibit the nuances and subtleties which may be discerned in the text. What remains an inevitable and inescapable conclusion is that different productions of *The Merchant of Venice*, even without the impress of any concept alien to the dialogue, will produce markedly different effects upon their audiences.

But, we may say, does all of this amount to anything more than

stating the obvious fact that there is diversity of critical opinion concerning the interpretation of this and other plays? Clearly, in one
sense it does not, yet clearly in another sense it means much more.
We observe the tremendous divergence between one critic's opinion
and that of another; we may decide that one critic gives a more
balanced or a more penetrating analysis of some selected drama than
does another commentator; if we are asked for advice we may refer
an inquirer to the interpretative volume we most admire; but we do
not commonly assume that only a reading of this particular study can
lead us to the truth. Yet that is precisely what we do when we declare
that the drama must be seen on the stage to be appreciated properly.
Within the context of the present inquiry into the relationship of
theatre and drama, such a declaration has no validity. To say
"Before you judge this play, you must see a performance—any performance—of it" is just about as sensible as it would be to say "Before you judge this play, you must read what a critic—any critic—
has written about it."

Stage and Study

We are, then, confronted by a dilemma, but it is a dilemma which
appears susceptible of a ready solution. We must hold firmly to the
initial concept of the drama as a work written in the first instance
for performance in the theatre; and we may go further than that—
recognizing that the strength of such a play as *Hamlet* is demonstrated by its enduring power to hold spectators in its grip. In addition, we must hold equally firmly to the realization that theatrical
performances continually serve to reveal qualities in the greater plays
which may readily be missed in perusal. The impact made by
Twelfth Night or *Hamlet* in a fine production, even while we acknowledge that the production cannot give us the whole of the play,
is something for which no substitute may be found; and even in less
accomplished productions we are constantly being rewarded by vistas
revealed to us by the realization of the scenes in theatrical form.

At the same time we have to bear steadily in mind the fact that a
great drama is a work of literature and that a careful study of its
lines can make apparent qualities we could not divine from witnessing either a single production or a series of productions. *Hamlet*
deserves to be read as minutely as we should read *La Divina
Commedia*.

Thus, only, it would seem, can the dilemma be solved. But one thing more must be said: since a play is primarily intended for the stage, the perusal of its text must be bound by thought of the theatre. Just as soon as this statement is made, however, we recognize that a peculiar and very serious problem arises in modern times. Recent literary criticism has developed a number of approaches which induce the reader to explore minutiæ and so to move ever deeper into what Lamb called the 'dream.' While in general this modern criticism, when applied to the drama, bows acknowledgment to the theatrical values, its explorations into the poetic content of selected plays tends to widen the gulf between stage appreciation and study appreciation. In the past the distance between the two was not so great. Those many nineteenth-century studies of Shakespeare's characters, culminating in Bradley's famous volume, even although they rarely referred to the plays in theatrical terms, and, indeed, habitually treated them purely as literary texts, came closer than many modern studies to the approach of the stage—since obviously it is upon characters that actors concentrate, and since audiences gain most of their impressions from hearing the actors deliver the lines assigned to those characters. Character studies, however, are rather out of fashion now, and it is chiefly other features in the texts upon which modern critics focus attention.

This matter is of such importance that perhaps it may be profitable to consider a few examples. In our own days the significance of myth has attracted a great deal of study, and thus the work of anthropologists and psychologists has been brought to bear on the drama. When Aristotle turned to analyse tragedy, as T. S. Eliot noted, he

> did not have to worry about the relation of drama to religion, about the traditional morality of the Hellenes, about the relation of art to politics; he did not have to struggle with German or Italian aesthetics; he did not have to read the (extremely interesting) works of Miss Harrison or Mr Cornford.[15]

That speculations based on the application to drama of these new areas of investigation colour a fair amount of modern criticism does not particularly matter: what does matter is that the criticism itself naturally influences many readers' attitude to the plays they are perusing and that thus they are being led to see things there of which no audience could be cognisant.

Along with this goes the current minute examination of imagery. As will be seen, there is some considerable justification for this, even from the point of view of audience appreciation, but there is an ever-present danger that the imagery which makes its impact on the auditorium may differ from the imagery discerned and interpreted by the single reader. In the study we may be apt to linger over a word or a phrase and to consider that word or phrase more important than a speech, a scene, or even the total effect of a whole play. Furthermore, the search for imagery has led towards a determination at all costs to find new 'meanings' for many qualities in older plays and hence to reach fresh assessments of these dramas. Take, for instance, the comedies written by Congreve. Hitherto, we have all observed and dismissed as a dramatic weakness their peculiarly tangled and obscure plots; critical assessment, based on reading, has gone hand-in-hand with audience assessment. Now, however, comes a modern critic, who, applying the current technique of exploring "contrast, parallelism, images, or symbols," determines that a meaning must be found even for this apparent fault. He admits freely that the playwright "has unduly complicated" the relationship, both of family and of emotion, among his characters, and that "in both cases some of the complications are not essential to the plot." He then proceeds:

> We must look for the reason. The confusion which is the prevailing atmosphere of the play becomes almost a kind of symbol for one of the points Congreve wants to make. That is, the confusion asks the question that underlies almost every facet of the play: What is the true interaction between these two kinds of relationships? To some extent, I think, we are meant to be aware simply of the idea "family" and the idea "emotion", without necessarily following through the involved details.

This, in turn, leads to an explanation of the 'meaning' of *The Way of the World*:

> The unraveling with its final clue, the deed, suggests the relation between the two complex realities of family and emotional ties: that the "real" reality is the inward, emotional nature; this reality is a changing flux that gives birth to a more stable framework of overt social facts (dynastic relations); when, for whatever reason, these social facts are not true reflections of the underlying emotional relations (Mrs Fainall's marriage, the projected "marriage" of Lady Wishfort to Mirabell's servant, and the like) a situation of power results in favor of one who knows the inconsistency; the antidote to such situations is to create an overt, social situation which will truly reflect the underlying realities. This interplay between two kinds of reality leads, naturally enough, to two kinds of action in the play. The first—I

will call it the *unraveling*—peels off bit by bit the surface appearances to get at the real facts of emotion underneath. The second, which I will call the *emancipating*, sets up a new social structure based on those underlying emotional realities.[16]

Is not this considering too curiously? It does certainly carry us far from theatrical experience.

Even if we do not go so far, problems constantly arise. *Hamlet*, as every one knows, offers a scene which, in reading, may appear to be a puzzle. When the Players present their Gonzago playlet before Claudius, they first show the plot in dumb show, and then they proceed to dialogue. Claudius is there on stage, but not until Lucianus' speech does he rise in confusion. When the tragedy is performed, it may be asserted with confidence that no spectators are aware of any serious difficulty or speculate concerning a concealed 'meaning' in the action. A reading of the play, on the other hand, has tempted various critics to interpret the scene as a comment on Claudius' character—showing him possessed of sufficient willpower to refrain from displaying any outward emotion during the mere miming, but of insufficient willpower to prevent his composure being shattered when the Player's words follow. These conjectures, arising from a reading of the text, seem to neglect making allowances for the dramatic necessity imposed on the dramatist; in effect, Shakespeare has to show the audience the plot of 'The Mousetrap' play, yet time forbids him to present this as a whole; and thus resort is made to a dramatic trick, with brief miming of the main action of the play-within-the-play and the subsequent provision of merely a few key-speeches.

Innumerable examples might be cited to illustrate the differences in approach and in interpretation which can make sharp cleavages between the audience and the reader. Often, perhaps, the differences are not of fundamental importance in themselves; but importance does attach to the fact that they may readily lead to differences in judgment and standard. In the course of reading we are often induced to find in individual dramas qualities beyond those experienced in the theatre and thus either to denigrate plays which make powerful impact on audiences or to claim as greater masterpieces plays which on the stage make lesser appeal. To exemplify this we need go no further than Shakespeare's works. During recent years we have been assured that *Hamlet* is an artistic failure and that certain other dramas, such as *Pericles, Timon of Athens*, and *Antony and*

D

Cleopatra, represent the topmost triumphs of his imagination. Yet these judgments run directly counter to the opinions of successive audiences. *Hamlet* stands out as the most appealing and successful among the tragedies, with a long and distinguished stage-history from its own time to ours; *Pericles* may have won popular success in its own age, but it possessed no lasting power to hold its position in the theatre; we cannot be sure that *Timon* ever was acted in Shakespeare's lifetime and its later revivals have been comparatively rare; there is no record of any early productions of *Antony and Cleopatra*, while it holds the unenviable distinction of coming, with a pitiful record of only six performances in 1759, at the very bottom of Shakespeare's dramas on the eighteenth-century stage. True, this last-mentioned play attracted some nineteenth-century actor-managers because of the opportunities it offered for scenic splendour, and in our own days it has witnessed a number of revivals; but it has not succeeded in displaying that power of attracting audiences which has been displayed by others among Shakespeare's works. Certainly it has failed to make an impact on audiences commensurate with the esteem in which it is held by to-day's literary critics.

These facts must be given full consideration, because clearly the recent high 'literary' praise given to *Pericles*, *Timon*, and *Antony*, taken in conjunction with the direct or implied strictures on *Hamlet*, means that literary critics are finding, or professing to find, qualities in these dramas which remain outside the scope of the audience. That such a cleavage is fraught with danger appears certain, and we shall stand on much securer ground if we decide that, while the greater dramas exist in the two worlds of literature and the theatre, while they demand for their full understanding both reading at leisure and witnessing on the stage, while it is justifiable to discover and to laud poetic, literary qualities enshrined in some play which, less than others, has succeeded in arousing audience interest, we should, in the end, recognize that the prime criterion, the essential standard, rests in the power of these plays to do what they set out to accomplish—the power to grip and stimulate a body of spectators in the play-house.

In saying this, of course, we are forced at the same time to admit that full allowance must be made for changing conditions. What has made appeal in its own time may have been conceived in terms such as could not possibly appeal to later audiences, accustomed to conventions of an entirely different kind and ignorant of the social circumstances out of which originally it grew. A good example is the Old Comedy of Aristophanes. Reading, either in the original Greek or even in translation, *The Birds* or *Thesmophoriazusæ* we cannot fail to discern the enduring qualities of these vigorous, vital, lyrical extravaganzas; but at the same time it is obvious that in form they belong so closely to the stage and conditions of their own time that any attempt to present them in their own shape to-day must be doomed to failure. Apart from this, the whole field of comedy, which has always inclined towards the presentation on the stage of scenes depicting or reflecting the social life of the times in which the various pieces were written, stands less chance than other dramatic forms of being able to preserve its original appeal. Comedy frequently tends to introduce topicalities, and even when some authors have succeeded, as Aristophanes did, in penetrating beyond the surface life of their ages and in exhibiting material of permanent human interest, the topicalities still remain to distract audiences living in other cultures and to make the comic scenes appear antiquated.

This no doubt explains why, while Aristophanes' comedies remain relatively unknown to-day, the *Œdipus Rex* of Sophocles, likewise using the now unfamiliar device of the chorus, can still make a powerful appeal, even when it has been translated from the open-air theatre of Dionysus to the restricted area of the present-day proscenium-arch stage. Perhaps revivals of this, or of any other ancient Greek play, are comparatively rare, but the very fact that there are revivals and that they still grip modern audiences, despite the complete difference between their forms and the dramatic forms to which the spectators are accustomed, testifies to the inherent skill with which their authors fulfilled the drama's first requirement.

Clearly, then, allowance has to be made for changing conditions; it would be folly to underestimate the dramatic worth of an Aristophanic comedy simply because its form, suited to the demands of its own theatre, makes it unsuitable for performance in ours. But, even when this qualification has been most amply admitted, the general standard of judgment must remain.

Public Stage or Private

The acceptance of this judgment means that, although drama belongs to the art of literature and although a play, unlike a ballet or an opera, can live a double life on the stage and in the study, the consideration of those auditors for whom dramatic works were in the first place intended becomes even more important in this sphere than it does in the sphere of theatrical representation.

Already an effort has been made to analyse at least some of the chief qualities manifested by the assemblages of persons who gather together in the theatre auditoriums. Now we must proceed to survey their significance for the playwright—and at the very start of this inquiry a pertinent question arises: what kind of audience do we have in mind? Aristotle had, of course, in view the only theatrical public existing in his age, the vast concourse flocking to the great Athenian playhouse; Castelvetro's *moltitudine rozza* seems to imply a popular assemblage; Shakespeare's audience at the Globe theatre was large and representative of divers interests and classes; when Maugham and Priestley speak of the audience they have similarly in mind the spectators who fill the auditoriums of ordinary public playhouses.

At various periods, however, there have been dramatists who, disturbed by the ordinary theatre's manifest crudity, even vulgarity, have felt impelled to seek groups of spectators less numerous and more refined; and this trend has assumed especial strength in modern times. As an extreme instance may be taken the complaints of W. B. Yeats. He describes how he had once been annoyed by overhearing a spectator, during the intermission, make some remarks on one of his plays. "Being sensitive," he explains,

> or not knowing how to escape the chance of sitting behind the wrong people, I have begun to shrink from sending my muses where they are but half-welcomed; and even in Dublin, where the pit has an ear for verse, I have no longer the appetite to carry me through the daily rehearsals.

Following this confession comes an even more significant avowal:

> My blunder has been that I did not discover in my youth that my theatre must be the ancient theatre that can be made by unrolling a carpet or marking out a place with a stick, or setting a screen against the wall. Certainly those who care for my kind of poetry must be numerous enough, if I can bring them together, to pay half-a-dozen players who can bring all their properties in a cab and perform in their leisure moments.[17]

This reflects the age-old problem voiced in *Hamlet*. "I heard thee speak me a speech once," says the Prince to the Player, but it was never acted; or, if it was, not above once; for the play, I remember, pleas'd not the million; 'twas caviare to the general. But it was—as I received it, and others whose judgments in such matters cried in the top of mine—an excellent play, well digested in the scenes, set down with as much modesty as cunning. I remember one said there were no sallets in the lines to make the matter savoury.

And Hamlet's comment on Polonius' objections to the lengthy speech from the Pyrrhus play summarizes the contempt felt by numerous poets towards the tastes of the general—"He's for a jig, or a tale of bawdry, or he sleeps."

At first glance it might appear as though no particular weight need be given to such views, since, we might say, the theatre's popular basis must be accepted by all who would write for it, and Yeats' timid avoidance of the public stage can be taken only as proving him more poet than playwright. We might thus dismiss his 'plays for dancers' as possessing little significance when we are engaged in considering the great sweep of the theatre in its totality. Two things, however, must make us pause.

The first of these is that the plea for the smaller, restricted audience has not by any means come only from poets such as Yeats, nor has it been motivated solely by the dramatists' sensitivity. From the time when the Freie Bühne was set up in Berlin and the Théâtre Libre in Paris, there has been a steady movement, diversely inspired, to establish 'little theatres' dedicated to aims different from those of the commercial playhouses, and all of these have been dominated by the thought that in the commercial playhouses, from the end of the nineteenth century onward, has reigned a spirit antagonistic towards finer dramatic effort. A few years ago Eric Bentley trenchantly sought to provide reasoned justification for this point of view.[18] The term 'public theatre,' he claims, means something different now from what it meant in earlier times; we cannot equate the ordinary playhouse of to-day with the Globe. The theatre has during the past fifty or sixty years become more and more commercialized as 'show-business,' while at the same time "the extension of literacy to the previously illiterate majority" has created "a nation of newspaper readers," fed on clichés, and, when they enter the theatre, incapable of appreciating anything save trivialities. "To be popular in an aristocratic culture," he avers, "like ancient Greece or Elizabethan England, is quite a different matter from being popular in a middle-class culture." Consequently he arrives at the "revolutionary conclusion" that we ought to repudiate

> the theatre as it is now financed and organized, which means, positively stated, the acceptance of a special, limited audience.

The argument appears cogent, but it requires very careful scrutiny. We may well question the application of the term 'aristocratic' to Athens' democracy,[19] and perhaps we might even balance Shakespeare's ballad-fed groundlings against to-day's newspaper-fed spectators. Certainly we must observe that the plea made here for special, limited audiences, so far from being revolutionary, is one which has frequently been expressed during the range of the theatre's history. During the early years of the seventeenth century there were playwrights who clearly found themselves happier when they were addressing the more privileged spectators who could afford to frequent the 'private' houses, and there were others who preferred even more restricted audiences attending amateur performances in country-house playhouses still more private. While, therefore, we may accept as a fact the development in our own times of a theatrical commercialism unknown in the past, we are compelled to acknowledge two other facts—that in earlier ages dissatisfaction with crude popular taste was by no means absent, but that the majority of dramatists whom we now recognize as outstanding were prepared, no matter how much they deplored this taste, to accept the prevailing conditions. Possibly Hamlet's critical comments may reflect some of Shakespeare's own thought, but, if so, the author of *Hamlet* showed himself ready to continue writing for the ordinary stage and to build his plays on what was wanted by the million. He remained content to savour his caviare as a luxury.

In considering this question three comments well put forward by Walter Kerr deserve attention.[20] The first is his observation that the dependence of dramatists upon mass audiences in the past did not prevent the creation of tragedies and comedies which we all recognize as literary masterpieces; the second is that "no genuine masterpiece has ever been rejected by the common audience before which it was first performed"; and the third is that "minority theatres never have produced important work." Although it might prove possible to offer a few qualifications to these generalizing statements, in essence they rest upon a firm basis; and they are supported by such relevant special studies as that which Alfred Harbage has devoted to the public and private theatres during the Elizabethan period. Harbage thus demonstrates that the mass audience attending the Globe encouraged a style of drama—Shakespeare's style—healthier and possessed of deeper qualities than that cultivated by the more select and intellectually superior spectators who patronized the Blackfriars.

The problem is a difficult one, and especially so in modern times; but, even when we do make full allowance for present-day commercialism and deplore the current prevailing literate illiteracy, we must, it would seem, refuse to abandon ourselves to a policy of despair. No doubt the existence of some minority theatres alongside the theatres of larger appeal can on occasion exert a useful and stimulating influence, since often these smaller ventures are associated with particular 'programmes'; quite frequently we find these programmes directed towards the promotion of objectives which are either fruitless or else inimical to the theatre's spirit, but occasionally they do have the effect of stimulating interesting and useful dramatic developments. For that reason they need not be discouraged; yet, at the same time, we must decide that, if we hope the theatre to flourish in the future, we have to look for its strength in the ordinary playhouses attracting the widest possible representation of community interests. In the small minority house the audience often is no more than a tiny collection of like-minded individuals, so few in number that they can hardly be styled an audience at all; the theatre's true power and differentiating characteristic lies in the immediacy of impact on such a gathering of diverse individuals as may associate them with a crowd. The very size of the gathering, apart from its composition, becomes of significance. In speaking, therefore, of the audience for dramatic literature, it is this general assemblage in ordinary public playhouses which we have to envisage.

The Dramatic Pattern

One important feature of the general audience, which, since it concerns the dramatist rather than the performer, has so far been referred to only by implication, must now be glanced at. In a small minority playhouse the audience-entity is, for the most part, composed of an assemblage of persons with kindred tastes and interests; in the larger theatres the assemblage is made up of men and women with sharply contrasting intellectual and social backgrounds and with markedly different powers of perception. Already it has been seen that, although the theatre's spectators do constitute a unity, the hundreds of individuals included within that unity succeed in preserving some of their own personalities; they are not absolutely submerged, as in a mob. Apart from this, however, they incline to divide themselves into sections, and most theatre-buildings have tended to emphasize these sections by formal separation of group from group. Even the large popular Athenian playhouse had its apportioned seats; even the Elizabethan public theatre had its yard, galleries, and gentlemen's rooms. Those many eighteenth-century prologues addressed to pit, box, and gallery recognized an ever-present fact, that the audience, although a unit, is never completely one, and that what will please one section may not please the others. David Garrick, actor and dramatist, well expressed this when he turned to speak to each part of the auditorium:

> *You* relish satire (*to the pit*), *you* ragouts of wit (*boxes*),
> *Your* taste is humour and high-season'd joke (*first gallery*),
> *You* call for hornpipes and Hearts of Oak (*second gallery*).[21]

All practising playwrights, of course, are fully conscious of this. In the majority of plays, material suited for the differing tastes or perceptive capabilities of the groups within the larger assemblage are freely introduced, although generally as almost separate elements: even in the hands of such a skilled dramatist as Bernard Shaw it is sometimes painfully evident how some piece of farcical business has been dragged in for the purpose of entertaining those whose attention might be flagging. On the other hand, it must also be acknowledged that, when the opportunities offered by the necessity of appealing to these divergent interests have been fully appreciated, a source of added strength is provided for the writer of plays designed for public performance. Shakespeare thus makes his different elements mutually reinforcing. The unlettered and naïve spectator who attends a production of *Hamlet* may succeed in grasping little more than the plot; but he does not come away from the tragedy with an impression fundamentally distinct from that created in the mind, let us say, of a spectator who by nature and training has been quick to grasp the deeper emotional qualities inherent in the more complex scenes. And the very fact that Shakespeare has been compelled in this manner to consider the requirements of the diverse levels within his audience partly at least explains the firmness, solidity, and enduring nature of his play.

Herein, perhaps, rests the prime power of the drama at its best. The conditions of dramatic literature are such that the playwright of genius, born in favourable circumstances, is enabled to produce work which, by its concreteness, its vitality, its variety, and its directness of appeal, may have a chance of endurance beyond that granted to only a few literary masterpieces. Even the greatest of non-dramatic poems tend to become the exclusive property of the initiated; *The Iliad* and *The Odyssey, La Divina Commedia, The Faerie Queene, Paradise Lost, The Prelude,* all acclaimed as outstanding achievements of the poetic imagination, cannot vie in any respect with the wide appeal of *Hamlet* and *Lear.* Somehow—and it is this somehow we are seeking—the dramatist has here succeeded in composing works built out of material popular in his own time yet incorporating qualities of enduring interest; and the power of the works themselves depends upon the fusion of these two elements.

This, however, the dramatist cannot do unless he realizes to the full the limitations imposed upon him by the fact that his work is presented to an audience and unless he seizes the chance of utilizing every opportunity and means offered to him by his medium. The limitations demand scrutiny first.

We may begin with three related physical facts which are so obvious that, were it not that they determine the very ground upon which the dramatist has to stand, we might almost deem it unnecessary to mention them: (1) an assembled group of spectators gathers to listen to a play, and, since these spectators have ordinary human frailties, the period of time during which they can be expected to remain in their seats is relatively short; (2) unlike individual readers who may read a few chapters of a novel, put down the book, and take it up again when they feel inclined, the auditors have to take in the whole work at one sitting; and (3) they have no chance, such as a reader may have, of referring back to scenes which have already been presented before them.

So far as the length of performance is concerned, it is true that occasions and habits sometimes differ. During those ages when the dramatic spectacles were periodical, festival, holiday affairs, it was but natural that they should tend to be of longer duration than the familiar performances in the theatres of to-day. As even the still-persisting productions at Oberammergau testify, holiday audiences may be induced to sit through performances far more widely extended in time than what normally we expect. The normal expectation, however, remains fairly constant, varying between a little more than two hours and, less frequently, a little more than three.[22] Deviations from this are rare; the exceptions are generally more apparent than real. *Man and Superman* is an outstretched piece, but actually it is composed of two parts—a play of usual length and an attached Hell-scene which may be omitted in production; and the majority of similar seemingly exceptional dramas may on analysis be found to fit themselves into the common pattern. *Strange Interlude* and *Long Day's Journey into Night*, it is true, drag their slow lengths along through many hours, but, happily, enormities of this sort occur but seldom.

It must, of course, be conceded that at times various playwrights have burst the time bonds by presenting connected dramas in series. Thus, for example, a typical Greek trilogy consisted of three virtually independent works which could be, and indeed were, also conceived as forming a larger whole—almost as though they were three extended acts of a single tragedy. The medieval mystery cycles were composed of thirty or forty short playlets, each with its own theme, but all combining to present to the audience a picture of the world from the creation to doomsday. In certain Chinese performances, it is said, something of the some kind occurs, and the practice forms part of the structure of the Japanese Nō. The Elizabethans had their two-part plays, such as *Tamburlaine* and *Henry IV*, which could be appreciated singly and which exhibited their own beginnings, middles, and ends, and yet which could be, as it were, taken together when they were played on successive afternoons. If certain modern critics are right, Shakespeare conceived his *Richard II*, the two parts of *Henry IV*, and *Henry V* as a tetralogy, and the three parts of *Henry VI*, with *Richard III*, as another. Shaw goes one better in *Back to Methuselah*, a set of five separate dramas all combining to make up one general totality.

None of these aberrations, however, take away from the normal concept of a play as a work designed for theatrical performance within a limited number of hours. By this restriction the author who essays this kind of literary endeavour is more or less strictly bound. As a result, he must inevitably abandon the freedom permitted to other writers. A poem may be as short as an epigram, as prolonged as an epic; prose fiction may extend from a short short-story to a compilation in many volumes. The dramatist is forced to confine what he has to say within a measure which permits of only slight adjustment.

This measure is small for what he has to do. He must tell a story, for plot forms an inescapable necessity, and he must provide convincingly delineated characters involved in that story, or through whose words and actions the story unfolds itself. Unlike a novelist, he cannot indulge in much description or direct comment, and, even if he restricts himself to a limited cast, he may assign to no one of his fictional persons more than a number of words which must appear pitifully meagre for his purposes.

The second and third physical facts noted above follow on from the first, and they are equally important. One of the principal causes of the difference between the assessment of a play in the theatre and its assessment in the study derives from the simple truth that, whereas theatre auditors have to grasp the import of the drama in one sitting, readers may, and often do, concentrate upon the text act by act or scene by scene. Indeed, it might almost be said that the only way in which a reader can approximate the impact which a play makes upon an audience is to peruse the text under the same conditions by taking it, at one time, from the beginning to the end. So far as the dramatist is concerned, clearly he must consider that the assemblage of spectators gathered to listen to his work consists of a miscellaneous collection of individuals representing widely different social strata, intellectual range, and interests. None of these must be permitted to become bored, and the significance of words and actions must be made immediately palpable. Furthermore, there is the third fact—that no opportunity is available for turning back to scenes already played. The impact of each passing episode has to be definite and clear if appreciation and comprehension of the whole is to be effected.

When we put these initial limitations, dependent upon the circumscribed time-scheme, alongside the other limitations which arise from the audience's characteristic approach, we realize that the dramatist's liberty has indeed clearly marked frontiers.

It follows from this that the only course the dramatist can take to achieve success is deliberately to make bold impact upon his auditors, to aim at an easily perceptible simplicity in the framework of his play, and to tell his story (or to present his vision) within a formally conceived pattern.

The Unities

Here, perhaps, it may not be without profit to turn for a moment from the present to the past and look briefly at the implications raised

by those 'Unities' about which there was so much pother in Renaissance critical writings. To-day, when the Unities are mentioned, we
are inclined to dismiss them with a superior smile or with a frown of
annoyance; the animated debate which once raged concerning them
may well seem to be a topic possessing none save historical interest
and unworthy of practical consideration. It does, indeed, embrace
much of folly, much that has no particular value, much that is
ridiculous; and yet, if we can delve below its external features, we
may possibly discern within it certain qualities of inner value.

The basic facts can easily be outlined in brief space. Aristotle, in
his *Poetics*, had emphasized that a play must have an organic unity
of action, with a clear focus, and he had further observed that, in
contradistinction to the epic, a play normally confines itself to a
restricted period of time. Renaissance theorists took over these two
comments, elevated them into the Unities of Action and Time, and,
from their reading of the Greek tragedies, invented a third Unity,
that of Place. Then the game began. What was to be the limit of
fictional time permitted? Some strict conservatives declared that

> the time of the representation and that of the action represented must
> be exactly coincident;[23]

some said it might extend to twelve hours, a single day; others were
prepared to interpret 'day' more generously. Milton thus averred
that

> the circumscription of time, wherein the whole drama begins and
> ends, is, according to ancient rule and best example, within the space
> of twenty-four hours.[24]

A few were brave enough to recommend a day or two. Exactly
similar was the discussion of the Unity of Place; one critic asserted
that

> the scene of the action must be constant, being not merely restricted
> to one city or house, but indeed to that one place alone which could
> be visible to one person;[25]

others allowed various scenes within a reasonably restricted area.

All the pettifogging arguments are stupidly absurd, and in the
eighteenth century it was quite easy for men like George Farquhar
to point out their worthlessness. "The less rigid Criticks," he said,

> allow to a Comedy the space of an artificial Day, or Twenty Four
> Hours; but those of the thorough Reformation, will confine it to the
> natural or Solar Day, which is but half the time. Now admitting this

for a Decorum absolutely requisite: This Play begins when it is exactly Six by your Watch, and ends precisely at Nine, which is the usual time of the Representation. Now is it feazible in *rerum Natura*, that the same Space or Extent of Time can be three Hours, by your Watch, and twelve Hours upon the Stage, admitting the same Number of Minutes, or the same Measure of Sand to both? I'm afraid, Sir, you must allow this for an Impossiblity too; and you may with as much Reason allow the Play the Extent of a whole Year; and if you grant me a Year, you may give me Seven, and so to a Thousand. For that a Thousand Years shou'd come within the Compass of three Hours is no more an Impossibility, than that Two Minutes shou'd be contained in one; *Nullum minus continet in se majus*, is equally applicable to both.

And so for Place:

Here is a New Play, the House is throng'd, the Prologue's spoken and the Curtain drawn represents you the Scene of *Grand Cairo*. Whereabouts are you now, Sir? Were not you the very Minute before in the Pit in the English Play-house talking to a Wench, and now *Presto pass*, you are spirited away to the Banks of the River *Nile*. Surely, Sir, this is a most intolerable Improbability; yet this you must allow me, or else you destroy the very Constitution of Representation: Then in the second Act, with a Flourish of the Fiddles, I change the Scene to *Astrachan*. *O, this is intolerable!* Look'ee, Sir, 'tis not a Jot more intolerable than the other; for you'll find that 'tis much about the same distance between *Egypt* and *Astrachan*, as it is between *Drury-Lane* and *Grand Cairo*; and if you please to let your Fancy take Post, it will perform the Journey in the same moment of Time, without any Disturbance in the World to your Person.[26]

Farquhar seems, in fact, to have the last merry word. Yet more can and should be said. The Renaissance debate about the Unities may be dismissed as being of no more than historical interest, that is true; but into this debate must come other considerations—for example, Shakespeare's well-known 'double clock.' When we see a performance of *Hamlet,* or when we read the play, our impression, actually inspired by some of the lines, is of a swiftly moving action. Only minute analysis demonstrates that the plot really presupposes the passing-by of weeks and months. Tear the plot of *Othello* to pieces in a similar way, and without doubt its progress must be regarded as hopelessly at variance with the shorter time-scheme which Shakespeare suggests to his audiences. While it is true that in some plays Shakespeare's fictional localities are made to change with an almost film-like variety, we must recall that the Elizabethan stage was bare and that consequently the spectators at the Globe were offered little or nothing in the way of visual alterations of scene; and we must also observe that, when scenic adornment became familiar in later years, the trend towards limitation in the number of settings was greater than the trend towards multiplication—partly inspired, no doubt, by practical, economic considerations, but owing something at least to other and inner claims.

It would, of course, be absurd to argue, as the Renaissance theorists did, that the Unities ought to be regarded as immutable 'rules'; indeed, for certain kinds of plays, such as romances and histories, extension in time and place becomes essential. On the other hand, there is much truth in Lessing's acute observation that, while the Unities were originally but logical requirements demanded by the presence of the chorus in the Greek theatre, they enshrined in themselves something of permanent worth. The Greeks

> submitted willingly to this restriction; but with an adroitness, with a sense of understanding, such that in seven cases out of nine they gained more than they lost. For they allowed this restriction to be the motive for so simplifying the action, carefully eliminating from it everything superfluous, that, reduced to its absolute essentials, it became simply an ideal of the action which was developed most felicitously in that form which demanded the least amplification from circumstances of time and place.[27]

T. S. Eliot's opinion is virtually the same. "The Unities," he says, "have for me, at least, a perpetual fascination. I believe they will be found highly desirable for the drama of the future. . . . The Unities do make for intensity."[28]

This brief examination of the Unities, then, although at first it might appear to be a digression, is not so. Ridiculous as the Renaissance discussions are, they were motivated by a realization of the concentration, patterning, simplicity, and boldness of approach ideally called for by the drama because of its peculiar nature. To exclude from our thoughts the implications that arise from a consideration of their significance may not be wise procedure. At the very least, even while we admit that the attempt to impose them as 'rules' was foolish and that Shakespeare paid no strict attention to them save in *The Tempest*, they serve to stress the principle of concentration normally required in all dramas which have hope of achieving more than immediate and temporary success.

The Impact of Realism

The Renaissance theory of the Unities illustrates one extreme—
the imposition upon the drama of conventional patterns so strict as
to become absurd when applied in an unimaginative manner. For a
complete contrast we have to move over the centuries and survey the
typical dramatic objectives of modern times—objectives which are
marked off sharply from those of all earlier dramatic writing.

Aristotle, the earliest and ultimately the greatest master of dramatic criticism, had before him a single basic form of drama, the
poetic—the fantastically lyrical Old Comedy of Aristophanes, and, in
particular, the poetic tragedy written by Æschylus, Sophocles, and
Euripides. For the moment comedy need not concern us, since it
inhabits a realm of its own; our attention has to be concentrated on
what for convenience may be styled the serious play. For Aristotle's
successors from the Renaissance onward to the eighteenth century
the serious play still meant fundamentally what it had meant to him
—poetic tragedy; but gradually a new concept began to emerge—
the serious play which is not tragedy, not comedy, not a mere
admixture of the two, and which, written in prose, seeks to reproduce on the stage the familiar surroundings, costume, speech of daily
life. Realism in the modern sense did not exist in ages past, was
indeed nowhere dreamed of; the majority of plays penned for our
theatres to-day are of this style.

This does not mean, of course, that from the very beginning drama
has not been accepted as a reflection of life. "Tragedy," declared
Aristotle, "is an imitation of an action that is serious, complete, and
of a certain magnitude." Although nowhere does he attempt to
define the word he uses—μίμησις, imitation—and although he seems
to employ it in a variety of senses, we can be reasonably sure that he
does not here imply a faithful representation of reality. When, for
example, he says that tragedy "seeks to imitate better" but comedy
"worse men than are," we realize that he is employing the word in
a very wide sense; and this realization is strengthened when we find
him declaring that "epic . . . and tragic poetry, and, moreover,
comedy, and dithyrambic poetry, and the greatest part of the art per-
taining to the flute and the lyre, are all entirely imitations." Indeed,
we might almost say that Aristotle is, in general, thinking either of
the utilization of real things—sounds and words—as opposed to the
reproduction of reality, or of the power which art has of creating
emotions such as might have been aroused by scenes of real life.

Since Aristotle's time his use of the word 'imitation' has been frequently echoed both by critics and by playwrights; Cicero thus described drama as "a copy of life, a mirror of custom, a reflection of truth," while Shakespeare, in the oft-quoted words given to his Hamlet, asserted that the drama's aim was "to hold, as 'twere, the mirror up to nature." At the same time, both playwrights and critics clearly refused to apply a narrow and literal interpretation to these words. Hédelin stated his opinion that "the stage does not present things as they have been, but as they ought to be"; all the 'rules' discussed by the neo-classic critics were conditioned by the thought that a play should be a carefully fashioned work of art; "the Poet," it was said, "must ... reform everything that is not accommodated to the Rules of his Art; as a Painter does when he works upon an imperfect Model."[29] Goethe gave fundamentally the same advice: "he who would work for the stage," he asserted, should "leave Nature in her proper place";[30] while Coleridge insisted that a clear distinction must be made between the concept of 'copy' and that of 'imitation' in a wider sense. Victor Hugo sought to make distinction between two senses of the word 'mirror':

> It has been said, 'The drama is a mirror in which nature is reflected'. But if this mirror be an ordinary mirror, a flat and polished surface, it will provide but a poor image of the objects, without relief—faithful, but colourless; it is well known that colour and light are lost in a simple reflection. The drama, therefore, must be a focusing mirror, which, instead of making weaker, collects and condenses the coloured rays, which will make of a gleam a light, of a light a flame. Then only is the drama worthy of being counted an art.[31]

And, finally, Sarcey demonstrated that mere nature set upon the stage would appear uninteresting and even false. "I hold," he declares,

> that reality, if presented on the stage truthfully, would appear false to the monster with the thousand heads which we call the public. We have defined dramatic art as the sum total by the aid of which, in the theatre, we represent life and give to the twelve hundred people assembled the illusion of truth.[32]

In opposition to such interpretations of 'imitation' and 'mirror,' however, a series of impulses gradually has led to the establishment in the modern theatre of a narrower concept of both. What, in fact, the stage has witnessed during the past couple of centuries is a series of waves each in its own way carrying the drama forward in the direction of realism. We can see one wave starting in the eighteenth century, producing Lillo's *George Barnwell* (1731) and various other sentimentally conceived dramas; a second, associated with Zola's naturalism in *Thérèse Raquin* (1873), wherein the author expressly states that he has "attempted continually to harmonize" his "setting with the ordinary occupations of" his "characters, so that they might not seem to 'play', but rather to 'live', before the spectators";[33] another taking shape in Ibsen's plays; still another in the plays of Chekhov. In all of these, although diversely, the dramatic writings spring from the attitude outlined by Beaumarchais in 1767; "if," he says,

> the theatre is a faithful picture of what happens in the world, our interest aroused thereby must of necessity have a close relationship to our manner of observing reality.[34]

Throughout its career, from its beginnings in eighteenth-century sentimentalism on to the present day, the realistic movement has ever directed itself towards a kind of drama distinct from the tragic. In an essay published in 1758, Diderot set the fashion by describing four sorts of play—(1) the 'gay comedy,' whose purpose was to ridicule and chastise vice, (2) 'serious comedy,' whose office it was "to depict virtue and the duties of man," (3) one kind of tragedy "concerned with our domestic troubles," and (4) another kind of tragedy "concerned with public catastrophes and the misfortunes of the great."[35] Thus was the *drame* established, and it has gone drifting on ever since, one peculiar feature in its history being that successive critics and playwrights, each enunciating a supposedly new 'realistic' aim, constantly have ignored the fact that that aim, instead of being something fresh and vital, was formulated a couple of centuries ago. Thus, for example, Eric Bentley, in 1946, can state that

> perhaps we have come to a stage when the nontragic drama may better represent us than tragedy; for our outlook is not tragic; and there is no adequate reason, I think, why it should be.[36]

This is almost exactly what Diderot was saying in 1758, and its sentiments underlie Beaumarchais' essay of 1767—

> The picture of an honest man in misfortune touches our hearts; the spectacle opens our hearts delicately, takes possession of them, and finally forces us to examine our own selves. When I see virtue persecuted, the victim of wickedness, and yet ever beautiful, ever glorious,

E

and preferable to all, even in the midst of misfortune—the effect of the drama in which this is displayed does not remain equivocal; it is virtue alone which holds my interest.... I have often noticed that a great prince, at the very height of happiness, glory, and success, excites in us nothing but the barren sentiment of admiration, which is a stranger to the heart.... What do I care, I, a peaceful subject in an eighteenth-century monarchy, for the revolutions of Athens and Rome? Of what real interest to me is the death of a Peloponnesian tyrant, or the sacrifice of a young princess at Aulis?[37]

Again and again have we heard these views echoed and re-echoed, always as though they were new and original thoughts: 'What do I care, I, a peaceful subject in an eighteenth-century monarchy—or an uneasy citizen in a twentieth-century democracy—for events outside the range of my own social life?'

Two or three basic assumptions are incorporated in this cult of the 'modern drama.' The first, expressed by Beaumarchais, is that in our age no real sympathy can be aroused for distant happenings and for those kings and princes who were the typical heroes of tragedy. The second is that, instead of admiration, sympathy in the narrower sense should be our objective. Hence the trend has ever been towards concentrating attention, first upon the Little Man, and next upon the Littlest Man. Dozens of playwrights have followed Galsworthy's lead in *Justice* (or, should we say, Lillo's lead in *The London Merchant?*), the hero of Arthur Miller's *Death of a Salesman* being only one of the latest among a long line of sentimentally conceived protagonists. And even when in our days figures from Greek myth are selected for dramatic treatment, the nobility of their surroundings is debased: Orpheus becomes shabby and Eurydice a tramp.

Diderot's emphasis upon "the duties of man" points to a final quality inherent in most of the 'modern' dramas. He dreams of a time when "the theatre will be the place where the most important moral problems will be discussed," and numerous dramatists, numerous critics, have gone on dreaming the same dream ever since. The 'drama of ideas' has become dominant, and more and more the ideas have tended to take precedence over the dramatic qualities. Twenty years ago Arthur H. Nethercot was lauding this development: comparing the later with the earlier playwrights working in the same tradition, he pointed out that

the difference between their use of such material and that of the modern dramatists of ideas is that until fairly recent times the ideas, problems, or themes were not chosen or presented primarily for their own sakes. They were used because they offered a striking character, a dramatic conflict, a good theatrical situation for comedy or melodrama, an opportunity to flatter or amuse an audience in its already established views or prejudices. Very seldom were they used as a challenge to society itself to reexamine its *mores*, to revaluate its motives, and to reform its methods and systems of thinking and behaving. It is in this last way that the 'drama of ideas' has become such a large part of the theatre today and has played such an important rôle in our modern culture.[38]

And only yesterday a prominent English dramatic critic, surveying the theatre of the fifties and searching for signs of encouragement, decided that the real sign of hope was to be found in

> a movement toward something fresher, something that was connected more intimately—more journalistically, perhaps—with daily experience.[39]

Discussion of plays in modern times thus regularly descends to examination of their social *milieux* and concepts.

This emphasis upon ideas, of course, assumes various forms. Almost every young and not-so-young playwright who aims at producing something more than a mere 'theatre-piece' begins by determining that his drama will put forward an 'idea' about a real or imagined error in contemporary social life. A few are content to follow Galsworthy's style as exemplified in such a play as *Strife*, shaping the rational concept in a fairly balanced manner; others may emulate Shaw's bouts of discussion, concentrating on diverse aspects of a selected thesis; more commonly, the author will deliberately enunciate his own conclusions in action and in dialogue, as Ibsen does in *A Doll's House*; and still more commonly will he intrude his own personality into his drama and make his work a piece of propaganda, wherein socialist or other concepts are of more consequence than any artistic values.

When the social ideas expressed in drama are invested with dominant importance and when the journalistic presentation of daily experience becomes the aim of the author, necessarily there is a complete regression from the sense of ordered form which we found in an extreme shape within the theory of the Unities. No doubt many modern plays are tightly constructed, but a taut framework is a thing wholly different from the sense of conventionality and pattern, which, in the past, had governed the minds of the playwrights. Thus the development of the realistic play of ideas has not merely brought in fresh content and a fresh general objective; much more significantly, it has substituted for the traditional an entirely different approach.

Ideas and Characters

Somerset Maugham, looking back on his career as a dramatist, has much to say about these plays of ideas and explains that he has thus enlarged upon the subject,

> because I think the demand for it is responsible for the lamentable decadence of our theatre.[40]

"The critics clamour for them," he says, adding that many critics, because they have perforce to stand aloof from the audience, may fail to discern what is truly best for the stage.

Maugham's opinion by no means stands alone. Indeed, many of those best able to take a wider survey have expressed the same sentiment in much the same terms. "Realism came in," remarked W. B. Yeats several decades ago, "and every change towards realism coincided with a decline in dramatic energy,"[41] and thirty years later Ronald Peacock, while recognizing that "the new realism cannot be divorced from powerful influences and beliefs of the time," decided that

> its expressiveness is achieved by a partial betrayal of the law of art, insofar as a 'truthful' or 'normalized' representation replaces the free working of the imagination.[42]

The realistic play of ideas purports to depict truthfully, but in fact it is concerned only with surface or external reality, so that "society" is "seen through blinkered eyes."

Clearly, these judgments require to be scrutinized with care, not only in general but in particular. Two aspects of the problem, form and medium, will demand fuller treatment later; but we may proceed immediately towards consideration of some other special questions—and at the very start this emphasis on ideas must have our closer attention.

From what has already been said, it becomes perfectly obvious that the playhouse does not provide a fitting arena for thought. "The fact," says Somerset Maugham,

> that the general mentality of an audience is so very much lower than that of its more intellectual members is a factor that the author must

deal with. I think it definitely reduces prose drama to a minor
place.... The only ideas that can affect them when they are welded
together in that unity which is an audience are those commonplace,
fundamental ideas which are almost feelings. These, the root ideas
of poetry, are love, death and the destiny of man.[43]

It is, of course, entirely possible to argue that the formal distinction
made here between thought and feeling is false. Thus, for instance,
Erich Heller refers to one of Hamlet's speeches:[44]

In so far as Hamlet's thought makes sense, Shakespeare must have
been thinking it, although not necessarily as the first to do so and
certainly in a manner of thinking which is more imaginative and
intuitive than rationally deliberate. To define 'thinking' in such a
way that the activity which Shakespeare pursued in composing the
speeches of Hamlet, or Ulysses, or Lear has to be dismissed as 'non-
thought', is to let thinking fall into the rationalist trap from which it
is likely to emerge as a cripple, full of animosity against that other de-
formed creature, mutilated in the same operation: the Romantic
emotion.

That is perfectly true, and it requires due emphasis in this age; but
fundamentally Heller's position is a philosophic, not a dramatic, one.
When Walter Kerr declares:

The playwright in our time has become a thinker. It often seems to
me that the best thing a playwright can do is put off thinking as long
as possible—[45]

he has in mind something entirely different. Doubtless it would be
foolish to deny that thought finds its place in Shakespeare's plays,
but the thought present there has two qualities: it does not obtrude
itself as a set of ideas cogitated in the dramatist's mind which he
wishes to impress on his auditors and it is thought which, as it were,
has been transmuted into an emotional form. The very language
which Shakespeare employs illustrates this. We are expected to react
emotionally, not to apply logic and reason. Hamlet's phrase about
taking "arms against a sea of troubles" is puzzling, if we try to
interpret it rationally; and in fact numerous commentators have been
so worried by it that they have been induced to postulate an error in
the text and to suggest some rather foolish emendations. Yet these
lines are emotionally evocative, precisely of the kind to make direct
impact on an audience.

This example of a single phrase has its bearing upon the wider approach: what is exhibited in the microcosm becomes a reflection of the macrocosm. The characteristic method of much modern playwriting is to build the drama's action upon and around an idea of the author's own and to keep the expression of this idea bound to rational terms. The result is commonly fatal. Pirandello was right in stating that "the new drama possesses a distinct character from the old: whereas the latter had as its basis passion, the former is the expression of the intellect."[46]

By its very nature, however, the theatre (and the drama) must depend upon emotion, and, as a result we are confronted by dozens, scores, hundreds of modern dramas in which war is being waged between what may be called the genuinely dramatic impulse and the non-dramatic intellectual purpose. Let us take Charles Morgan's *The Burning Glass* as an example. The preface to the printed text shows that the author was intent upon expounding an intellectual thesis—that recent inventions are more dangerous for mankind in peace than in war. The preface is brilliantly written; but on the stage the 'idea' which Morgan sought to express conflicted with the dramatist's power over character and in any event was far too 'intellectual' for an audience easily to grasp. "One of the most fascinating struggles to watch in the contemporary theater," remarks Kerr,

> is that between the upsurging artist and the stubborn dialectician in the same man. Ibsen was surely an artist, but an artist who stumbled on a dialectical time and a dialectical form. He had an instinct for character, and a passionate determination to make points. The two are in eternal conflict.[47]

The plain truth, then, is that the drama reveals itself as a literary form which, precisely because it addresses itself to an audience, is unfitted to convey the 'thoughts'—the 'messages,' the propagandist beliefs—of its author. That is why the modern cult of the dramatist as thinker is inimical to the very being of the stage. What an audience wants is what Shakespeare gave it and what Shakespeare's contemporary, Thomas Dekker, described in his prologue to *If It be not Good, the Devil's in It*: "Give me that man," he said, who

> Can call the banished auditor home and tie
> His ear with golden chains to his melody—
> Can draw with adamantine pen even creatures
> Forg'd out o' the hammer on tip-toe to reach up
> And from rare silence clap their brawny hands
> T' applaud what their charm'd soul scarce understands—

That man give me whose breast, filled by the Muses
With raptures, into a second them infuses,
Can give an actor sorrow, rage, joy, passion,
Whilst he again, by self-same agitation,
Commands the hearer, sometimes drawing out tears,
Then smiles, and fills them both with hopes and fears.

And the extraordinary fact is that, in our own days, the banished auditor, who, rightly bored with the dull realistic plays of ideas, had given up his attendance at the theatre, is now being called home by Shakespeare. So outstanding has been the recently growing vogue of his dramas that even *Time*, always intent upon the topical, has of late devoted a lengthy centre article to the theme.[48] Noting the hundreds upon hundreds of Shakespearian performances being witnessed by hundreds of thousands of spectators, this article sets out to determine the cause. Sir Isaiah Berlin's contrasting symbols of the hedgehog and the fox provide a starting-point:

> The hedgehogs are the great systematic thinkers, and, since life is not systematic, they are also the great excluders. The great men of feeling, of whom Shakespeare was the greatest, are the great includers. That may be why men turn to Shakespeare, as they seem to, in especially troubled times.[49]

Beyond that, however, there is something else. Shakespeare's tragic characters are great-souled; they claim and they deserve much:

> One reason why the Willy Lomans, the Blanche DuBoises and the poor, driven people of O'Neill are pseudo-tragic and fail to exalt an audience is because they are small-souled. They claim little and deserve little. They cannot fall because they are already down.

Time is not a 'highbrow' magazine, and, just because it is not, its realization that Shakespeare has something to give to audiences which they cannot get in the modern drama becomes a matter of prime significance. Furthermore, its comments stress the essential fact that it is Shakespeare's work which appeals and not simply the efforts of the producers. Those directors who approach Shakespeare's plays with the thought that something must be done to render them 'popular' or who strive to make them exemplify social 'meanings' betray their own lack of sensitivity to what the public is craving for. An American commentator recently referred to the television *Hamlet* presented in the United States in 1959. "The director," he remarks, decided to emphasize 'melodrama and action'. When he was asked why, he declared, "Frankly, to get a bigger rating. While it's fine to stimulate interest among the Shakespearian societies, the schools and colleges, I believe our big guns should be trained on the larger audience, the people who are afraid of longhair, egghead and Shakespeare, and who associate these things with everything dull.

But, as *Time's* analysis shows, this is precisely the theatrical method likely to destroy what may well be the theatre's most glowing hope in the present; this director's words display his insensitivity, his unsuitability for the task to which he had been assigned, and his lack of understanding of what has caused to-day's upsurge of interest in Shakespeare's works.

If *Time* is right in its assessment, then the realistic play of ideas and its associated methods of production have been banishing auditors from the theatre not only because those auditors are not and never have been interested in 'ideas,' not only because the modern styles in production have laid emphasis on the physically material, but also because the auditors could not find in these plays or productions the boldly conceived characters and the imaginative power which, when not reduced to terms of 'melodrama and action,' *Hamlet* and its companion dramas can offer them. "Have we not been in error," ironically inquires W. B. Yeats,

> in demanding from our playwrights personages who do not transcend our common actions any more than our common speech? If we are in the right, all antiquity has been in error.[50]

"It has been justly remarked," Gustave Le Bon declares,

> that on the stage a crowd demands from the hero of the piece a degree of courage, morality, and virtue that is never to be found in real life.[51]

And Francis Fergusson makes the interesting observation that, in Continental drama, with the development of realism, the tragic characters of Racine faded away while the confidants (who in the Racinian plays had been the repositories of logic, reason, and fact) were elevated into their rôles.[52] The same observation might have been even further extended. All that seems to remain of *Hamlet* in the hands of some modern playwrights is the rational Horatio and the hysterical Ophelia.

The Modern Way and the Ancient

The realistic play of ideas, then, is working against the theatre's grain. It is quite true that among the rationalistically conceived dramas of our time there are numbers which deal with their subjects in an emotional manner, but for the most part they do so in the wrong way. The theatre demands of the serious dramatist what may be styled controlled, extroverted passion; in a large degree the great playwright becomes a god looking down upon the creatures his imagination has fashioned, breathing passions into them, sympathizing with them, but remaining himself always above them. When emotion intrudes into the modern realistic drama, only too often it is merely the involved, introverted emotion of the author himself, and consequently for passion is substituted a kind of sentimentalism, vacuously mild or hysterical according to its intensity. Intellectual 'idea' and sentimental approach have characterized this sort of drama from the days of Richard Cumberland down to the present.

Apart from all of those considerations, there are others. The intellectual and realistic endeavour tends in various ways to make the dramatist concentrate upon inessentials and to neglect the exploitations of opportunities offered by the theatrical form. Thus, for instance, the modern dramatic author becomes mightily concerned about consistency; but inconsistency on the stage not only does not matter but also may prove positively valuable. The reason is not far to seek. Since the audience has to accept a play as it flows on through its two or three hours and since there exists no chance of turning back to earlier episodes, the impact of each scene has peculiar force in and for itself. To aim at absolute consistency in matters of fact between scene and scene is a waste of energy and possibly of precious words; more importantly, it deprives the author of an instrument apt to his hand.

In perusing the text of *Othello*, for instance, the solitary reader may be struck by the fact that, while Cassio greets with palpable astonishment the news of Othello's marriage, he is described elsewhere as a kind of go-between, acting for the Moor in his wooing. No audience has ever noted the discrepancy, precisely because the impact of each scene, being direct and strong, has the effect of concentrating attention upon it and upon it alone. And for the impression to be created in each of these scenes the inconsistent treatment of Cassio's association with Othello is of definite value. Thus the drama can, as it were, take short cuts. In writing *Macbeth* Shakespeare does not want to complicate the action by introducing any children belonging to the guilty couple; but, when he needs to, in one scene he may refer to Lady Macbeth's having given suck, in another scene he may cause Macbeth to utter words implying that he has a son, and in yet another scene he may make Macduff declare that the tyrant has no children. Thus, a dramatist like Shakespeare, working with and not against the stage, can, through inconsistency, gain effects which otherwise he could not achieve.

A further extension of the stress on fact, consistency, and logic appears in the method of delineating the characters. Clearly, a dramatist, although he does not possess the novelist's wider scope or power of direct comment, has one important asset—the fact that his persons are interpreted, or are intended to be interpreted, by actors. The audience, seeing the actor or actress on the stage, immediately is induced to accept the fictional character as 'real.' Insofar as this process is concerned, certainly, there exists no difference between the Elizabethan spectators' reception of Hamlet in the person of Burbage and a later audience's reception of St Joan in the person of Sybil Thorndike. Unfortunately, however, there is a wide and inescapable difference between the opportunities offered to a Shakespeare and the opportunities offered to a Shaw. Nowadays, a playwright may pen some work with a particular star-actor in mind, but Shakespeare, writing for a more or less permanent company, had the advantage, while actually composing a play, of mentally casting most of the parts for the members of his company. Their 'lines of business' were known to him, and we can actually catch glimpses in the original text of *Much Ado* of the way in which his mind produced a kind of superimposed image of Dogberry–Kemp and Verges–Cowley: we may believe that when he was penning *Hamlet* he saw the Prince as Burbage and had an image of some other actor as Polonius.

That the modern dramatist does not have Shakespeare's opportunity is regrettable, nor can he be blamed for not having it. Here we are confronted with one of those theatrical conditions which we can do no other save accept. But one important conclusion follows from the observation of Shakespeare's apparent practice. Shakespeare has not formed in his mind concepts of 'living' persons to serve as the characters in his plays; rather has he fused together in his imagination fictional images and the semblances of living actors. His characters, then, are conceived theatrically; they are not living beings or even the direct reflections of actual men and women. There is an anecdote which declares that Dogberry was created out of a village constable whom Shakespeare had encountered in his journeys from Stratford to London. Possibly this story may be true; but it seems far more likely that the Dogberry of *Much Ado* arose from the author's imagining how Kemp would behave had he been in the constable's office.

Shakespeare is not alone in this. In effect, all the persons in the greater, more enduring plays are nothing but emblems of characters. We may, if we care, express this truth by saying that the fictional persons, ultimately, are not human at all, but purely symbols of a poetic vision[53]—although such phrasing seems to carry us rather far from the theatre. Better is it to think of these figments of the imagination as if they were akin to, yet soaring far beyond, the familiar figures of the *commedia dell' arte*—the masks vitalized by the actors, each contributing to the general design. The *commedia dell' arte*, indeed, provides us with a useful pointer towards appreciating the way in which the fictional persons in a drama take their place on the boards. Harlequin appears in a wholly formalized costume, a dark mask covering half of his face; manifestly he has nothing to do with the actual world of the spectators. Yet, if Harlequin is skilfully acted, these spectators, within a few minutes, will be sharing a double impression: the masked figure and the fictional person will have fused into one, and at the same time the audience will go more than half-way towards endowing the conventionally clad figure with a living soul, accepting him imaginatively as a human being, laughing with him, sympathizing with him. The process is exactly the same with a character such as Macbeth. What Shakespeare has given is merged with the actor's personality, and for the audience there is, on the one hand, a constant awareness of the performer-pretending-to-be-Macbeth and a desire imaginatively to accept Macbeth as a living person.

Naturally, even within the sphere of the older drama, the mask-like quality differs from playwright to playwright. In the tragedies of Æschylus, for example, ordinary personal relations among the *dramatis personæ* hardly exist at all; the characters are presented in monumental simplicity, the emblem or mask is all; Sophocles permits himself to introduce more 'human' touches in his dialogue, so that the mask-quality is already modified in the lines of the play even before an actor-interpreter takes it over; in the plays of Shakespeare these 'human' touches are so frequent as almost to cheat us into ignoring the presence of the mask entirely.[54] Perhaps there exists some justification for Yeats' view that comedy allows more of this humanization than tragedy. "Character," he avers, "is continually present in comedy alone":

> There is much tragedy, that of Corneille, that of Racine, that of Greece and Rome, where its place is taken by passions and motives, one person being jealous, another full of love or remorse or pride or anger.

In Shakespeare's tragedies, however, an element of comedy enters in; these tragedies present character,

> but we notice that it is in the moments of comedy that character is defined, in Hamlet's gaiety let us say; while amid the great moments, when Timon orders his tomb, when Hamlet cries to Horatio 'absent thee from felicity awhile,' when Antony names 'of many thousand kisses the poor last', all is lyricism, unmixed passion, 'the integrity of fire.' Nor does character ever attain to complete definition in these lamps ready for the taper, no matter how circumstantial and gradual the opening of events, as it does in Falstaff who has no passionate purpose to fulfil, or as it does in Henry the Fifth whose poetry, never touched by lyric heat, is oratorical.[55]

In many respects, the dramatist, even in the sphere of comedy, works rather as an illusionist does, cheating the willing spectators into seeing things which, both because of the limited framework of the dramatic form and because of the bold, enlarged effects which the audience demands, are not really there. "The dramatist's characters exist in their scenes and nowhere else"[56] is a truth always to be remembered, and for Shakespeare the stress, as we have seen, is often upon the word 'scenes.' He, and other masters of the dramatic working under conditions propitious to their art, can sacrifice factual consistency to effect, since they know that an audience "is careless of probability if the situation excites its interest."[57]

Probability, however, is one of the things about which the realistic play of ideas worries most. The contrast between the two attitudes may well be exemplified by reference to the opening scene of *King Lear*. It may confidently be asserted that no audience finds any puzzlement in the terse manner of Shakespeare's exposition—unless, perchance, the production is so bad that it permits individual spectators to start asking questions. The situation excites interest; the persons are there materially before us; we do not ask why, if the division of the kingdom has been made, there should be this discussion of the question now, nor do we seek for motivations in the characters beyond those immediately offered to us. When, however, Tolstoi turned to this tragedy both as a reader and as an exponent of the 'modern' style in drama, he found himself puzzled and dismayed. Contradictions loomed up before him, and he came to demand explanations for the actions of the characters which no audience asks for. Turning to the old tragi-comic *King Leir*, which carefully outlines the events preceding Shakespeare's first scene, which tells us that Lear has been so much engaged in governmental business as not to have had the opportunity of knowing his daughters, and that the evil sisters had engineered a situation wherein Cordelia would be forced to anger her father—Tolstoi decided that Shakespeare's dramatic technique falls far short of that exhibited by his anonymous contemporary.

There are few readers of the two plays dealing with Lear's story who would be prepared to endorse this view; Tolstoi's essay thus remains an oddity. Yet in itself it stands as a warning against the application of intellectually conceived judgments and factual considerations to a form of literature where they have not, or should not have, any pertinence.

In general, the modern realistic play of ideas has led towards three main kinds of character-drawing, all mutually contradictory yet all concurring in pursuing a false path. The first is the common subordination of the fictional persons to the 'thesis' which the play sets out to expound. In the Shakespearian drama characters are often subordinated to the emotional, imaginative visions which form its core; but that is vastly different from the modern method, especially since this modern method, based on the factual and on supposedly consistent rationality, tends, as the Shakespearian method does not, to draw attention to any character falsifications consequent upon anxiety to emphasize an idea.

The second shows itself in the application of modern psychological studies, sometimes ill-understood, to the drama, leading both towards the style of composition associated with the work of Jean-Jacques Bernard, and towards those theories of theatrical interpretation which urge actors to regard as real the persons they play. The approach savours greatly of such deservedly ridiculed essays as the nineteenth century's *Girlhood of Shakespeare's Heroines* and encourages a kind of stage-interpretation which *Time* typically pillories:

> As for acting, Method-mad U.S. actors swallow a character like medicine and then release him through their pores in involuntary shudders.[58]

The comment might well be applied to many modern playwrights as well.

The third way is that of Bertolt Brecht. According to him the actor ought to utter his lines not "like an improvisation, but like a quotation," so that the audience should develop a "critical" attitude to the fictional character—a critical attitude which is to be deliberately encouraged by the performer in his interpretation. This resembles many other modern theatrical theories—the imposition of concepts alien to the quality of the stage upon dramatic composition and upon histrionic method. Actually, however, Brecht's own creative method in his best plays contradicts his critical, theoretical precepts.

All of these approaches are potentially destructive because they are built upon intellectually conceived propositions and because they assume that, being modern, they must be improvements on the old. In spite of our present-day social and philosophical doubts and anxieties, we are, in these realms, strangely self-confident and self-satisfied. We are sure that the Greek tragic dramatists and Shakespeare "are newly legible in our time,"[59] that we understand them as they have never truly been understood before. And we tend to look upon artistic forms as though they were scientific in nature—implying that, just as modern science is better than Greek or Elizabethan science, so the modern theatre must be better than the old. In a recent discussion engaged in by the radio 'Critics'[60] the question arose concerning why present-day spectators do not find Charlie Chaplin's early films as amusing as they once were; and the conclusion was arrived at that mime and ballet are 'primitive' theatrical forms and that "we must grow out of them." This is typical of our whole attitude: 'We are modern and therefore what we have is better than what people had in the past.' And a remark made by Sartre in an address which he delivered at the Sorbonne is equally typical of its complement. Drama, in his opinion, deals with the efforts of a politically minded individual or group to translate a wish into an accomplishment; the drama thus becomes simply an instrument designed to serve a social purpose.

If we have hopes that the theatre will endure and recover its ancient strength these comments and judgments are ill auguries for the future.

NOTES TO CHAPTER 2

1. J. E. Spingarn, *Creative Criticism* (new and enlarged ed. 1931), p. 23.
2. J. E. Spingarn, *op. cit.*, p. 25.
3. L. C. Knights, *How Many Children had Lady Macbeth?* (1933), p. 34.
4. J. E. Spingarn, *op. cit.*, p. 23.
5. J. E. Spingarn, *op. cit.*, pp. 29, 31.
6. J. E. Spingarn, *op. cit.*, pp. 55–56.
7. *The Twentieth Century*, clxix, 1961, p. 214.
8. W. Somerset Maugham, *The Summing Up* (1938), p. 131.
9. J. B. Priestley, *The Art of the Dramatist* (1957), p. 3.
10. J. L. Styan, *The Elements of Drama* (1960), p. 7.
11. Theodore Hoffman, 'An Audience of Critics and the Lost Art of "Seeing" Plays' (*Tulane Drama Review*, iv, 1959, p. 41).
12. Letter to Robert Lloyd, July 26, 1801.
13. 'On the Tragedies of Shakespeare.'
14. L. C. Knights, *op. cit.*, p. 34.
15. T. S. Eliot, 'A Dialogue on Poetic Drama,' *Selected Essays* (1932), p. 44. For discussion of the application of myth to the study of drama see Francis Fergusson, *The Idea of a Theater* (1949), pp. 26–32, and T. R. Henn, *The Harvest of Tragedy* (1956), pp. 80–92. Clifford Leech has an excellent essay, 'The "Capability" of Shakespeare' (*Shakespeare Quarterly*, xi, 1960, pp. 123–136), in which he stresses the dangers inherent in modern critical trends in the interpretation of Shakespeare's plays.
16. Norman N. Holland, *The First Modern Comedies* (1959), pp. 179–180.
17. *Plays and Controversies* (1923), p. 416.
18. Eric Bentley, *The Playwright as Thinker* (1946). Complaints about the evils of the present-day commercial theatre, the 'Entertainment Industry,' are widespread and are voiced by both dramatists and critics. Particular note may be made of the remarks on this subject in Francis Fergusson, *The Idea of a Theater* (1949), pp. 64–66.
19. See, however, J. A. Moore, *Sophocles and Aretê* (1938), where stress is laid on Sophocles' pursuit of aristocratic 'virtue.'
20. W. Kerr, *How not to write a Play* (1955).
21. Prologue to Arthur Murphy, *All in the Wrong* (1761).
22. We may, of course, omit from consideration here the shorter pieces which at certain periods have proved theatrically popular—the eighteenth century's 'afterpieces' and the nineteenth century's 'curtain-raisers.' What we are concerned with is the upward, not the downward, limit.
23. H. B. Charlton, *Castelvetro's Theory of Poetry* (1913), p. 84.
24. *Samson Agonistes*, preface.
25. H. B. Charlton, *op. cit.*, p. 84.
26. George Farquhar, *A Discourse upon Comedy* (1701).
27. G. E. Lessing, *Hamburgische Dramaturgie*, no. 46.
28. T. S. Eliot, "A Dialogue on Dramatic Poetry," in *Selected Essays* 1932), p. 58.

29. *The Whole Art of the Stage* (1684), p. 65.
30. *European Theories of the Drama* (1919), p. 339.
31. *Cromwell* (1828), preface, p. xl.
32. F. Sarcey, *A Theory of the Theatre* (1916), p. 31.
33. *Thérèse Raquin*, preface, p. 11.
34. *Essai sur le genre dramatique sérieux* (1767).
35. *De la poésie dramatique* (1758).
36. Eric Bentley, *The Playwright as Thinker* (1946), p. 241.
37. *Essai sur le genre dramatique sérieux* (1767).
38. A. H. Nethercot, *The Drama of Ideas* (1941), p. 15.
39. Kenneth Tynan in *The Observer*, December 27, 1959.
40. W. S. Maugham, *The Summing Up* (1938), p. 140. For a director's views on the subject see Tyrone Guthrie, *A Life in the Theatre* (1960), pp. 175–192.
41. W. B. Yeats, *Plays and Controversies* (1923), p. 127.
42. Ronald Peacock, *The Art of Drama* (1957), pp. 210–211.
43. W. S. Maugham, *The Summing Up* (1938), pp. 134–135.
44. Erich Heller, *The Disinherited Mind* (1952), p. 121.
45. Walter Kerr, *How Not to Write a Play* (1855), pp. 74.
46. Quoted in Eric Bentley, *The Playwright as Thinker* (1946), p. 180.
47. W. Kerr, *op. cit.*, p. 56.
48. *Time*, July 4, 1960.
49. Sir Isaiah Berlin, *The Hedgehog and the Fox* (1953).
50. W. B. Yeats, *Plays and Controversies* (1923), p. 121.
51. G. Le Bon, *The Crowd* (1897), p. 37.
52. Francis Fergusson, *The Idea of a Theater* (1949), pp. 66–67.
53. See J. L. Styan, *The Elements of Drama* (1960), pp. 163–169.
54. On the characters in the plays of Æschylus and Sophocles, see H. D. F. Kitto, *Form and Meaning in Drama* (1956).
55. W. B. Yeats, *Essays* (1924), p. 297.
56. J. B. Priestley, *The Art of the Dramatist* (1957), p. 17.
57. W. Somerset Maugham, *The Summing Up* (1938), p. 132.
58. *Time*, July 4, 1960, p. 46.
59. Francis Fergusson, *The Idea of a Theater* (1949), p. 196.
60. June 4, 1960.

3

The Dramatic Kinds

IF ANYONE takes the trouble to look through the pages of the
annual *Era Almanack* from 1860 onwards—or, better still, if
anyone examines year by year the dramas submitted for licensing
to the Lord Chamberlain's Office—one must at once be struck by a
peculiar fact. Up to the close of the nineteenth century, almost all
these dramatic compositions were classified by their authors in
categories; many of the categories, it is true, were of then recent
coinage—such as 'extravaganza' and 'comedietta'—but the majority,
'comedy' and 'tragedy' in particular, were of time-honoured an-
tiquity; and the more recently invented terms owed their being
obviously to the general trend towards the classifying principle.
When, however, we move on past the year 1900, the majority of
such works are simply labelled 'plays' or 'dramas'; occasionally,
'comedy' is applied to them; 'farce' occurs with less frequency;
'melodrama' lingers on sporadically; 'tragedy,' for all practical purposes, disappears.

At first glance it might seem that thus the modern drama has won
a new freedom, and there are many critics who would endorse this
view. "A classification of plays by types," it has been said,

> is today supremely unhelpful; to stamp a play as a tragedy or comedy,
> a melodrama or farce, is to bind it by rules external to itself and
> illegitimately borrowed.[1]

This sounds eminently reasonable, yet the tendency towards classification by kinds requires to be very carefully explored not only in
connexion with those antique Greek and Elizabethan dramas specifically called tragedies and comedies, but also in connexion with the
modern theatrical works levelled under the one general term of
'play.'

To begin with, we must fully admit that the history of the theatre
shows two forces at work; the one, which might be styled the conser-

F

vative, tends to keep plays in strictly marked groups, of which tragedy and comedy stand as prime representatives, while the other tends to induce playwrights to break away, to mingle elements appropriate to the various groups and to establish new forms. Thus, even in the days of the Greeks we find a New Comedy supplanting the Old Comedy and in the plays of Euripides there is clearly evident an attempt to deviate from the established tragic pattern. Some centuries later Plautus styled his *Amphitryon* a tragi-comedy because it introduced characters properly belonging to the tragic realm and set them in an amusing adventure. Later, during the Renaissance period, tragicomedy assumed diverse shapes, often mixing together scenes of tragic import and scenes of hilarious fun; and Fletcher could reach a stage where he confessed he did not know what to call one of his dramas:

> I dare not call it *Comedy* or *Tragedy*; 'tis perfectly neither; A Play it is.[2]

Thus was the vague designation 'play' adumbrated, although a couple of centuries were to pass by before it became familiarly established.

At first glance, we might feel prepared to believe that in this development appears nothing save an entirely proper sloughing-off of ancient and useless traditionalism. Our argument would be that tragedy and comedy came into being as part of the religious atmosphere associated with the Greek stage, that because of the strong influence of the classic authors these categories continued to be maintained during periods when their true force had evaporated, that in any case the retention of specific descriptive terms was due largely to the traditionally conservative pronouncements of later critics, and that therefore there is no real reason why the terms themselves should be preserved. A play, we might continue, exists in and for itself; to describe it by a generic name is foolish, useless, and even distracting. In any event, life does not separate itself into watertight compartments; a drama is a mirror of life; and consequently it cannot, and ought not to be, more narrowly defined than by the simple use of the term 'play.'

All of such argumentation sounds persuasive: yet several other considerations must be taken into account. One thing which attracts our attention is that, among literary forms, drama is peculiar in its generic nomenclature. For the most part, poems are presented to us without any distinguishing labels, and many novels—which are, of course, the nearest relatives of plays—are published merely with their own specific titles. Throughout the whole history of the theatre, on the other hand, there has been this steady trend towards the indication of dramatic categories.

Apart from this salient fact, there is another. Within the realm of non-dramatic poetry, if and when generic descriptions are employed, these tend to refer rather to the external shape of the verse than to the attitude of the poet towards his subject matter. No doubt we can speak of an 'epic' approach or spirit; no doubt a 'dirge' can be nothing save a song of lament; but most of these terms, such as 'sonnet,' are concerned with the outward lineaments rather than with inner qualities. A sonnet is a poem of fourteen decasyllabic lines riming in one of half a dozen established ways; any particular sonnet may be light or monumental, serious or gay, a song of praise or a song of grief. We recognize a sonnet by its structural shape, not by its particular tone.

Something else reveals itself when we turn to prose fiction. Here the generic terms generally apply to the nature of the subject-matter rather than to the manner in which this subject-matter is dealt with. We speak familiarly of an historical, a domestic, a detective novel, indicating that the first deals with life in a past age, the second with ordinary situations and characters, the third with crimes and their exposure. No attempt is made here to suggest the attitudes of the authors towards their themes; the terms employed remain bound and restricted by the nature of the contents of the works themselves.

Most of the terms applied to drama are of a completely different kind. True, we find in the Elizabethan period such a description as 'history,' which does not in any respect point to the approach which has been taken towards the historical material itself; and in the modern period 'detective play' parallels the 'detective story' of prose fiction. Usually, however, the theatrical terminology possesses an import of its own, stressing the way in which the author has looked upon his plot and characters. It is not merely that ancient classical terms have been carried on traditionally through the ages; even when generic names unthought of by the Greeks find their way on to the stage they are generally either expressive of an attitude or, if originally they sprang from another source, become modified in time so that they are used to express an attitude.[3]

To make this clear, it may be well to take a particular example, and none could be more appropriate than that term of comparatively recent vintage, 'melodrama.'

Melodrama

Originally the word 'melodrama' crept in on the Continent during the early years of the seventeenth century to describe the musical plays designed by some enthusiasts in imitation of the musical dramas of the ancients. In effect, modern 'opera' was thus born, and in Italy the word *melodramma* long has continued in this particular sense.

The employment of the word in the significance of 'opera,' however, is only part, and the least important part, of the story. Towards the close of the eighteenth century and the beginning of the nineteenth century, France and England saw the re-introduction of the term in the sense simply of a play which had some musical accompaniments, and as such it was in origin nothing save a convenient theatrical description based on purely external features. Thus, for example, in the special conditions of the English theatre at that time, when theoretically only the larger patent houses had the right to produce plays with spoken dialogue, and when the minor theatres succeeded in evading the statutory restrictions by the performance of shorter pieces, in which the dialogue was uttered against a background of instrumental music and was accompanied by some songs, for a time the word 'melodrama,' associated with another word 'burletta,' came to be used, not for the purpose of indicating the style and content of a play, but merely for that of outlining its external shape. Shakespeare's *Hamlet* thus was a 'tragedy'; but, if a playwright took Shakespeare's work, cut it down to three acts instead of five, caused the actors to speak the lines against a musical background and provided five or six songs, the resultant piece was properly styled a 'melodrama.'

Then something very interesting occurred. It was found that the shape of the melodrama influenced its style, that this style was of a kind which could be found elsewhere in the theatre's history and that no term had as yet been invented to apply to such plays. The result of this was that in England, even when a new act of 1843 released the minor theatres from their earlier limitations, and when thus the term itself no longer had any technical significance, the word 'melodrama' was retained with a special inner meaning. When men spoke of melodrama in the late nineteenth century, or when we use the term to-day, the original implication of musical accompaniment is absent. 'Melodrama' now suggests a particular approach to dramatic material and a particular way of handling that material. We have no hesitation in saying that some of Euripides' plays exhibit melodramatic features, of stating that *Macbeth* is a tragedy based on a melodramatic theme, of differentiating *Hoffman* as in essence a melodrama.

The important things to observe here are the facts that the need for the term has been felt, and that even the modern period, when playwrights are breaking away from the original dramatic kinds, has thus been impelled to establish a new kind of its own, or at least to find a name for a kind which had hitherto remained nameless.

Nor is the word employed in any careless sense. We have to acknowledge that, when we use it, it serves to describe and delimit a dramatic form we instantly recognize, even if we may find it difficult to put our impressions into precise rational shape. Thus, T. R. Henn quotes an anonymous "philosopher, with a classical background," writing on the subject of tragedy. After discussing the element of spectacle in the performance of such a drama, this author comments:

> The chief danger is perhaps that the scenic manager will turn the play into a melodrama, a situation which may perhaps be defined as one in which emotions are depicted on the stage, or suggested through décor and scenery, that are disproportionately greater than those likely to be more than momentarily aroused in the audience, even when the play is given an otherwise good performance. Melodrama may thus be either the fault of the author (in which case the play 'is' a melodrama) or of the performers (in which case it 'becomes' one).[4]

This statement is confused and lacks clarity in expression, but it demonstrates at least the awareness of a quality in what we call melodrama which marks it out as distinct. Henn's own definition, that melodrama is

> that type of play which attempts to produce the emotions appropriate to tragedy on insufficient emotional pretexts: through *inorganic* conceptions of character and plot,[5]

clearly comes much closer to an adequate description of the effect produced, and it is interesting to observe that, despite the differences in the forms of these two definitions, the same general impression manifestly lies behind both.

Maybe, instead of a formal definition, an effort to determine and list certain salient features of the melodramatic form will provide a better approach. First, when we speak of melodrama we always think of something with hardly any 'literary' quality, offering dialogue which does no more than provide the bare minimum necessary for an understanding of the plot and the positions of the persons involved. Its structure, therefore, is crude; no attempt has been made to individualize the characters, and consequently we think of melodramatic characters not in terms of separately imagined persons but in terms of types. In each example of the species we have the same performers—innocent heroine, noble hero, hero's faithful friend, villain, villainess; it does not matter what their environment may be or what names are given to them, they remain always the same. This leads to a second observation, that melodrama is ever conceived in our minds as being 'theatrical.' Not only are the characters not individualized, they take shape as stock stage figures which, in the text, only rarely show living persons behind the masks. Iago may be a puzzling character, but we believe in him; no villain in melodrama can really be credible. Our emotions in witnessing a melodramatic performance, therefore, are, as it were, purely fictional; we are always conscious of the make-belief, never immersed in it. The villain may be hissed and the hero applauded, but hissing and applause are both part of a game played between performers who do not try to make their impersonations intimate and spectators who only half-pretend for the moment to accept these impersonations. A third quality consists in the element of exaggeration. Even during the time of the nineteenth-century domestic melodramas, the wicked squires and the violent incidents generally existed in the realm of the completely improbable; the later Drury Lane melodramas, in which the heroine often spent three hours in moving from imminent destruction to imminent destruction as the scenes unfolded, were but a more blatant exhibition of a feature which ever formed the melodramatic core. And with this, finally, is to be noted the determination on the part both of writers and performers to keep the audience constantly supplied with a series of thrills.

If we take all these qualities together, we realize that melodrama means for us the type of play and performance which is bound entirely to the limits of the stage, which reaches its effects almost always by crude and generally physical means, which never seeks to persuade an audience that the actors and actions are related to life outside the theatre's walls. If, therefore, we say that some tragedy has a basis in melodrama, we intend to imply that certain parts of the plot are so violent or that certain characters are conceived in such exaggerated terms as to make us think of melodramatic devices; on the other hand, we recognize that the play in question is not a melodrama precisely because the author, by the exercise of his literary power, has transformed the physical into the spiritual and the improbable into the imaginatively credible.

Farce

The really important consideration here is, of course, that the development of the concept of melodrama came from an unconscious feeling for the need of determining a dramatic category on the basis of an audience emotion and of giving this category a precise name.

Much the same may be said concerning farce. At the beginning, farce seems to have had little if any definite significance. Presumably, when it was introduced into the French theatre in late medieval times, it meant no more than a short comic play suitable for performances in the midst of other festivities, such as a banquet. Later, it came to be more widely applied in that country, and during the Restoration period it was transplanted into England.[6] Confusion for long raged in its use. Generally, the term was applied to an afterpiece, or else to a piece inserted within an evening's performance; generally, it tended to be associated with short plays, not more than three acts in length. Rarely were any firm attempts made to define its qualities, although there is no doubt that, as the form became more and more a familiar feature of the theatre's offerings, the same process exhibited in the growth of the term 'melodrama' can be traced; and by the nineteenth century a category 'farce' had come into being both for general purposes and for the specific purposes of critical study.

To a large degree, an investigation of the qualities we now associate with the term itself indicates that it bears the same relationship to comedy as melodrama does to tragedy. It is, in the first place, unliterary and theatrical. We do not expect in a farcical entertainment to be regaled with brilliant sallies of wit or to meet any but stock stage figures. As in watching melodrama, our concern in the play never leads us to pass in imagination beyond the platform on which the players move. We expect, and are given, a rapid series of scenes in which improbability rules and exaggeration triumphs.

When John Dryden refers to "unnatural events" and to things "monstrous and chimerical,"[7] and when John Dennis speaks of "Monstrous Extravagance,"[8] they indicate a feature which has always been associated with this kind of dramatic entertainment. Lastly, just as in melodrama the public is provided with a constant series of thrills, so in farce they are provided with a constant series of laughs. In a comedy laughter is present, but within measure; indeed, only seldom do we find any of the great comedies keeping the house continually in a roar of merriment, which is precisely the effect aimed at in any farcical entertainment.

Thus, once more, when we say that every comedy should be based on farce, we mean simply that the rough physical framework provides an excellent skeleton for comedy's richer qualities and that without this it is in danger of becoming too delicate and refined for the common theatre's daily food. And so, when we say of the performance of some comedy that the production has made it farcical, we mean that an insensitive producer, thinking in terms of farce's physical knock-about merriment, has destroyed comedy's spirit by resorting to a series of interpolated pieces of business simply for the sake of raising a few cheap laughs.

The Classification by Kinds

The invention both of 'melodrama' and of 'farce,' therefore, demonstrates the theatre's continued craving for categories, and the same craving can be seen in the retention of older terms which we might well have thought would have vanished in modern times. Tragedy and comedy were technical words belonging to the ancient Greeks; the modern playwrights, as we have seen, tend towards the use of the indeterminate word 'play'; yet the extraordinary fact is that, both within the theatre itself and within the field of criticism, tragedy and comedy continue to bear as strong a force as they ever did. The terms are among the commonest in ordinary use; anxiously we seek to determine the exact nature of tragedy and to inquire whether the tragic spirit can find expression in the modern theatre; we debate whether a particular play can properly be placed within comedy's realm or whether it belongs to the sphere of farce.

In considering the underlying cause, several comments and considerations may prove of service. First, our attention is caught by a judgment expressed by J. W. Krutch concerning recent American drama.[9] "It is worthy of remark," he says, that the playwrights whose names most persistently reappear in any discussion of the possibly permanent achievements of the contemporary drama are those in whose work the formal element is conspicuous. It is true that Eugene O'Neill, Maxwell Anderson and S. N. Behrman have all dealt sometimes with current topics. It is also true that they could not have been so important as they are had they not been unmistakably of our day. But it is not primarily of their timeliness that one thinks; they are, first of all, a writer of tragedies, a poetic dramatist and a creator of comedies, respectively. That means that each has thought his way through his material with such thoroughness that he has been able to give it one of the forms eternally appropriate to the drama. It also suggests that such a process is necessary before any play can achieve permanent interest and that we have, perhaps, been too ready to assume that intellectual honesty in the presentation of contemporary themes is in itself all-sufficient.

While it may be argued that Krutch's classification of tragedy, poetic drama, and comedy lacks precision, since poetic drama is not descriptive of any particular kind of play, it is certain that he has here stressed an essential truth and that there are indeed "forms eternally appropriate to the drama." "These persistent forms of drama," comments Ronald Peacock,

> are natural and organic because they pertain to its profoundly communal character, and are based on salient general features of experience.[10]

For the peculiar force of the several dramatic kinds a theatrical explanation can readily be found. The drama, because of the conditions of its art, ideally demands a clarity, perhaps even a conventionality, of approach. What we get from the greatest plays is not a photographic, phonographic record of ordinary life, but an image of life viewed, as it were, through some magical glass interposed by the playwright between ourselves and the so-called real world—a glass which may be dark and sombre or light-coloured and gay, relatively plain or so polished and curved as to contort what is seen through it. Thus all enduring plays, whatever variety may be introduced into their scenes, exhibit a vigorously controlled imaginative vision, an apperceptive concord. Within the extended scope of a long novel we do not necessarily demand this special kind of uniformity; but in the theatre's two hours' traffic, if a play is to make a deep and lasting emotional appeal, harmony of approach becomes essential.

At first thought we might be prepared to say that the possible approaches must be infinite, corresponding in number to all the plays that have ever been written; yet, when we consider the audience's special character, and, in particular, its call for bold and clearly outlined scenes, we must acknowledge that, in fact, these approaches are strictly limited, and are to be seen not so much as individual attitudes adopted by single writers, but rather as compass-points which are selected for orientation by many authors. Thus, for example, Shakespeare, who may never have known more of Sophocles than his mere name, has viewed his characters in *Hamlet* by the same light as that which illumined for his Athenian predecessor the characters in *Antigone*.

To a large degree, the realization of this quality in the drama forms the core of Sarcey's essay on the audience:

> To be strong and durable, an impression must be single. All dramatists have felt this instinctively; and it is for this reason that the distinction between the comic and the tragic is as old as art itself.
>
> It would seem that when drama came into being the writers of ancient times would have been led to mingle laughter with tears, since drama represents life, and in life joy goes hand in hand with grief, the grotesque always accompanying the sublime. And yet the line of demarcation has been drawn from the beginning. It seems that, without realising the philosophic reasons we have just set forth, the dramatic poets have felt that in order to sound the depths of the soul of the audience they must strike always at the same spot; that the impression would be stronger and more enduring in proportion as it was unified.[11]

Sarcey's "unity of impression" is the same as Krutch's "eternally appropriate forms" and as Freytag's "unifying idea," through which, he states, "unity of action, significance of the characters and, finally the whole structure of the drama are produced."[12]

The employment of the word 'idea,' however, tends to lead us astray. What we are concerned with are emotional impressions, imaginative attitudes, and of these the definable number is limited. Ideas are legion; passions tend to be few. Possibly help comes to us here from the interesting development in Sanskrit criticism of the theory of *rasas*, which might well be called impressions, emotional attitudes, or passions aroused by the drama—the æsthetic 'relish' resultant upon sharing in a performance. Thus the Sanskrit theorists rightly concentrated not upon the emotions inspiring the dramatist, but upon the emotions aroused in the audience by his work. Altogether, eight such *rasas* were commonly recognized—the emotions of love (*sringar*), anger (*rudra*), heroic ardour (*vira*), disgust (*vibhatsa*), laughter (*hasya*), pathos (*karuna*), wonder or admiration (*adbhut*), and fear or terror (*bhayanak*); to these eight is sometimes added a ninth—*shanta*, or *vatsalya*, which might be defined as tranquil, tender affection. According to this theory, these *rasas* might be savoured in their pure forms or they might be combined and interwoven in a single work; at the same time, it was insisted that, if there were intermingling of two or more *rasas*, no worthy and successful play could be composed without dominant emphasis on one of them. A further development of the theory suggested that the audience could, when witnessing a play of this kind, reach an emotional-imaginative state of universal sympathy in which the individual personalities of the spectators became lost in the *rasa* they were experiencing. In this area of Sanskrit critical thought the truly significant concepts are the recognition that these 'poetic relishes' are limited, and that an audience needs to be directed towards one or another if complete satisfaction is to be attained.

To a large extent, this analysis agrees with the general approach made by Aristotle. When he speaks of tragedy acting to create "pity and fear" or refers to its events as "inspiring fear or pity" or suggests further that admiration, wonder, should form part of the tragic pattern, he is, in effect, expressing in a different manner and more simply what the Sanskrit theorists later worked out independently into a complex pattern.[13]

Putting this in a variant way, we might perhaps say that many basic stories are capable of distinctly separate approaches, and that an audience, gathered for a short space in the theatre, needs to know or to sense the dramatist's fundamental attitude. This attitude might be defined as the way of looking at the events chosen for each play and as the means of giving it form. We can see these events in the light of infinity and experience fear, wonder, awe; but we can see them in the light of infinity and feel that the whole of life is a colossal jest; we can think of the events in the light of society, finding laughter and delight in our acceptance of whatever they possess of joyousness or absurdity; we can become animated by disgust when satirically the playwright presents his events or persons in ridiculous shapes. The thing that is important is that the attitude should be unmistakable.

When we think of the drama in this way, the reasons why some plays, even those which are well written and include interesting characters, fail to have the enduring qualities of others, seem to become apparent. *All's Well That Ends Well* provides a good example. This has never been popular among Shakespeare's works and on its revivals audiences habitually exhibit a considerable amount of uneasiness. Almost certainly the disturbance of spirit arises from the fact that the author has not given us a clear lead; we do not know how he wants us to receive the manifestly conflicting and confusing elements incorporated in his work as a whole. A similar unease prevails in performances of *Measure for Measure*; its values are obscured; fairy-tale improbabilities jostle with scenes realistically treated; emotions potentially tragic are offset by a glib handling of theatrical intrigue. Thus, even although we feel this to be one of Shakespeare's most interesting dramas, the stage-life of *Measure for Measure* has never been thoroughly secure. Perhaps the suggestion may be made that the comparative paucity of theatrical presentations of the Roman plays, excluding *Julius Cæsar*, is similarly to be explained. It is, of course, perfectly easy for a producer to provide an 'attitude' towards *Coriolanus*, either by underlining the greatness of the hero or by stressing his enormities; but at performances where an effort has been made to follow the text, the spectators must remain at a loss to know the drama's purpose. An individual critic, reading the play, can draw our attention to its admirable ambivalence; but, unless it be resolved, ambivalence is a quality likely to perplex an audience and leave them dissatisfied. *Coriolanus* has never proved a truly popular drama.

The failure to preserve unity of impression was strongly marked in the later 'Elizabethan' theatre, not in the manner illustrated by these Shakespearian plays, but more blatantly by a violent admixture of attitudes or kinds. This usually took the form of the provision of double plots, one tragic and one comic. Occasionally the latter was used to dramatic effect by contrasting with and thus emphasizing the former, but only too often the pair remained distinct. Middleton's *The Changeling* will serve as a convenient specimen. Here a powerfully conceived tragic plot involving a proud, self-willed girl and a villain who draws her ever deeper into the toils of sin is set cheek-by-jowl with a series of dismally would-be comic scenes having a distinct theme of their own. The tragic and the comic may be mingled in various ways, but not in this. Another aspect of the failure of these seventeenth-century dramatists results from a false desire, on the part of the shallow-pated spectators who flocked to the small 'private' playhouses, for thrill and surprise. Thus the familiar technique exemplified in so many of the 'Beaumont and Fletcher' plays, wherein an apparently 'tragic' story is suddenly brought to a happy conclusion through the discovery of some secret, titillated the interest of contemporary audiences, but took from these works the possibility of enduring popularity. While *A King and No King* is on the whole ably written, in its structure it lacks the balance, directness, and sureness of impression which alone makes for lasting quality.

With the advent of the realistic style in drama this essential unity tended to be ignored still further. As Krutch has observed, those dramatists in whom we feel the presence of greatness display an ability to think things through and to subordinate their plot-material to a central concept; on the other hand the general modern trend has led to the production of hundreds of plays wherein the anxiety on the part of their authors to impose an intellectual 'idea' on the events chosen for dramatic treatment, combined with the general mistaken confusion between the unordered variety of life and the order essential in successful dramatic work, has resulted in the production of theatrical pieces of inchoate style.

A couple of examples may here be cited. Harold Brighouse's *The Odd Man Out* (1912) may be selected as being by no means among the poorer early plays written in the 'modern' realistic manner. Reading it now, however, we recognize that it could never make appeal to an audience of to-day; the passing of a few decades has shorn it of its value. Examination of its structure suggests that this is due to the fact that no clear impression has been provided by the author, or rather, perhaps, that the author has muddled together his various 'modern' elements in an unordered manner. He has his intellectual idea—that happiness forms the greatest moral good; he calls his play a 'comedy,' but the characters are stock types lifted directly from melodrama—Jonas, the sanctimonious villain, Barbara, the impossibly innocent heroine, Dick, the bronzed, athletic, clean-living hero; from melodrama, too, he borrows a number of thrills—revolvers brandished in the air and the sudden unexpected appearance of a glamorous South American Dolores; at times the action moves into the sphere of farce; yet the over-all endeavour is to make the piece realistic. The result is a drama possessed of a certain minor historical interest, but completely lacking the qualities necessary for endurance.

One wonders how many plays of our own time may not similarly be judged in the future. Although he does not specifically refer to unity of emotional impression, Walter Kerr seems to be thinking along this line in his comment on *Death of a Salesman*:

> Presumably Mr Miller started out with a precise social moral he wished to drive home. Mr Miller has told us, in effect, that this is his principal interest in the theater. It is apparent enough that this moral had something to do with the rightness or wrongness of that American phenomenon, salesmanship. But the play worked out oddly. I have talked with people who regarded it as anti-American propaganda. I have also talked with people who regarded it as a disinterested work of art. There were people who were outraged by it, there were people who were deeply moved by it, there was the man who was heard to mutter, in the men's room during intermission, "Well, that New England territory never was any good, anyhow". So far from leaving a single, didactic impression on its audiences, *Death of a Salesman* seemed susceptible to various, and seriously divergent, interpretations. There was agreement on one thing, though: that the lonely, tormented salesman Willy Loman was a believable, heartbreaking man. Once more a character had taken on stature and independence; in the process he could not help but burst the tidy boundaries that may have been set for him. He is enough of a person to make the play's meaning personal rather than socially prophetic. At the end of the evening, if we pause to work over its "message' at all, we find ourselves asking, "Is this the tragedy of an individual—is it Willy's own fault?" or "Is this a social tract—is Willy the helpless victim of forces outside himself?" We aren't sure.[14]

NOTES TO CHAPTER 3

1. J. L. Styan, *The Elements of Drama* (1960), p. 254.
2. Prologue to *The Woman-Hater*.
3. The preceding three paragraphs have been adapted from an article 'Tragical-comical-historical-pastoral: Elizabethan Dramatic Nomenclature' (*John Rylands Library Bulletin*, xliii, 1960, pp. 70–87).
4. Quoted in T. R. Henn, *The Harvest of Tragedy* (1956), p. 278.
5. T. R. Henn, *op. cit.*, p. 278.
6. Leo Hughes, *A Century of English Farce* (1956), pp. 3–20.
7. J. Dryden, *Evening's Love* (1668), preface.
8. *Critical Works of John Dennis*, ed. E. M. Hooker (1939–43), ii, p. 385.
9. J. W. Krutch, *The American Drama since 1918* (1939), pp. 311–312.
10. Ronald Peacock, *The Art of Drama* (1957), pp. 190–192. See also Northrop Frye, *Anatomy of Criticism* (1957), p. 246.
11. F. Sarcey, *A Theory of the Theatre* (1916), pp. 41–42.
12. G. Freytag, *Die Technik des Dramas* (1863), p. 7.
13. S. M. Tagore, *The Eight Principal Rasas of the Hindus* (1879). I am indebted to Dr R. S. Varma for further information on this subject.
14. Walter Kerr, *How not to write a Play* (1955), p. 57.

4
Tragedy

ERR's two questions make it imperative to turn to a consideration of what is implied by the term 'tragedy.' "Is this," he asks, "the tragedy of an individual—is it Willy's own fault?"—suggesting that for him tragedy takes its being from human error; in the second question he equates the position of a man who is "the helpless victim of forces outside himself" with a "social tract," and yet the Greek drama regularly presents precisely such a situation in plays we recognize as tragedies. Maybe a third question should be put: "Is it proper in any way to relate such a drama as *Death of a Salesman* with tragedy at all?"; and that, of course, raises the basic question: "What do we mean by tragedy?"

An approach towards answering the final question can be made in one of two ways. We may start from the common, familiar use of the words 'tragedy' and 'tragic,' often not applied to dramatic works but to events in actual life, seeking to deduce from such usage the emotional connotations of the words; then we may refer our conclusions to those theatrical writings which are styled tragedies. Or we may work from within outwards, starting with consideration of a limited number of acknowledged tragedies, endeavouring to assess their common qualities, and, as it were, delimiting their confines.

Of the two approaches, the second appears to be the more potentially fruitful, although consideration of the results to be obtained from the first will serve both to prevent our conclusions from becoming too narrow and to illuminate the emotions aroused in an audience by dramas of this kind.

We begin, let us say, with *Œdipus Rex* and *Antigone*; for the Greeks these were tragedies. We then turn to *Hamlet* and *Macbeth*; for the Elizabethans these were tragedies. And when we put them together we find that, in spite of the separation in time and culture between the two pairs, the same kind of emotional, imaginative impress is made upon most of us. True, some critics take Croce's path and declare that "there is no such thing as Shakespearian Tragedy: there are only Shakespearian tragedies,"[1] that it is unprofitable to attempt to define any 'tragic' quality shared by *Antigone* and *Hamlet*. While, however, each play must be considered in its own right and all care taken not to impose the image of one work upon another, the differences between these dramas cannot conceal an inner kinship between them.

At the same time, three observations have to be made. Although the word 'tragedy' comes so freely to people's lips, and although this word is carelessly applied in a dramatic sense to almost any play which deals with distressing incident, those who have most deeply thought on the subject are inclined to see the true tragic emotion as an exceedingly rare and precious thing, exemplified in only a very few plays in the theatre's history. Bradley, after careful scrutiny, confined his attention to Shakespeare's four major dramas; one critic gives the title 'deep tragedy' to this selected, limited group, another, with the same idea in mind, retains the use of 'tragedy' for the limited group, but dismisses the rest as 'pseudo-tragedies.'[2] There is the sense that tragedy, the highest reach in the drama, incorporates a vision which but seldom can be attained.

Along with this goes the fact that, although most of those who have endeavoured to analyse the nature of the vision concur in defining its main qualities, and although a general agreement exists concerning the choice of plays in which it is exhibited, not all would agree in particular. Thus, for example, G. B. Harrison, admitting that *Lear*, *Othello*, *Hamlet*, and *Macbeth* all "stand out above the rest" in this kind, proceeds to make a distinction:

> *Lear* and *Othello* are in the highest degree deep tragedy; *Hamlet*, though it remains the most fascinating play ever written, is not deep tragedy; and *Macbeth* falls far short.[3]

There are many other readers and spectators, however, who would not agree with Harrison's division; for them, if they were asked to select the two greatest of Shakespeare's tragedies and those of deepest quality, the choice might well have been, not *Lear* and *Othello*, but *Hamlet* and *Macbeth*. Paradoxically, therefore, while there is a large measure of concurrence as to the general nature of the tragic emotion, individual predilections occasion disagreement in the choosing of those dramas wherein the tragic sense is thought to be most powerfully expressed.

A further element of contradiction arises concerning the precise application of the term, 'tragedy.' One man will limit it strictly to the realm of theatrical art, another will be prepared to find it within that of prose fiction, speaking of "the tragedy of Hardy" exactly as he would speak of "Shakespearian tragedy" or "the tragedy of Sophocles." Thus we are concerned, not merely with an endeavour to determine the essential features of an established form of literature, but also with the problem of deciding as exactly as we may what that form of literature includes.

All of this means that it is fruitless to hope for a formulation of any definition which would be universally accepted. Even that presented by Aristotle, although it is constantly being quoted and taken as a basis, has been modified, qualified, or expanded by almost every one who has accepted its general terms. Nevertheless, the fact that tragedy cannot be precisely defined in a simple, rationally conceived statement need not lead, and ought not to lead, either towards the view that the effect created by great tragic dramas lies beyond the possibility of determination, or towards the application of the term 'tragedy' to works from which the genuine tragic experience manifestly does not arise.

The whole subject of this tragic experience is a vast one, the exploration of which inevitably carries us far beyond the consideration of purely dramatic qualities: it bears us into the regions of philosophy and metaphysics, of psychology and myth. Even a cursory perusal of recent writings on the theme—and these are numerous— will demonstrate at once the complexities and the intricacies of the problems involved. Within the context of the present survey it would be inappropriate, and, if only because of limitations of space, impossible, to go so far. We are occupied here with considerations bearing directly upon the theatre and the drama, and consequently it is necessary to restrict attention to a few fundamental aspects of this kind of play and to keep 'dramatic' qualities strictly in mind. The discussion, however brief it must be, is essential precisely because within the field of tragedy are to be found the drama's finest achievements. If we wish to have a clear image of what the drama can attain to, we must establish and assess the qualities inherent in this genre.

The Tragic Qualities

Throughout the range of critical writings on tragedy from the later classical days down to the eighteenth century, there was a

G

general trend to concentrate attention upon external rather than upon inner aspects. Tragedy, for the critics, was a type of play which showed an illustrious man passing from happiness towards a miserable end: Chaucer's words, although not applied specifically to drama, may be taken as a fair representation of the general attitude:

> Tragedie is to seyn a certeyn storie,
> As olde bokes maken us memorie,
> Of him that stood in greet prosperitie
> And is y-fallen out of heigh degree
> Into miserie, and endeth wrecchedly.

Usually, to such a description of the determining events was added a declaration concerning tragedy's supposed moral value; the critics averred that its mission was to show either the punishment meted out to the man who disobeyed God's commands or else the instability of a world ruled by Fortune's whims.

Such a description of the tragic form, since it deals solely with outward characteristics and binds the tragic experience within the limits of a rationalistically appreciated 'moral,' must needs be deemed unsatisfactory. Nor is it strictly exclusive. Many plays closing in disaster and introducing persons of "heigh degree" can certainly not be accepted as invoking the tragic vision. Clifford Bax's *A Rose without a Thorn*—to take a single modern example—satisfies both conditions, but no one would seek to associate it with the kind of play which we are at present considering. At first glance, therefore, we might well be prepared to say that, in our search for the tragic qualities, no help can come from the long series of definitions and descriptions which prevailed during the renaissance and neo-classical periods. On the other hand, even if we firmly reject these definitions and descriptions as providing a criterion, they may provide us at least with a start.

(1) That all tragedy deals, in some way or another, with peculiarly dark events is something we accept as self-evident; thought of death is its constant preoccupation. The fact of death, however,

> is as common
> As any the most vulgar thing to sense;

and tragedy characteristically treats of matters neither common nor vulgar. If thought of death is its constant preoccupation, the sort of death upon which it most focuses its gaze is death unnatural or at least violent. In the minds of the Elizabethans, indeed, the connexion between murder or suicide and tragedy was so definitely established that for Shakespeare and his companions the two could almost become synonymous. Not only did the word 'tragedy' imply a work involving murder, in its familiar common use it could actually be used to refer to murder itself. Thus in *Jack Drum's Entertainment* Pasquil uses "tragedy" for the murder he is about to commit; "Arden's Tragedy" in *Arden of Feversham* means his death by criminal hand; "Thy tragedie" in *The Spanish Tragedy* means 'thy death by violence.' In the induction to *A Warning for Fair Women*, tragedy is "Murthers Beadle." The prologue to *The Devil's Charter* sums it all up:

> Our subject is of bloud and Tragedie,
> Murther, foule Incest, and Hypocrisie.

Dozens of examples could be adduced to show that it was the manner of death and not simply death itself which occupied men's minds when they thought of this term; and the more murders there were in a play the more intense a tragedy it seemed to become. In the first part of Thomas Heywood's *The Iron Age* a stage-direction informs us that

> *They are all slaine at once,*

whereupon one of the survivors comments:

> Why, so so, this was stately tragicall.

Almost the only notable tragic drama of the time which does not emphasize this element in the plot is *Romeo and Juliet*; all the other tragedies written by Shakespeare focus upon it—Macbeth murders Duncan, Banquo, and Lady Macduff, *Hamlet* begins with the ghost of a murdered man and closes on a composite scene of murder, *Lear* shows the virtual murder of hero and heroine, Othello murders Desdemona and himself commits suicide.

The emphasis upon murder among the Elizabethan dramatists was, of course, extreme, but among the Greeks the same general trend may be observed. Antigone goes to a forced death and Haimon takes his own life; *Œdipus Rex* is as dark in its events as is *Hamlet* or *Macbeth*; when we think of the slaughtering of Agamemnon, of the revenge taken upon Ægisthus and Clytemnestra, of the terrors associated with the story of Medea, we realize that the Greeks and the Elizabethans were working within the same imaginative atmosphere.

Usually, and with manifest justification, modern studies of the tragic begin with discussion of metaphysical questions, and it may appear somewhat strange to launch the present exploration by reference to something which, after all, is physical and material. Quite clearly, the mere fact of murder is not 'tragic,' nor does the tragic experience arise from contemplation of events alone. At the same time, since we are approaching this subject specifically from the point of view of drama, there may be a certain virtue in examining briefly the implications of the prevailing emphasis upon unnatural death. First, there is the fact that, drama being what it is, the nature of the plot possesses initial significance. Drama starts with an action and expands upon it. The action forms the driving impulse in the play; and the tragic authors have found in themes involving unnatural death a force apt to stimulate the imaginative vision they seek to exemplify in their works. Secondly, observance of this persistent theme of murder draws our attention to a peculiar paradox in tragedy. In the greatest of these plays the commonplace is avoided; the audience is presented with things outside the experience of the majority; and yet the very substitution of the extraordinary for the familiar has the power of delving down to the primeval roots of humanity. By removing men from the cluttering, trivial affairs of their own practical existence, these plays make possible an awareness of deeper truths. It is only one man among millions who discovers that his father has been murdered by his uncle and that his mother is married to the criminal; that does not prevent Hamlet from being regarded almost as Everyman; indeed, the plot's exceptional nature in itself contributes towards its impress of universality. The more ordinary and familiar are the events selected for dramatic treatment, the less chance is there of releasing the mind for contemplation of those issues which tragedy seeks to exhibit and explore.

(2) Nearly all the early definitions of tragedy, besides stressing the "heigh degree" of the principal characters, laid stress upon the use of historical material. In origin, this stress derived from a remark made by Aristotle, in which he argued, in effect, that the extraordinary events introduced into these plays would make deeper impact upon the audience if, instead of being presented as imaginary situations, they appeared as theatrical representations of events which once had occurred in actuality. Among Aristotle's followers, this passage in the *Poetics* was generally reduced simply to a bare and unexplained statement that the themes of tragedy should be selected from actions in the historical past; and a kind of virtue came to be

attached to their authenticity in and for itself. Thus, for example, when Ben Jonson sought to outline the estimable qualities of his *Sejanus*, he placed special weight upon the play's "truth of argument," which, he claimed, all "tragic writers" should aim at incorporating in their works.

Now, quite clearly no particular value can be attached to authenticity for its own sake, and indeed the more 'authentic' is the presentation of an historical setting in a play, the more its spirit seems to veer away from the genuinely tragic. There exists, it is true, a certain justification for Aristotle's belief that the utilization of historical material may induce in an audience an immediate willingness to allow the fictional scenes to assume an imaginative reality; but even this explanation fails to reach down to an ultimate truth.

If we look at *Œdipus*, *Antigone*, *Hamlet*, and *Macbeth* from the point of view of their settings, we realize that they are all akin: every one of them introduces us to an 'historical' story, but at the same time to a story placed in a remote past. For the Greeks the tale of Thebes was part of the national heritage; when first it was published, *Hamlet*, set in ancient Denmark, was styled a tragical history; Macbeth's story came from Holinshed's account of early Scotland, just as that of Lear was taken from a corresponding account concerning early Britain. What binds these plays together is not simply the employment of historical or of legendary-historical material, but rather the selection of such tales as may permit the dramatists to put before us a stark atmosphere of primeval grandeur and simplicity; even *Hamlet*, which in places comes close to actual Elizabethan life, has in its bleak sea-girt castle of Elsinore a background which, in its own way, harmonizes with the megalithic impress made by *Lear* and *Œdipus*.

To say that without the treatment of historical matter tragedy is impossible must, of course, be regarded as an erroneous statement; yet, when we consider the question carefully, and especially when we make survey of the greater plays within this realm, we are forced to conclude that when a tragic dramatist deviates from such procedure he essays a task of truly tremendous difficulty. We may be inclined to believe that even *Othello*, despite its triumphant verve and profound emotional intensity, suffers from the fact that its setting has a vaguely contemporary, if distanced, flavour—a setting which gives to the drama as a whole an almost domestic spirit. And domesticity in a play is apt to destroy the emotion which it is the mission and object of the tragic author to arouse. Of a recent production of *Lear* one critic wrote that it was a "suburban *Lear*," and his choice of adjective negatively indicated the quality missing in the performance and without which the true tragic experience cannot be invoked. If we were to imagine *Macbeth* treated by some realistically inclined author, we might well see at a glance what Shakespeare owed to his selection of material from the more ancient sections of Holinshed's volumes. For such a modern author, *Macbeth* could readily become *The Macbeths*, with a psychological study of husband and wife, set in familiar domestic surroundings, suffering from a fashionable inferiority complex and murdering their uncle for the sake of the football-pools' winnings which he keeps hidden under his mattress. Critics, of course, would acclaim the piece because it dealt with contemporary problems; and without doubt it would be utterly forgotten a year or two after its composition. The spirit of tragedy would not shine in it, and it could not arouse in us the passions which are conjured up by Shakespeare's drama. For tragedy to make its full impact upon us, we seem to require the presentation of strange events calculated to inspire the mood expressed in the last lines of *Lear*:

> The weight of this sad time we must obey;
> Speak what we feel, not what we ought to say.
> The oldest hath borne most; we that are young
> Shall never see so much nor live so long.

(3) With this element of antique grandeur in the setting goes an accompanying sense of grandeur in the persons represented. At times, we may feel inclined to believe that Aristotle devoted disproportionate space to his discussion of the nature of the tragic hero and that subsequent criticism has suffered from following his example; yet, when we cast our eyes over the tragedies written from Æschylus' time onward, we must be struck by the fact that nearly all take their titles from the name of a single hero and that in the plays themselves this hero dominates all. We think of Œdipus, Antigone, Hamlet, Lear, elevating these far beyond any of the other characters in the action. Aristotle has said that the hero "must be one who is highly renowned and prosperous—a personage like Œdipus, Thyestes, or other illustrious men of such families," and for the most part critical opinion and common practice long continued to support this judgment, often simplifying it into the statement that, whereas comedy properly dealt with ordinary persons, the heroes

of tragedy ought to be kings. In 1536 Daniello declared that "familiar and domestic occurrences" were the stuff of comedy, "while the tragic poets treat of the deaths of high kings and the ruins of great empires." "Those of high rank," thought Minturno, alone were fitted to walk the tragic stage; the influential critics, Scaliger and Castelvetro, agreed that "the actions of kings are the subject of tragedy."

Unquestionably, of course, the neo-classic critics were wrong in their endeavour to define tragedy by reference to the rank of its characters; and Dr Johnson was correct in casting ridicule upon those who opined

> that nothing was necessary but that they should crowd the scene with monarchs, and generals, and guards; and to make them talk, at certain intervals, of the downfall of kingdoms, and the rout of armies.[4]

Nor can it be said that anyone believes that a man born to be king is greater, or better, or grander, than any other man. Nevertheless, these neo-classic critics were groping towards the truth. Tragedy must, if it is to produce its proper passions, be vast. By going to a remote and legendary past, Sophocles and Shakespeare were aided in reaching towards the appropriate atmosphere, and in the selection of men in high positions they were further assisted towards investing their heroes both with a kind of symbolic force and with an aura of grandeur. Emotionally, the contemplation of Lear the monarch, of Macbeth nobly born, of Hamlet the prince, and of Othello descended from men of "royal siege" aids in engendering what Sidney styled the combined "effects of admiration and commiseration." It has been rightly said that "the hero must be generally superior to most men," because otherwise "he cannot awaken that intense concern for man's plight which is certainly essential to tragedy."[5]

While it is true that even in Shakespeare's lifetime there were some dramatists, such as the author of *Arden of Feversham*, who deserted the exploitation of high scenes and characters in favour of common-place stories of murder such as journalists delight in, this tradition remained constant up to nearly the middle of the eighteenth century. During that period George Lillo essayed a so-called tragedy in which the hero was an apprentice, and, more significantly, Beaumarchais reached the conclusion that, so far from arousing emotion, kings in tragedy prevented it. "The genuine heart-interest," he wrote, the true relationship, is always between man and man, and not between man and king. And thus, instead of the exalted rank of the tragic characters adding to my interest, on the contrary it diminishes it.[6]

This pronouncement laid the foundation-stone for a long series of similar declarations which still are being repeated in our own times. But one significant fact has to be remembered. In effect, Beaumarchais was engaged in an attempt to destroy the tragic drama; the title of his essay speaks of *"le genre dramatique sérieux,"* and it was this serious drama which he sought to establish in tragedy's place. For that reason, he rejected the emotions of "admiration and commiseration," which hitherto had been regarded as the prerogative of tragedy, and laid stress upon "heart-interest," by which he meant pity. In order to evoke that pity, he sought for "serious" plays which presented ordinary characters, set in familiar surroundings, with whom we might immediately sympathize. For Beaumarchais thus to plead for the cultivation of a new kind of play was entirely justifiable; but it is not legitimate for his followers to cloud the issue by endeavouring to interpret 'tragedy' in the terms which he applied to his *"genre dramatique sérieux."*

(4) Beaumarchais speaks of the relationship between man and man; but basically all the great tragedies, directly or by implication, are religious and not social in tone.[7] They are not religious in the sense that they preach any particular creed or exemplify any form of theological argument; they are religious in that, directly or indirectly, they set men, or at least one man, against infinity. If thought of death, and particularly of unnatural death, is one of tragedy's preoccupations, another, and even more significant, preoccupation is thought of the gods. Concerning the Greek dramas it has been argued by some that the constant introduction of the divine was due to the fact that these plays formed part of a religious ceremonial; the only opportunities which the authors had for the performance of their works, it is said, was at the great festivals, and thus they were compelled to infuse into their scenes religious concepts which otherwise might have been omitted. This view, however, is manifestly erroneous; and a recent writer on this subject is absolutely justified in declaring that the idea

> that it was a traditional dramatic apparatus which, by restricting the dramatist, dictated the form of the tragic drama, is one that cannot be entertained. On the contrary, the dramatists invented and moulded

this form because it enabled them to do exactly what they wanted to do; not to represent life in all its dynamic variety, but to present their conception of the principles or forces that operate in life.[8]

And when we move down the centuries to Shakespeare, writing not for religious festivals but for the daily offerings of the public stage, we recognize that we inhabit the same imaginative world. In *Lear* references to the gods are continuous as the action progresses: the villainous Edmund may reject them entirely; in his despair Gloucester may see them as inimical forces, cruelly sporting with men—

> As flies to wanton birds are we to the gods,
> They kill us for our sport;

later he can assert that

> This judgment of the heavens, that makes us tremble,
> Touches us not with pity;

and Edgar finds in the torment that has fallen on Gloucester an awe-inspiring example of a justice which, being divine, passes man's comprehension—

> The gods are just, and of our pleasant vices
> Make instruments to plague us:
> The dark and vicious place where thee he got
> Cost him his eyes.

In *Hamlet* allusions of similar sort, although less direct, are no less potent; and *Macbeth* is enveloped in the murky air of hell.

When we consider tragedy in these terms, the position occupied by the hero and the emotions we feel in contemplating that central figure fall into perspective. In tragedy we are confronted by infinity and the finite, by the unseen pressure of unfathomable forces and by men. These forces, being infinite, have a power which far exceeds the power of humanity and they express themselves in ways which pass beyond, or operate on a plane different from, the ordinary morality governing our own lives. They may bring a universal doom upon an entire house; they may permit the humanly worthy to perish; they may destroy the very instrument used to effect their purposes; they may measure out death for faults which to our eyes seem either trivial or for which the individual cannot be held responsible.

Yet central upon the stage stands a man of such magnitude that we feel the infinite is almost being matched by the finite. This man may exhibit faults and be guilty of errors, even of crimes; but the very presence of these errors or crimes serves merely to emphasize his humanity, and, because we as spectators see and know more than do the characters upon the stage, to bring finite and infinite together. Contemplating the hero, we regard him as a man more grandly drawn than ourselves, yet still a man, and at the same time, set within a serried audience, we are for the moment transformed into gods.[9]

The result of this metaphysical approach makes the hero in tragedy at once great and small. From one point of view, in the integrity of his spirit and in his unequal battle against the infinite forces, he arouses a feeling of wonder, admiration, awe; from another, precisely because he is contrasted with the infinite and because we see his inability to cope with the problems confronting him, he appears incredibly minute.

The Tragic Attitude

All of this explains why, in attempting to analyse the tragic structure and emotion, we are always compelled to concentrate upon opposing elements, and it is entirely proper that almost every attempted definition of tragedy should include these. Aristotle will say fear and pity; another will say terror and pride;[10] others will speak of sorrow and pain, of awe and understanding.[11] Shakespeare himself seems to have thought in terms of woe and wonder;[12] some modern critics have stressed good and evil;[13] or have developed the antithesis in psychological manner. Thus, for example, I. A. Richards, adopting the terms pity and terror, explains that

> Pity, the impulse to approach, and Terror, the impulse to retreat, are brought in Tragedy to a reconciliation which they find nowhere else, and with them who knows what other allied groups of equally discordant impulses. Their union in an ordered single response is the *catharsis* by which Tragedy is recognized, whether Aristotle meant anything of this kind or not. This is the explanation of that sense of release, of repose in the midst of stress, of balance and composure, given by Tragedy, for there is no other way in which such impulses, once awakened, can be set at rest without suppression.[14]

The phrase "set at rest" is important. In presenting his vision of the gods or of the universe, the tragic dramatist sometimes suggests that beyond our human ken there exists a power which is not inimical to man, and always he deals with the basic problem of evil, never succumbing to the belief that evil is simply a figment of the imagination. More commonly, however, he treats his material in such a way as might lead us to think that the power beyond us is fundamentally opposed to human aspirations and joys. "Because of the apparent absence of a kindly or just disposition of things in the world," it has been said,

> and because of his disregard of a future life, the tragic dramatist inevitably sees the gods as remote, if not as beings actively hostile to men,

so that "the end is not peace, neither with nature nor with men."[15] There is truth in this observation, and yet, when we have witnessed an adequate performance of a great tragic drama, we do not leave the theatre cast down and in despair. There may be no 'reconciliation' for the central hero, who stands as an image of mankind; Macbeth may go to his death a man utterly damned and Othello may be forced to take his own life; but, even so, our spirits are not made despondent. Even although we may be left with a feeling of waste, a great sense of emptiness, there comes a reconciliation for ourselves, if not for persons in the play; and the source of this reconciliation seems to arise from the fact that, amid the contrasting passions aroused by the tragic action, we are left with a profound impression of the universe, not as kindly or inimical or indifferent towards man, but rather as something inscrutable, obeying laws of its own beyond our imperfect understanding. It is the mystery of the world which tragedy presents to us—not the feeble and facile mystery beloved by a Maeterlinck, but a mystery strong and profound.

In many ways, the choruses of *Antigone*, reflecting the vaster implications of the simple story outlined in that drama, may be taken as reflecting what tragedy has in general to offer. The background first is set, dawn rising on the field of battle where the two brothers are lying dead:[16]

> Now the long blade of the sun, lying
> Level east to west, touches with glory
> Thebes of the Seven Gates. Open, unlidded
> Eye of golden day! O marching light
> Across the eddy and rush of Dircê's stream,
> Striking the white shields of the enemy
> Thrown headlong backward from the blaze of morning!

Then comes the first ode, celebrating man's greatness:

> Numberless are the world's wonders, but none
> More wonderful than man; the stormgrey sea
> Yields to his prows, the huge crests bear him high;
> Earth, holy and inexhaustible, is graven
> With shining furrows where his plows have gone
> Year after year, the timeless labour of stallions.

Birds and fish, the noblest animals, yield to him. His is the power of words and intelligence.

> From every wind
> He has made himself secure—from all but one:
> In the late wind of death he cannot stand.

The mood evoked is almost identical with Hamlet's

> What a piece of work is a man! How noble in reason! how infinite in faculties; in form and moving, how express and admirable! in action, how like an angel! in apprehension, how like a god! the beauty of the world! the paragon of animals! And yet, to me, what is this quintessence of dust?

The second ode of *Antigone* strikes a new note. The doom of the gods, not the wonder of man, forms its theme:

> What mortal arrogance
> Transcends the wrath of Zeus?
> Sleep cannot lull him, nor the effortless long months
> Of the timeless gods: but he is young for ever,
> And his house is the shining day of high Olympos.
>   All that is and shall be,
>   And all the past, is his.
> No pride on earth is free from the curse of heaven.
>
>   The straying dreams of men
>   May bring them ghosts of joy:
> But as they drowse, the waking embers burn them;
> Or they walk with fixéd eyes, as blind men walk.
> But the ancient wisdom speaks for our own time:
>   *Fate works most for woe*
>   *With Folly's fairest show.*
> Man's little pleasure is the spring of sorrow.

In the third ode the measure changes to sing of the power of emotion, which in man's life wields power even greater than intellect. And then the fourth ode turns to give examples of the manner in which the gods have thwarted men's desires and best-wrought plans—this leading at the conclusion to a pæan of praise to the deities, not without ironic connotations, but still celebrating the "God of many names."

If we were to take these choruses of *Antigone* alone, maybe we should be able to find enshrined in their contrasting themes the inner core of the tragic spirit. We start with a background image of primeval grandeur, Thebes of the Seven Gates—or Lear's antique court, or Danish Elsinore, or Macbeth's battlements. Man's greatness is sung, and his littleness; his intellect, highly vaunted, can yet come within the grip of emotion, and the power of the gods remains illimitable, beyond comprehension.

The vision itself is noble, and we may well believe that Kierkegaard judges rightly when he sees that the modern age, tending to reject the gods and holding "every individual responsible for his own life," inevitably has lost the sense of the tragic and thus has deprived itself of something infinitely precious:

> One might now believe that this must be a kingdom of the gods, this generation in which also I have the honor to live. On the contrary, this is by no means the case; the energy, the courage, which would thus be the creator of its own destiny, aye, its own creator, is an illusion, and when the age loses the tragic, it gains despair. There lies a sadness and a healing power in the tragic, which one truly should not despise, and when a man in the preternatural manner our age affects, would gain himself, he loses himself and becomes comical. Every individual, however original he may be, is still a child of God, of his age, of his nation, of his family and friends. Only thus is he truly himself. If in all this relativity he tries to be the absolute, then he becomes ridiculous.[17]

Tragedy shows us the prince Hamlet and the princess Antigone; all that the untragic vision can offer us of greatness is a Hitler, the Little Man swollen up with a ridiculous, dangerous, and desperate vanity.

Dramatic Ritual

The choral odes in *Antigone* draw our attention to one particular aspect of the tragic drama which has been much discussed within recent years. Myth obviously has predominated in this kind of theatre, and from Æschylus to Racine a ritual element has influenced its shape. From the store of what Yeats calls 'The Great Memory,' tragedy, it is argued, draws its material, and in it the basic themes of myth are presented—the dominance of the leader or hero, the slaying of the Old King, sacrifice, the dying hero who takes upon himself the sins of his people, the hero slain—all arousing a conflict of sorrow and hatred, a concept of man and the forces of the universe surrounding him.[18]

In all of this there resides a truth, but the truth is perhaps only partial. We may believe that the attempt thus to relate tragedy with such mythical material as has played so large a part in our consciousness ever since the publication of *The Golden Bough* at once tends to go too far and applies only to certain tragic themes. The mythical elements which have been listed do make their appearance in some tragic dramas, but the treatment of tragedy simply as the reflection in dramatic form of mythical content still leaves much unsaid, and those who endeavour to argue in this way frequently are compelled to force rather than to find parallels. *King Lear* fits perfectly, but not all tragedies obey the pattern.

What is certain, however, is the presence in the dramatic structure of a ritualistic tone, and we might almost be prepared to say that without such a ritualistic element the arousing of the tragic experience must prove impossible. Ritual implies ceremony, and ceremony in turn implies ordered beauty. Unless a drama incorporates within itself an element of the beautiful the higher and deeper passions cannot be stirred by it. The whole question of style in drama must be reserved for later discussion; but here stress has to be laid on what appears to be an obvious fact—that for tragedy the employment of a poetic form of expression is essential. We might even go further and say that a tragic drama demands the use of a poetic style so formal that the audience is made fully conscious of its presence. Just as the actions and the atmosphere have to be exceptional in order that they may, paradoxically, release the imagination for the contemplating of basic human problems, so the language requires to be removed from the common familiar speech of every day. In plays of other kinds the dialogue, even although patterned, may be of such a sort that the auditors are not consciously aware that they are listening to anything save conversational prose, but tragedy's train needs to be ceremonially borne and her words must be framed in formality.

Ritual and ceremony remind us also that the effects secured by a tragic performance arise from a contrasting detachment from and sharing in the display. At most great non-dramatic ceremonials just such detachment and involvement are fundamental. During a coronation, a monarch, in rich and glittering garments, surrounded by representatives of Church and State, likewise gloriously clad, provides the centre for a mysterious, solemn, and symbolic pageant; the privileged public watches this pageant and yet, at the same time, forms part of it. In saying this, we realize that the attitude of those attending a coronation ceremony and those who watch the performance of a great tragedy is in essence the same; even although the final emotional experiences differ, the imaginative processes are alike. Still further, we recognize that these imaginative processes represent in finest form what the theatre is most qualified to offer.[19]

For the pleasure we derive from tragic drama many explanations have been offered, extending from didactic interpretations, which assume that Aristotle's catharsis implied that these plays are like doses of medicine, cleansing our emotions, through theories involving reference to sadism and masochism,[20] on to those which suggest, with Timocles, that at a tragic performance the spectator "is reminded that all his calamities, which 'seem greater than mortal man has ever borne,' have happened to others, and so he bears his own trials more easily."[21] The emotion experienced certainly is complex and cannot be reduced to logical terms. Perhaps we can do no more than say that it arises from watching and sharing in a solemn, and yet vigorous and variegated, ceremonial performance, which gives us a vision of grandeur and of littleness, paining our senses and yet stimulating them by its beauty. In tragedy the theatre rises to the heights, providing us with "the most general, all-accepting, all-ordering experience known."[22]

"It is not necessary for there to be blood and corpses in a tragedy," said Racine wisely;

> it is enough that its action be great, its actors heroic, that the passions be excited in it; and that the whole give that experience of majestic sadness in which the whole pleasure of tragedy resides.[23]

And with this "majestic sadness" goes a strange exhilaration as we are brought into association with an expansive, mighty, and boundless world beyond our common experience:

> If the real world is not altogether rejected, it is but touched here and there, and into the places we have left empty we summon rhythm, balance, pattern, images that remind us of vast passions, the vagueness of past times, all the chimaeras that haunt the edge of trance.

Thus,

> it is in the supreme moment of tragic art there comes upon one that
> strange sensation as though the hair of one's head stood up.[24]

The "supreme moments of tragic art," as we have seen, come to
us but rarely. Most of the plays to which the term 'tragedy' has been
attached at various times fail to reach the summit, yet, even when
we recognize that properly the term itself must specifically belong
to the greater works in this kind, there is justification for extending
its use to apply more widely to numerous dramas, which, although
they cannot wholly satisfy, aim at conjuring up the essentially tragic
experience. That experience, however, cannot be evoked without the
arousing of a feeling of admiration, in its Elizabethan sense, of
wonder, of awe; nor can it take shape in the consciousness unless
cosmic issues are directly or indirectly introduced into the development of the action. The assumption, frequently expressed by some
modern critics, that tragedy depends merely upon the presentation
of a man in conflict with a force outside himself, and therefore that
we may have a modern 'tragedy' which depicts man struggling
against his social environment, is a tempting one, but it agrees in no
wise with what the Greeks and Shakespeare, in their greatest plays,
have to give us. Consequently, there is no justification for arguing
that such a drama as *Death of a Salesman*, with its pitiful hero
and its emphasis on social values, touches even the fringe of tragedy's
robes. The concentration in so many plays of this kind, first upon
the Middle Man and then upon the Little Man can hope to arouse
no more than sentimental tears. If we contrast the facile emotions
aroused by this drama or by *A Streetcar Named Desire* and the
dreary pretentiousness of the suitably titled *Long Day's Journey into
Night* with the course of *Antigone*, as expressed both in its main
action and in its choruses, we are bound to admit that an impassable
chasm separates the Sophoclean tragedy from the others. All of this
appears self-evident now, yet stress must be laid upon it since certain
movements in the drama from the time of Ibsen onward made it
indeed very tempting to believe that perhaps the modern theatre
might evolve a genuinely tragic form distinct from and yet inwardly
allied to what had been exhibited by the Greeks and by Shakespeare.
Many of us have argued in the past that the theme of such a play as
Ghosts approached the tragic form by substituting for the ancient
Athenian gods forces in life which harmonized with more modern

concepts, and that numerous playwrights since then were at least dimly manifesting a tragic approach to their material even when their minds were intent mainly upon social elements.

Many decades, however, have passed by since Ibsen's time, and during this period the course of the realistic drama has indicated that our views must change. This becomes the more necessary because the wider application of the word 'tragic' to the drama tends towards two confusing results: on the one hand, we are inclined to reduce its significance to its common, familiar, journalistic use, when, for example, some one's death in a motor accident is described as tragic merely because it was sudden and unexpected; and on the other hand, we are inclined to attach to its dramatic significance elements which do not belong properly to this genre. As an example of the second result, we may, for instance, take a comment made in a recent thoughtful study of the twentieth-century drama. The author is referring to Pirandello's *Right You Are (If You Think You Are)* and he says:

> As in *Think of It, Giacomino*, the message seems to be live and let live. It is a tragedy, a revolt against wanton interference by others with what we wish to keep to ourselves, our hidden truths.[25]

The easy, careless journalistic use is avoided here, but there is something else which in the end may be more hazardous. Tragedy, as exemplified in the masterpieces of the past, has nothing to do with any "message"; nor is it a "revolt" even when the doom of the gods bears down most ponderously upon mankind; nor is it basically concerned with matters political and social. What it does offer us is a vision of those profoundest problems which, since we are all so immersed in the immediate questions of daily living and so much distracted by trivialities, we often ignore. The vision is one which may be expressed in other forms of literature, but only in dramatic literature, through its peculiar artistic means and through the communion of the theatre, can it reach ultimate perfection of utterance.

For that reason, those of us who may previously have been induced to apply the terms 'tragedy' and 'tragic' to certain plays belonging to the realistic tradition will perhaps decide that these terms, because they define and so clearly belong to the other and older tradition, must more fittingly be restricted to the realm made glorious by Sophocles and by Shakespeare.[26]

H

NOTES TO CHAPTER 4

1. Kenneth Muir, *Shakespeare and the Tragic Pattern* (1958).
2. G. B. Harrison, *Shakespeare's Tragedies* (1951), p. 271; I. A. Richards, *Principles of Literary Criticism* (1925), p. 247.
3. G. B. Harrison, *op. cit.*, p. 271.
4. *The Rambler*, No. 125.
5. W. G. McCollom, *Tragedy* (1957), p. 48.
6. *Essai sur le genre dramatique sérieux* (1767).
7. This is particularly stressed in H. D. F. Kitto, *Form and Meaning in Drama* (1956).
8. H. D. F. Kitto, *op. cit.*, p. 219. W. G. McCollom, in *Tragedy* (1957), pp. 9–20 conveniently summarizes the dramatists' prevailing attitudes towards these "principles or forces."
9. To say, as D. D. Raphael does in *The Paradox of Tragedy* (1960), p. 27, that "some of the peculiar satisfaction of tragic drama comes from a feeling that the sublimity of the hero's spirit is superior to the sublimity of the power which overwhelms him" seems a false assumption. The balance maintained in tragic drama is much subtler than such a statement would suggest.
10. Clifford Leech, *Shakespeare's Tragedies* (1950), p. 16.
11. Søren Kierkegaard, *Either/Or* (revised edition, 1959), i, p. 145.
12. *Hamlet*, v, ii, 355. See J. V. Cunningham, *Woe or Wonder* (1951).
13. Una Ellis-Fermor, *The Frontiers of Drama* (1945), pp. 127–147.
14. I. A. Richards, *Principles of Literary Criticism* (1934), pp. 245–246.
15. Clifford Leech, *op. cit.*, pp. 11, 158.
16. Dudley Fitts and Robert Fitzgerald, *The Antigone of Sophocles* (1939).
17. Søren Kierkegaard, *Either/Or* (revised edition, 1959), i, p. 543.
18. On this aspect of tragedy T. R. Henn (*The Harvest of Tragedy* (1956), pp. 80–92) has some excellent comments.
19. While it is perhaps not proper to relate closely the tragic experience with the experience which may be gained at a religious service, 'Mr E' in T. S. Eliot's 'A Dialogue of Poetic Drama' (*Selected Essays*, 1932, p. 47) does not go too far astray when he speaks of the prime "dramatic satisfaction" arising from hearing "a high Mass well performed."
20. For a summary of these see Chu Kwang-Tsien, *The Psychology of Tragedy* (1933), pp. 48–57.
21. Athenaeus, *Deipnosophistae*, vi, 233.
22. I. A. Richards, *Principles of Literary Criticism* (1925), p. 247.
23. J. Racine, *Bérénice*, preface.
24. W. B. Yeats, *Plays in Prose and Verse* (1922), pp. vii–viii.
25. F. Lumley, *Trends in 20th Century Drama* (1960), p. 26.
26. George Steiner's *The Death of Tragedy* (1961), which appeared after this chapter was written, is an important contribution to the consideration of tragedy in the modern world and provides still another example of the anxious inquiry which has been devoted during recent years to this theme. Basically, Steiner argues (1) that the tragic attitude assumes the existence of a "hidden or malevolent God" or of "blind fate" mocking and destroying mankind, and (2) that such a concept, essentially Hellenic, is alien both to Christian philosophy and to the ideas of Marxism, the two basic concepts in our culture. Hence, he concludes, tragedy cannot exist to-day. It may, however, be pointed out that the basing of the tragic experience upon the operations of divine malevolence or blind fate narrows and falsi-

fies the tragic concept as a whole, that Shakespearian tragedy, while not specifically Christian, is at the same time not anti-Christian; that Racine, with his Jansenist leanings, evoked the tragic mood out of Christian ideas; and that the Marxist myth, while pervasive in our times, manifestly still leaves men groping for an answer to the ultimates. Perhaps the most significant part of Steiner's impressive study is his discussion of the loss of poetry in the modern drama and his linking of this to the position of poetry generally in our time. "Literature moves out of the theatre," he says, "as poetry withdraws from the centre of moral and intellectual activity." Expressive language among us shows a "stiffening of the bone," and words have become "weary." "Sociologists, mass-media experts, the writers of soap operas and politicians' speeches, and teachers of 'creative writing' are the gravediggers of the word. But languages only let themselves be buried when something inside them has, in fact, died." (pp. 311–314.)

5
Comedy

THE other great dramatic category which throughout the ages has ever stood alongside tragedy is, of course, the comic. When we are dealing with tragedy we always feel oppressed by doubts and uncertainties, but we always have the comfortable impression that at least we know what comedy is. That impression, however, is illusory and deceptive: theatrical practice and critical theory combine in offering us in this realm admirable variety, confusion, and contradiction.

For this several explanations may be adduced. In the first place there is the fact that, while Aristotle devoted the greater part of his *Poetics* to tragedy and thus stimulated others, from his own time until the present, to devote attention to its problems, he dismissed comedy almost in a few sentences. As a result, most of the various later treatises based on his example concentrated on the tragic form, and comedy, when alluded to, tended to receive but perfunctory treatment. During the past few years there have been signs that attempts will now be made to redress the balance, but H. B. Charlton unquestionably has justification for his statement that a very great deal of work, a great deal of exact thought, must be applied to this subject before "the criticism of comedy can reach the same stage of development as the theory of tragedy had already reached in Aristotle's treatise."[1]

A second cause of confusion rests in the fact that until very lately there has been a failure to recognize the existence of several distinct strains or kinds within the general field of the comic. Not only has this resulted in the production of hundreds of plays marred by uncertainty on the author's part concerning fundamental objectives, it has also created confusion within critical disquisitions on the theme. With their minds set on some limited group of comedies, theorists have sought to define the comic spirit according to that one pattern, and they have either ignored or harshly attempted to crush into their definition other comedies conceived in different terms. Thus, the writings on comedy have habitually shown the application of preconceptions which cannot be justified by the range of comic plays themselves.

A third cause arises from the common, almost universal, equation of comedy with laughter. Obviously, when we think of the comic in the field of drama, the idea of merriment must come to our minds, yet just as it is wrong to use 'drama 'and 'theatre' with the assumption that these are identical, so it is conducive to error if we employ 'laughter' and 'comedy' as exact synonyms. This is constantly being done. Meredith in his notable essay not only fixes his regard upon one single manifestation of comic drama, the comedy of manners, but also makes laughter and comedy almost interchangeable terms. *Le rire* forms the title of Bergson's famous philosophical analysis, and here too we encounter both concentration upon one style of comic expression and indiscriminate use of the two words. Many books on Molière or the English playwrights of the Restoration period are preceded by introductory chapters framed similarly to that which forms the preface to H. Ten Eyck Perry's *The Comic Spirit in Restoration Drama*:

> 'The Comic Spirit' has been an accepted term in literary criticism ever since George Meredith celebrated it in his famous *Essay on Comedy*, originally delivered as a lecture on February 1, 1877; but a philosophic attitude towards laughter is as old as Plato and Aristotle.[2]

True, the interchangeable employment of the two words might be, and indeed has been, defended on various grounds. Perry thus continues:

> Comedy fares best in the open. Laughter is essentially a social thing and flourishes where private feelings must be temporarily effaced for the public good. Personal joy and grief cannot always be indulged in the arena of life, where an infinite number of impersonal encounters make up so large a part of human activity. And it is these very impersonal relationships that in the multiplicity and variety of their details furnish the richest material for the Comic Spirit; it observes them constantly, combines them incongruously, and allows the onlookers to draw their own conclusions. Hence the stage is the proper habitat of the Comic Spirit.

Leaving aside for the moment Perry's reference to "the public good," we may readily agree with his argument. Laughter is indeed pre-

dominantly social. We do not commonly laugh when we are by ourselves, or, if we do, we imagine the jest shared with some one else.
A witty remark read in a play will attract our interest, but generally
we do not indulge in such outward laughter as the same remark
might cause in the theatre; a humorous character may, in the reading, make an appeal to us, but again his imagined presence will not
occasion the hilarious merriment with which the appearance of the
same character on the stage would be greeted. Even when full allowance is made for the actor's skill in accompanying his words with facial
movements and amusing gestures, the truth is the laughter itself
arises mainly from the fact that in the theatre we become part of an
assembled audience, that we are set in the social atmosphere in which
laughter luxuriates. Some recent studies of audience psychology,
indeed, seem to demonstrate that what might be called the force of
the laughter is conditioned by the very size of this audience. Thus,
for example, a counting of actual 'laughs' and a measurement of
their duration at several performances of the same play has shown
a definite correspondence between these and the number of persons
in the auditorium. Where the audience amounted to some six hundred persons, a chosen play offered over a hundred such 'laughs,'
extending over a total of three and four hundred seconds; where the
audience was half the size, the corresponding 'laughs' were down in
the sixties and seventies, the 'laugh-seconds' dropped to little over
150.[3]

All of this is true, but the fundamental facts remain. Certainly
some comedies, such as *The Importance of Being Earnest*, exist
primarily for the laughter stimulated by their series of witty lines,
but, as we well know, most of the greater comedies in the theatre's
history do not have such a constant series of laugh-lines. We expect
to laugh frequently during the course of the performance; we do
laugh; but we cannot describe the entire production in terms of
laughter alone. The laughter itself forms merely part of a larger
whole. No one will deny that *As You Like It* is a comedy, but anyone who cares to take the trouble to examine the dialogue from this
point of view may be surprised at the limited number of lines which
are designed in themselves to arouse laughter; and, lest it be argued
that *As You Like It* is a special case, let it be said that the same
observation might be made concerning most true comedies from
those of Terence onward. On these grounds alone, therefore, the
common equation of comedy = laughter becomes both dubious and

hazardous; if we apply it, our sum is not likely to come out right.

Apart from this, the use of the equation completely ignores a significant observation made by Sir Philip Sidney nearly four hundred years ago. In his *An Apologie for Poetrie* he offered a pregnant distinction between two kinds of pleasure to be derived from comic entertainments. "Our comedians," he said,

> thinke there is no delight without laughter, which is very wrong, for though laughter may come with delight, yet commeth it not of delight, as though delight should be the cause of laughter; but well may one thing breed both together; nay, rather in themselves, they have as it were, a kind of contrariety: for delight we scarcely doe, but in things that have a conveniencie to ourselves, or to the generall nature: laughter almost ever commeth of things most disproportioned to ourselves, and nature. Delight hath a joy in it, either permanent or present. Laughter, hath onely a scornful tickling.[4]

Although critical theory, and especially the theory of laughter, has gone far beyond Sidney's level, we may well believe that his words express a permanent truth—that comedy, in contradistinction to farce, neither needs nor commonly depends upon continual laughter for its enjoyment, and that in nearly all the greater comedies are combined elements "most disproportioned to ourselves," apt to call forth laughter, and other elements which have "a conveniencie to ourselves," equally apt to summon forth a feeling, which, for lack of a better word, we may designate delight.

The Comic Realm

In seeking to explore this comic realm, while the basically important thing is to remain ever aware of its variety, perhaps within the multiplicity of forms certain fixed characteristics may be discerned.

The critics of the Renaissance agreed in making a formal distinction between comedy and tragedy by asserting that, whereas the latter was concerned with kings and personages of high estate, the former introduced characters of "middle or low condition." How firmly this concept was implanted in men's minds is shown by a comment made by Pierre Corneille in 1660:

> When one puts on the stage a simple love intrigue between persons of royal birth, and when these run no risk either of their lives or their states, I do not think that, even though the characters are illustrious, the action is of such a sort as to raise the play to tragic levels.[5]

The very fact that such a remark had to be made tells its own story.

Clearly, the hide-bound theorists were wrong in making rank by itself a definite criterion; yet in a sense they were right. Comedy's sphere belongs within the world of the ordinary. The majority of comedies known to us do deal with persons of "middle or low condition," and when princes disport themselves on this stage it is, as it were, in undress. We do not expect here either the robes or the ritualistic paraphernalia appropriate to tragedy.

Moreover, the characters presented in comedy are 'ordinary' in another way. They tend to be set in familiar surroundings and thus we are given the illusion that they are more real, rounded persons than tragedy offers. There is, therefore, justification for Yeats' remarks concerning the presentation of 'character' in comic situations. At the same time it must be recognized that the impression thus created is, indeed, generally an illusion, that comedy for the most part concerns itself with figures which, however real they may seem at times, are types rather than individuals, and that this type characterization may go so far as to make the characters three-dimensional stage embodiments of abstract concepts.

These characters are almost invariably set before us in groups and in a social environment; and the kind of titles usually given to comedies stresses this feature. Nearly all the great tragedies, and most of those in which lesser authors have essayed to capture the tragic emotions, have their titles determined by their heroes, so that Œdipus, Antigone, Hamlet, and Lear give their names to the plays devoted to them—and rightly so, since each of these characters not only forms the focal point in the drama wherein he appears, but also soars in stature above all his or her companions. In the field of comedy, on the other hand, the commonest titles are those which have a general colouring, either, like *The Way of the World* or *Thesmophoriazusae*, suggesting the presence of a social group, or turning, like *She Stoops to Conquer, As You Like It*, or *Measure for Measure*, to proverbial and similar phrases which indicate rather the tone or subject of the play than a central figure. When the title does concentrate upon a single prominent character, the trend is to avoid the use of a proper name and to refer, instead, to this person's chief quality or to his position in the plot: thus, in place of a *Macbeth* and *Othello*, we have *The Plain Dealer, The Man of Mode*, and *The Merchant of Venice*. It would somehow seem inappropriate for *Macbeth* to be styled 'The Ambitious General' or *Othello* to be called 'The Jealous Husband'; equally inappropriate would be 'Manly,' 'Dorimant,' and 'Antonio' for the three comedies mentioned. When occasionally a comedy has a personal title, such as *Volpone* or *Tartuffe*, in general the author is found to be veering away from comedy proper. The comedies which we recognize as coming within the normal range advertise themselves as *The School for Scandal*, *The Confederacy*, or *You Can't Take It With You*.

Comedy, then, is usually, indeed almost invariably, concerned with human society, and effects its purpose by filling its stage with society's representatives. This leads to a further observation. The characteristic close of tragedy is death; the familiar ending of comedy is a wedding. While it is true that tragedies exist wherein love passions are exploited—as, for example, *Medea*, *Othello*, *Bérénice*—these are comparatively rare. The typical tragic plots concentrate on other matters, and, if love intrudes, it tends to be kept merely as a subsidiary element. Although Haimon dotes on Antigone and Ophelia on Hamlet, neither *Antigone* nor *Hamlet* assumes form in our minds as a love tragedy. Comic dramatists, on the contrary, but seldom deviate from the presentation of this theme; love, youthful love, provides the core of nearly all their essays in this kind. Now and then a purely masculine or a purely feminine comedy will make its appearance, but we feel that these are aberrations and none of this kind has attained more than a temporary success. Audiences never seem to tire of watching young lovers overcoming the obstacles set in their path and moving on to the sound of wedding-bells at the final curtain.

This further means that comedy habitually balances and contrasts what might be called the eternal masculine and the eternal feminine. In tragedy, as a rule, the sex of the dominant figures is not important. Although an added poignancy enfolds the spectacle of a frail young Antigone opposed to the middle-aged King Creon, she might as easily have been a hero instead of a heroine; Lady Macbeth tempts Macbeth, but not specifically as a woman; indeed, precisely the same situation appears in *Julius Cæsar*, with Brutus in Macbeth's place and Cassius, a man, in Lady Macbeth's. In comedy, however, the difference between the sexes forms the very stuff of the plays. The eternal masculine in Benedict, Orlando, Dorimant, and Mirabel stands juxtaposed with the eternal feminine in Beatrice, Rosalind, Harriet, and Millamant. And every endeavour is made by the dramatists to see that stress shall be laid on the essential qualities we associate with men and women; Millamant's whole being is feminine, Mirabel's all masculine.

The Comedy of Manners

Beyond these general comments it would appear that we cannot go. Although there are exceptions, the features indicated briefly above seem to be generally characteristic of comedy as a whole, but when we try to move beyond them we enter into a sphere of uncertainty, and particularly into a sphere which includes elements applicable only to individual kinds of comedy. As has already been observed, numerous critics who have written on this subject have in fact directed their attention to one of these kinds only and have sought to give their findings a universal application; but such procedure leads to confusion rather than to clarification. The essential thing is to recognize the existence of a number of entirely different and distinct strains manifest in this area of dramatic endeavour.

That style of comedy which has captured most attention is the style which first took shape in the Greek New Comedy, was passed on to Terence, and thence to the comedy of manners. Fundamentally, this form of comic expression demands an apparently 'real' framework. Again and again the authors set before their audiences familiar scenes, sometimes places like Hyde Park or St James's, sometimes merely fictional drawing-rooms or boudoirs furnished in the current taste.

Its dialogue craves for the use of prose, the normal speech-forms of the characters inhabiting this fictionally 'real' world, and as we watch the evolution of the comic dialogue, we may easily trace the gradual sloughing-off of verse and the establishment of a means of expression more fit for its own special objectives.

The use of prose, however, has a double value. From one point of view it harmonizes with the fictionally 'real' atmosphere; from another, it offers opportunities for that display of wit which provides this style of comedy with one of its most characteristic features. As Meredith argued, the finest development of the comedy of manners demands the background of a society in which men and women act according to a set of unwritten laws, in which men and women have equal freedom, and in which the game of sex may be conducted with the precision, the decorum, and the ordered pattern of a dance. With this harmonizes the play of wit, the balanced, delicately poised fancies of the society reflected in the comedy, but made still more refined and polished.

The characteristic interplay of wit in this style of comedy occasions three observations. The first is that it subtly modifies, or at least is instrumental in modifying, the outward appearance of realism. This comedy seems to exhibit contemporary life on the stage, but the spirit of its scenes delineates a world which is highly selective and rendered finer than that of actuality. Thus Lamb's central thesis in his paradoxical essay 'On the Artificial Comedy of the Last Century' may be defended. Etherege and Congreve, even although they permit references and actions hardly in Victorian taste, aim at giving the more refined aspects of the society to which they belonged —its gaiety, its wit, its decorum. While, therefore, it is perfectly correct to describe the comedy of manners as offering a picture of current life in definitely metropolitan surroundings, we must qualify the statement by observing that the picture includes only certain facets of society's behaviour and that it presents these facets as more polished and scintillating than they ever could have been in actuality.

A second point concerns the relationship between the authors' attitude to this society and the wit they allow to play over the comic action. Beyond the society itself and beyond thoughts of the present moment they do not go. In the conduct of their plots they normally avoid raising considerations of any world other than that in which they live. The tragic playwright makes free use of the supernatural with the precise object of stimulating such considerations; we are asked truly to credit the ghostly presence of the elder Hamlet and to allow our imagination to range beyond the actual scene into the dark regions from which he has come for a space to revisit the glimpses of the moon. When, however, in this kind of comedy a god descends to earth, as Jove does in *Amphitryon* or in *Amphitryon 38*, he is made domestic and social; his divine attributes are left in some cloak-room on Olympus. When Bridie writes *Mr Bolfry* he does not expect us to credit the diabolical reality of the spirit conjured up by magic; the devil masquerading in the sombre attire of a Scots minister is nothing more than a colossal joke. Nor does Coward anticipate that we shall be thrilled by supernatural fears as we watch his *Blithe Spirit*; this elegant ghost behaves too humanly and with much too graceful feminine felinity for that.

All metaphysical concepts, therefore, are alien to this world, a world frankly accepted for its own pleasures. The very fact of acceptance has prime importance. In the comedy of wit, society is viewed as excellent in itself and, in particular, it is viewed as peculiarly excellent for youth. There may be a measure of opposition between the ways in which it is interpreted by the elderly and by the sprightly youngsters respectively, but no desire for a change finds expression in its scenes. An admirable conservatism rules here, and such ridicule as appears directs itself at elements apt to endanger society's perfection—at fops who carry its affectations to absurd lengths, at middle-aged women who will not accept the rules of the game, at misers who will not take pleasure as it comes, at elderly men who would interfere with the joys of the young.

On such persons wit plays freely and most of the laughter in the comedies emanates from this source. Once more, however, stress must be laid on the fact that the equating of this laughter with the total comic effect causes nothing save confusion. Looking at the laughter alone, those who write on the subject continually repeat a single phrase, 'comic detachment.' If the laughter which comes from the display of wit forms the sole object of our attention, then assuredly such comic detachment becomes of prime importance. Sensibility clearly may destroy laughter. Should we feel sympathy for a wretched old miser in some comedy of manners, the barbs of wit directed at him by the airy young gentlemen might well appear to us so cruel as to stifle any inducement to laugh. In fact, of course, the comedy of manners keeps sympathy for characters of this sort at a minimum; the oddities which are ridiculed hardly seem real at all; they are little more than pegs upon which jests may conveniently be hung.

Here, however, a word of caution has to be expressed. If we carry this observation concerning comic detachment from the limited realm of laughter to the larger field of this comedy as a whole, we shall be falsifying the latter. Most of these comedies have at their centre a group of persons who are not oddities and commonly they are involved in love plots. No doubt amusement comes to us from the scrapes in which they become involved, from the conflict between social manners and the desires of natural humanity, and from the duel between the sexes; but audiences would not suffer this constant repetition of love plots did they not emotionally sympathize with them. The prevailing spirit of wit may be intellectual, but it can hardly be denied that Mirabel's perplexed pursuit of Millamant stirs the emotional interest of the audience and that the final words of

The Man of Mode, in which the gay Dorimant expresses himself prepared to suffer the torments of country dullness for love of his Harriet, stimulates a similar sympathy. That the comedy of manners builds itself upon a prevailingly intellectual attitude to life is certain, but to assert that our reception of it in the theatre demands complete comic detachment falsely describes its impress upon us. The emotions may not be deeply aroused, but the entire effect of the comedy depends upon the interplay of a prevailingly intellectual approach and an undercurrent of sensibility.

One final comment may be made. In discussions of this style of comedy there has been a constant attempt on the part of critics, and sometimes of dramatists, to argue that such comic dramas have a real moral value. "Comedy,' declares Sidney,

> is an imitation of the common errors of our life, which he representeth in the most ridiculous and scornefull sort that may be. . . . There is no man living, but by the force truth hath in nature, no sooner seeth these men play their parts, but wisheth them in *Pistrinum.*[6]

The assumption is that in these plays ridiculous characters are put before us in such a manner as either to make us despise and reject similar characters in real life or else, if we sense their errors in ourselves, to cause us to mend our own ways. Such was the plea put forward by the Restoration comedians when Jeremy Collier fluttered their dovecots towards the close of the seventeenth century, and the plea continues to be made. "Laughter is essentially a social thing," says Perry, "and flourishes where private feelings must be temporarily effaced for the public good."[7] "Comedy," declares Northrop Frye,

> is designed not to condemn evil, but to ridicule a lack of self-knowledge. . . . The essential comic resolution . . . is an individual release which is also a social reconciliation. The normal individual is freed from the bonds of a humorous society, and a normal society is freed from the bonds imposed on it by humorous individuals.[8]

Unquestionably, the very facts that in the comedies of wit men are presented as members of a human society and that common sense receives continual emphasis imply something of this kind; but it must seriously be doubted whether any thought of "the public good" enters our minds when we laugh at the oddities, or whether any playwright within this sphere consciously essays in writing a comedy "to ridicule a lack of self-knowledge" or to effect "a social reconciliation." The comedy of wit exists for its delight rather than for any sense of moral purpose.

The Comedy of Satire

The raising of this question, however, draws attention to the presence alongside the comedy of wit of another kind of comedy, the comedy of satire. Here the dramatist assuredly has an object in view beyond the mere giving of delight, but his basic approach, instead of being urbanely conservative or at least acceptive, assumes a destructive tone. The desire to satirize obviously springs not from approval of existing forms but from condemnation, although commonly the condemnation itself is motivated, not by moral judgments and disinterested concern with the common good, but by a sense on the author's part of intellectual superiority to his fellows and by incentives which are personal. For that reason, satire often moves forward from a moderated balance, in the expression of which laughter exercises a chief rôle, to a bitter stridency, and sometimes, even when it starts with relatively good-natured merriment, it ends in despairing malevolence. The movement from Jonson's *Every Man in His Humour* to *Volpone* is as typical in drama as is Swift's movement from the Lilliputians to the Yahoos in non-dramatic satire. Detachment certainly rules in this realm, for the satirist feels himself above the thing he attacks; and yet, despite this, the passions are apt to be heavily aroused—not in the sense in which they are aroused in tragedy, generating sympathy, but expressing themselves in an ever fiercer and even frenzied lashing of the objects despised by the author, with the loss of all magnanimity and with indulgence in cruelty. In *Volpone* there is no hope, only despair: Volpone himself, his self-seeking servant Mosca, the screeching crew of Corbaccio and the rest, the very judges at the close, are all revealed as creatures falling far below what we might have expected from rational humanity.

Volpone offers us practically nothing of a norm; the only persons who might be considered in this way are mere shadows and are given only a few lines in the dialogue—and this fact well illustrates the vast chasm separating Jonson's play from, say, *The Man of Mode* or *The Way of the World*. These comedies do include ridiculous persons conceived in the Jonsonian manner, but they are balanced by the others. Although Congreve's play has its Witwoud, Waitwell, Foible, and Mincing, it is Mirabel and Millamant who form its centre; in Jonson's satirical comedies the monsters provide the dominant core.

Because no sympathy exists, this satirical comedy tends to work in the 'humours' tradition, with the introduction of dramatic persons created by the author as though they were automatons. Now, automatons, unless we include within this sphere the eccentrics of farce and the stock types of melodrama, are not well adapted to appeal on the stage, and when we add to this the fact that in the typical comedies of satire no real focus is offered for an audience's sympathy, we understand perhaps why Jonson, in spite of his skill and literary quality, has not endured in the theatre. His plays, as it were, set a caricature before the audience which they are asked to watch and not become involved in, and as a consequence such elements of a laughable nature as have been incorporated in the scenes are apt to become dull and dry, while the caricature itself, which might have entertained for half an hour, grows wearisome and even distasteful. Only when, as in *The Alchemist*, a lively plot keeps the spectators' interest alert can we endure with any pleasure the author's exaggerated and machine-like figures.

In general, satire is not well fitted for the stage. Its atmosphere may successfully form an incidental part of a comedy, but its basis in a sense of self-conscious superiority, its lack of sympathetic warmth, and, above all, its openly expressed sense of purpose make it a dangerous style for any playwright to attempt. After all has been said, an audience wants to enjoy itself.

The Aristophanic Comedy

In some of Jonson's works there are signs that, had he possessed the ability, he would have liked to pursue a path leading elsewhere than towards the 'realistic' comedy of abnormalities: when he professed esteem for the '*vetus comœdia*' and when he wrote such a play as *Cynthia's Revels*, he seems to have had in mind the spirit of the ancient Aristophanic drama—and this offers us a form of comic expression of a sort entirely different from that exemplified either in *The Way of the World* or in *Every Man in His Humour* and *Volpone*. With rich lyrical abandon and buoyant merriment, Aristophanes revels in the wholly impossible. A couple of Athenian citizens, ill-content with their way of life, essay to copy the birds, take feathers upon themselves, and build a city-state between heaven and earth; in order to halt a war, the women of Athens stage a sex-strike;

an embarrassed Hercules descends to the nether regions and becomes involved in the frog-chorus of the Stygian lake. Fundamentally for Aristophanes individuals do not matter, nor is he concerned with the relationship between the citizen and the society to which he belongs. His gaze is set upon mankind as a whole, and in one sense we might almost think of him as reaching close to the metaphysical concept of tragedy—save that his gods are not mysteriously majestic and inscrutable, they are merely fools. His laughter is not subtle, social, and refined, nor is it narrowly bitter; it is almost cosmic in its uproariousness.

After Aristophanes, the tradition of the Old Comedy virtually vanished; yet periodically in the theatre's history its spirit has reappeared. We might almost say that, while it does not exhibit itself as a continuing force, its mood finds occasional expression through the impulse of individual authors, who, sometimes quite independently, receive glimpses of the Aristophanic vision. There is a touch of it in Gozzi's *fiabe* and in the fantasies of Raimund; and, if there had been sufficient literary quality among the dramatic writers of the time, we might have witnessed a great recrudescence of the Aristophanic in nineteenth-century extravaganza. Within this Victorian atmosphere, the farthest possible reach was only the Savoy operas of Gilbert and Sullivan. In these, however, the atmosphere of the Old Comedy does find reflection, if but in milk-and-water form; the world presented on the stage is an impossible one, and the spirit animating the whole series of extravaganzas finds its symbol in Gilbert's final effort, *Utopia Limited*, in which, like Aristophanes, he looked upon humanity as a whole and let loose upon it his lyric barbs and the sparkle of his wit. One further rejuvenation of the style seemed to be promised in New York during the thirties of this century with the appearance of such fantastic extravaganzas as *Let 'Em Eat Cake* and *Of Thee I Sing*; but these pieces unfortunately were political rather than cosmic, and in any case they were not the forerunners of any continuing tradition.

Something of the mood that inspired the Aristophanic comedy may perhaps be traced in another type of play which has developed in the twentieth century—the serious or tragical farce, now commonly described as 'the theatre of the absurd' and sufficiently far exploited to be receiving its own theoretical expositions. Already in 1907 a critic spoke of a play, *Amongst the Brigands*, as one in which the author dealt "with serious issues of life and death, even to the

point of bloodshed, in an aggressively farcical manner." Some of the
French surrealists took a similar approach. In 1922 W. J. Turner
wrote *The Man who Ate the Popomack*, presenting a character, Sir
Philo Phaoron, who, after partaking of a strange, rare, legendary
fruit, exudes a disgusting stench and goes about, quite happily,
encased in a diving-suit—a concept fully as absurd as any imagined
in our own times by Ionesco or F. N. Simpson. While, however,
there seems to be an outward kinship with the Aristophanic vision
exhibited in these farces, a considerable measure of difference separates the two. Where Aristophanes introduces the impossible, the
modern authors stress the absurd; where Aristophanes employs the
impossible for the purpose of opposing new-fangled, revolutionary
ideas and of inculcating conservatism, the modern authors are inclined to use the absurd with the object of demonstrating an almost
despairing philosophy; and where Aristophanes, no matter how
deeply moved in spirit, never ceases to abandon comic laughter, the
modern authors dally with the absurd in an attempt to intensify the
'tragic' bitterness of their concepts. Apart from these distinctions,
one other is of particular importance: fundamentally the Aristophanic
comedy is lyrical, its impossibilities and seriousness of purpose en-
wrapped in an ecstasy of poetic expression, whereas the recent plays
of the absurd exist in a dramatic world bound within the limits of
prose.

The Comedy of Humour

In the history of comedy neither the extravaganza nor the comic
satire has played a particularly significant rôle, yet it is important
not to lose sight of these two areas of dramatic endeavour or to
ignore their qualities. Even more important is it to bring within the
picture the extensive field of what may be called the Shakespearian
tradition.

For earlier writers who interpreted 'comedy' as meaning only the
familiar comedy of manners, Shakespeare's contributions always
proved embarrassing. Some critics were inclined deliberately to leave
them out of consideration altogether; others, conscious of their significance and yet equally conscious of the fact that their prime
features are at variance with those of the 'Comic Spirit' as expressed
by Molière or Congreve, sought by subterfuge to evade the issue.
Typical is the close of Meredith's essay: after having described this
Comic Spirit in ecstatic terms, he feels it necessary to acknowledge

I

Shakespeare's greatness; that he does, but hastily he adds that these Elizabethan plays belong to the sphere of the "poetically comic." Quite clearly, the use of such a phrase has no critical validity, nor does it serve in any way to solve the essential problem—the existence of a number of admittedly great comedies which yet cannot be brought within the proposed definition of what is so often called the 'Comic Spirit.' For one particular kind of comedy the definition is satisfactory; an attempt to make it extend over all the kinds must inevitably result in tangled judgments. When, for example, a critic argues (*a*) that a comic dramatist always isolates his material, (*b*) that *The Merchant of Venice* is a comedy, and (*c*) that therefore Shylock must be viewed with comic detachment and without sympathy,[9] then something is wrong with the critical approach.

During the past few years the subject of Shakespearian comedy has come to attract a fair amount of attention, and various efforts have been made to determine its special qualities, but we still await a comprehensive analysis. Every one agrees that in two respects these plays harmonize structurally with those written in the style of Molière, Etherege, or Congreve. Like the latter they lay stress upon a group of persons; like them, they introduce characters who are 'ordinary,' in the sense that they are not intended to excite our admiration. But beyond this measure of similarity, they remain markedly and perplexingly different.

In search for their distinguishing characteristics, much stress has been and is being laid on the romantic elements in these plays, so that the Shakespearian comedy tends to be described as the comedy of courtship. Certainly it is so; yet one wonders whether concentration upon that single feature determines its singular tone. After all, love-making has been one of comedy's chief preoccupations at all times, and love-making, if universal, varies from age to age. The Roman comedians' scenes, which show the various intrigues designed to satisfy the sexual appetite, seem far removed from the adventures in the wood near Athens or the strange wooing of Rosalind and Orlando; yet the Roman and the Elizabethan English plays concur in displaying the way of a young man with a maid, even if, in the latter, the pattern is sometimes reversed and we are confronted instead with the way of a young maid with a man. The young Roman's way differs from the young Elizabethan's only in so far as the social manners of the two ages differ.

Perhaps, on the whole, an earlier approach to the problem was better. Since at least the beginning of the nineteenth century it has been emphasized that, whereas Congreve flourishes in the world of wit, Shakespeare flourishes in the world of humour. "Humour," says Hazlitt, "is the describing of the ludicrous as it is in itself; wit is the exposing it, by comparing or contrasting it with something else."[10] For Bergson, humour presents an inverse of irony. In irony we pretend to believe what we do not believe; in humour we pretend to disbelieve what we actually believe. Humour, as analysed by Sully, exhibits

> a quiet survey of things, at once playful and reflective; a mode of greeting amusing shows which seems in its moderation to be both an indulgence in the sense of fun and an expiation for the rudeness of such indulgence; an outward, expansive movement of the spirits met and retarded by a cross-current of something like kindly thoughtfulness.[11]

These attempted definitions obviously lead us towards an understanding of its quality. It is certainly intellectual, indeed more deeply so than normally appears in the expression of wit; and yet all its greatest exponents have been men of feeling. If insensibility and detachment are demanded for most ordinary laughter, sensibility and sympathy are essential for humour. Humour often is related to melancholy of a peculiar kind—not a fierce melancholy savage in its black darkness, but a melancholy that arises out of pensive thoughts and a brooding on the ways of mankind. The man of wit is apt ruthlessly to mock everything different from himself: the humorist is himself an eccentric who sees the fun of his eccentricity. Wit aims at brilliance, humour rarely so. Wit is clear and refined and cultured; humour is whimsical. Wit tends to live in the present; humour often casts a half-wistful glance at the past and frequently extends its gaze into the future.

In entering this realm of humour, then, we are breathing an air entirely at variance with that in the realm of the comedy of manners. The latter assuredly permits a slight play of emotion to modify its prevailing rationalism; but the former, despite the thought which lies behind it, primarily arises out of emotional sympathy. The important thing to acknowledge is that we must make room for this in our general concept of comedy. "The fault of Shakespeare's comic Muse," asserts Hazlitt, "is that it is too good-natured and magnanimous," and he goes on: "I do not, in short, consider comedy as exactly an affair of the heart or the imagination, and it is for this reason only that I think Shakespeare's comedies deficient."[12] Hardly could we find a better example of the danger inherent in restricting the concept of "the comic Muse" or the oft-repeated "Comic Spirit" to a single kind of drama and hence of failing to appreciate the virtues of other kinds. Reading Hazlitt's words we might almost think of Shakespeare as trying to write like Congreve, and, because of his deficiencies, falling far below that master.

Emphasis on romantic courtship and on humour, however, does not in itself serve sufficiently to distinguish the two kinds of comedy. Here a return must be made to the question of romance, and again an example may be taken to illustrate the danger of looking at these plays with preconceived ideas. A recent commentator has drawn attention to two elements which Shakespeare deliberately added to the Roman plot-material used in his *Comedy of Errors*—the introduction of Luciana and the introduction of Ægeon. Being concerned with the theme of romance, this critic declares that of the two additions, Luciana is the more significant.[13] That the incorporation of Luciana into the plot is important no one can or should deny; yet, before we admit the force of the adverb "more," consideration must be given in particular to the first scene of the play. Here is Shakespeare setting out to write a farce-comedy based on Plautus, and, not content with merely following the Roman comedian's example, actually doubling the improbabilities which keep the acts swiftly moving in a tangle of merriment. The author picks up his quill and starts his play. How? By introducing a wretched old man with a gaoler at his side, placed before a Duke of Ephesus, who stands as symbol of implacable law. The very first two lines, spoken by the prisoner—

> Proceed, Solinus, to procure my fall,
> And by the doom of death end woes and all—

with their emphasis on "fall," "doom," death," and "woes" provide the opening keynote, and the Duke's following speech, together with Ægeon's replies, echo and re-echo the same note:

> A doubtful warrant of immediate death. . . .
> Happy were I in my timely death. . . .
> Thou art adjudged to the death.

And the refrain is caught up again at the close of the play, when, after all the confusions and laughter, Ægeon

> Comes this way to the melancholy vale,
> The place of death.

Reading these lines, can we truly aver that Luciana is the more significant addition? Surely the answer must be that the solemn note struck by Ægeon, with its emphasis upon death, far surpasses it in importance. Our confidence in the rightness of this judgment receives confirmation as we observe that this scene in *The Comedy of Errors* by no means stands alone. *Love's Labour's Lost* is a comedy in which the witticisms of lively young intellectuals play a dominant part, yet suddenly a messenger, Marcade, makes an unheralded entry to interrupt their merriment:

> I am sorry, madam; for the news I bring
> Is heavy in my tongue. The King your father——
> PRINCESS: Dead, for my life!
> MARCADE: Even so, my tale is told.

A harsh discord, this, the whistling flail of death's scythe stilling the laughter. Nor does Shakespere leave it at that. "Oft have I heard of you, my Lord Berowne," says Rosaline,

> Before I saw you; and the world's large tongue
> Proclaims you for a man replete with mocks,
> Full of comparisons and wounding flouts,
> Which you on all estates will execute
> That lie within the mercy of your wit.
> To weed this wormwood from your fruitful brain,
> And therewithal to win me, if you please,
> Without the which I am not to be won,
> You shall this twelvemonth term from day to day
> Visit the speechless sick, and still converse
> With groaning wretches; and your task shall be,
> With all the fierce endeavour of your wit,
> To enforce the pained impotent to smile.
> BEROWNE: To move wild laughter in the throat of death?
> It cannot be; it is impossible;
> Mirth cannot move a soul in agony.
> ROSALINE: Why, that's the way to choke a gibing spirit.

And that Shakespeare was fully conscious of what he was doing is shown by the following line,

> Our wooing doth not end like an old play,

as well as by the concluding duet of Spring and Winter. This is a new kind of play he seeks to write. A critic may ecstatically declare that "the World is made of Life and Hope: the Shakespearian Comedy is a portrait of the World";[14] but not only Life and Hope appear here, Death and Despair are not forgotten.

As in inevitable consequence, thoughts of the past and the future are mingled in this comedy with the immediate present. The permission that Shakespeare gives Death to peer round the sides of the stage, thus providing an unseen force of which the characters are conscious, means that we cannot remain comfortably within a time-space bounded by the first and the last scenes of the play. *Twelfth Night* will begin with a sister's mourning for her dead brother and end with the humorous-merry, yet inherently sad, sound of the searing wind and the rain that lashes—

> A great while ago the world began,
>   With hey, ho, the wind and the rain.

Still more importantly, the introduction of this note qualifies and indeed transmogrifies the seemingly 'real' atmosphere proper to the comedy of wit. We have seen that whereas tragedy ever pines for the past, the comedy of manners characteristically disports itself in an immediately perceptible present. The Shakespearian comedy is as characteristically timeless. The very obviousness of this quality sometimes leads us to ignore the integral part it plays in Shakespeare's comic world and the deliberate use he makes of it. Save in the aberrant *Merry Wives of Windsor* (which, in any case, is supposedly set in the reign of Henry IV), choice is made of localities unfamiliar to the audience—in Illyria, not London, these comic characters move. Certainly, Shakespeare can place in Illyria persons who are recognizably Elizabethan, but this only adds to the timelessness of the general atmosphere, and it finds balance in the equally deliberate introduction of elements which carry our imaginations far from the contemporary world. Shakespeare was not so unlearned as to be ignorant of the incompatibility of classical Dromios and medieval Abbesses, or of the incongruity of presenting Theseus of Athens to Bottom the Weaver and to Oberon, king of the fairies, or of the discrepancy between an antique Delphic oracle and a living Giulio Romano. The incongruities are introduced of set purpose.

The timelessness and the placelessness of the Shakespearian comedy find their appropriate background in the arousing of an atmosphere which continually hovers between life's phenomena and the phantasmagoria of the dream—the one inextricably mingled with the other.

Throughout the plays, from the earliest to the latest, we can trace this. We start with the queries in *The Comedy of Errors*: "What, was I married to her in my dream? Or sleep I now?" and "If this be not a dream I see and hear"; we proceed with the almost identical phrases, now made positively emphatic, of *The Two Gentlemen of Verona*: "How like a dream is this I see and hear!" *The Taming of the Shrew* is set in a framework of a drunkard's 'dream,' and Bottom's 'dream' in *A Midsummer Night's Dream* similarly has the content of the actual misconstrued as the figments of sleep. Or is it? "It seems to me that yet we sleep, we dream," remarks one of the lovers, but we in the audience have seen him and his companions involved in a confused reality. And the play itself? What of that?

> This weak and idle theme,
> No more yielding than a dream.

"If it be thus to dream, still let me sleep!" forms a motto for *Twelfth Night*, and the original question finds reiteration in *Much Ado*: "Are these things spoken, or do I but dream?" So the foundation has been laid for the final apotheosis: "We are such stuff as dreams are made on."

Inevitably, all of this means that the characters in Shakespearian comedy assume a form utterly different from those in the other types of comedy. Even although the persons are ordinary and appear before us in a crowd, the play of humour, associated with the other elements dependent upon it, offers us the illusion of a living quality in its very strangeness. No English Restoration dramatist, hardly even the French Molière, could have conceived, or, if he had conceived, could have admitted, the retort of the ridiculous schoolmaster Holofernes to the courtly, witty circle within which he has been an object of mirth: "This is not generous, not gentle, not humble." Nor could such a dramatist have allowed Costard's comment on Sir Nathaniel: "There, an't shall please you, a foolish mild man; an honest man, look you, and soon dash'd. He is a marvellous good neighbour, faith, and a very good bowler; but for Alisander—alas! you see how 'tis— a little o'erparted." Precisely by these and other kindred lines does the breath of life enter into Shakespeare's comedy. It enters, too, in another way. Not only does the author look upon his characters in this manner, they themselves at times exhibit a similar humorous attitude. Falstaff is fat, and he jests at his own fatness. There is more than a hint that he runs away at Gadshill partly at least for the delicious pleasure of indulging in his prevarications. In a sense he is the butt of his own wit. Such a person would be impossible in a comedy of manners; neither a hero like Mirabel nor any one of the ludicrous persons who are made the subjects of comic attack could ever be made to see the fun of his own being.

The exercise of this humour demands consummate skill, for Shakespeare is aiming at illusion, not at the semblance of reality. Like a conjuror he has at one and the same time to convince us and to avoid misleading us. The conjurer saws a lady in half; were this real it would be decidedly painful for the lady; were we to think it real, painful it would be for us. Between the acceptance of the illusion and disbelief the conjurer holds his balance; and Shakespeare works in almost the same way. He gives us the illusion of reality, presenting characters whom we might almost take for living beings, and yet constantly he shatters the illusion. Just as we imagine we are in the presence of actuality, some incredible incident or impossible motivation intrudes to show us that this is, after all, only a play, a game. In effect, the course of Shakespeare's comedy is the inverse of the course of his tragedy; in the latter we may start with an incredible presupposition, but after that everything becomes logically believable; in the former we commonly start with an easily accepted premise and move on to impossibilities. *Othello* and *Much Ado* have basically the same plot, but their movements are at odds with each other. In *Othello* we have to begin by accepting an almost incredible fact—that Iago's villainy has never been for a moment suspected by anyone, not by Othello, his general, not by his wife, Emilia, not by Cassio, his fellow-in-arms. After we do accept that almost incredible premise, the tragic plot moves forward with a terrible inevitability. As *Much Ado* opens we are confronted with scenes, which, in their ease and domesticity, put no strain upon us; nothing out of the ordinary confronts us here; and then suddenly we are swept away into a realm where the almost incredible rules.

These two balanced forces exhibit themselves, too, in still another manner. Romance is here, the world of the ideal; here also is the common world of reality. Launce can laugh at the lovers and they themselves can exhibit foolish affectations; yet love is real. In *As You Like It* Silvius may indulge in a highly patterned, almost artificial love-lament; Rosalind may comment that these words recall her own wound; Touchstone may utter his ridiculous rustic story of Jane Smile, concluding that

We that are true lovers run into strange capers; but as all is mortal in nature, so is all nature in love mortal in folly—

while Rosalind's "Thou speakest wiser than thou art ware of" draws the little symphony to a close. It has been said that Shakespeare is "a genial sceptic," introducing love-sickness but treating it as worthy only of kindly mockery. That is true, but the mockery comes from within and not from without. "And I," cries Berowne, "forsooth in love!"—

> What! I love, I sue, I seek a wife—
> A woman, that is like a German clock,
> Still a-repairing, ever out of frame,
> And never going aright, being a watch,
> But being watch'd that it may still go right!

Benedict's soliloquies have precisely the same tone, with their humorous conclusion:

> Shall quips, and sentences, and these paper bullets of the brain, awe a man from the career of his humour? No; the world must be peopled.

Theseus in *A Midsummer Night's Dream* is commonly taken to be Shakespeare's mouthpiece; he is not a man likely to mistake a bush for a bear; but we who have been watching the play know that the bears were not bushes, that the fairies were truly fairies. H. B. Charlton has said that "worldly wisdom" is "the philosophy of comedy"; but Shakespeare's comedy has a philosophic basis deeper than merely worldly wisdom. Theseus would wish to reject the poet; and Shakespeare was a poet.

The extraordinary complexity of intellect and emotion, of the real and the imaginary, reminds us that these comedies pursue a path far more perilous than that of the comedy of manners. All depends here on the exquisite sense of balance possessed by a tight-rope walker. Death must be introduced, but just so much and no more; timelessness is essential, yet the timely must not be forgotten; placelessness too is essential, but the local habitation and the name also are required; the persons have to be seemingly real, yet they are associated with incredible circumstance and lack of motivation. Few such comedies, clearly, can be perfect; even Shakespeare at times fails to tune his instrument aright; and, in view of its subtlety, we need not wonder that truly successful examples of this kind of comedy are rare. Nevertheless, we encounter its spirit in numerous plays from Elizabethan times, through Goldsmith's *She Stoops to Conquer*, down to our own times. Quite clearly, an understanding of Christopher Fry's work demands an understanding of its essential principles. His own account of what he has sought to accomplish might indeed well stand as a description of the typical comedy of humour:

> The bridge by which we cross from tragedy to comedy and back again is precarious and narrow. We find ourselves in one or the other by the turn of a thought; a turn such as we make when we turn from speaking to listening. I know that when I set about writing a comedy the idea presents itself to me first of all as tragedy. The characters press on to the theme with all their divisions and perplexities heavy about them; they are already entered for the race to doom, and good and evil are an infernal tangle skinning the fingers that try to unravel them. If the characters were not qualified for tragedy there would be no comedy, and to some extent I have to cross the one before I can light on the other. In a century less flayed and quivering we might reach it more directly; but not now, unless every word we write is going to mock us. A bridge has to be crossed, a thought has to be turned. Somehow the characters have to unmortify themselves: to affirm life and assimilate death and persevere in joy.[15]

Tragicomedy

Comedy and tragedy have been, since the days of the Greeks, the two outstanding forms of drama—the serious play in its greatest excellence, tragedy, and its companion, the play of gaiety—the drama of death and majestic sadness and the drama of life and delight. Always, however, there have existed intermediate realms. The Greeks had their satyric plays, distinct both from the one and from the other, and this satyric drama proved to be the far-off ancestor of the pastoral of Renaissance times. The pastoral in itself does not possess much importance; apart from a very few pieces such as Guarini's *Il pastor fido* and Fletcher's *The Gentle Shepherdess*, few writings in this form have any particular value; but the intermediate realm, to which the satyric play and the pastoral belonged, has pursued an important rôle in the history of the stage.

Already in Roman days Plautus, as we have seen, used the term 'tragicomœdia' for his *Amphitryon* because Jove, a god, and Amphitryon, an heroic general, were its chief persons. This well illustrates one way by which the elements usually thought of as belonging by right to tragedy could be mixed with material proper to comedy. There were, however, many other ways even more commonly used than that followed by Plautus. The early Elizabethan drama mingled clowns and kings. Sometimes, as in Shakespeare's tragedies, the comic matter was restricted to a few scenes, sometimes it was expanded in such a manner that a tragic plot ran alongside an equally important comic plot. Sometimes a playwright like Fletcher wrote a drama which for four-fifths of its length promised nothing save a disastrous conclusion, and then, by the introduction of some trick, brought his events to a happy ending. Sometimes an author like Shakespeare deliberately created an atmosphere distinct alike from the tragic and the comic, and yet dependent upon both, expressed in a spirit of romance; or else he penned such a play as *Troilus and Cressida*, the fundamental objective of which has been rich matter for question and debate. These and many other varieties of the mixed form were common in the Renaissance theatre.

For the most part the early critics opposed this trend. Occasionally there appeared a 'modernist' of the persuasion of Giraldi Cinthio, who sought to establish a new kind of dramatic writing, but the majority were inclined towards the position taken by Sir Philip Sidney, who spoke of

> these grosse absurdities... neither right Tragedies, nor right Comedies: mingling Kings and Clownes, not because the matter so carrieth it: but thrust in Clownes by head and shoulders, to play a part in majesticall matters, with neither decencie, nor discretion.[16]

Nearly a hundred and fifty years after Sidney wrote these words, Joseph Addison described tragicomedy as

> one of the most monstrous inventions that ever entered into a poet's thoughts. An author might as well think of weaving the adventures of Æneas and Hudibras into one poem, as of writing such a motley piece of mirth and sorrow.[17]

These ideas are based evidently on the classical doctrine of 'Kinds,' interpreted strictly. In England, however, the dramatists of the Elizabethan age had succeeded in producing several effective plays of this mixed sort, and, as these were universally acknowledged to be good theatrical pieces, English critics in general came to see the necessity of so adjusting their severe 'classical' standards as to find for such plays an adequate excuse. This they did by appealing from the 'ancients' to 'nature.' Thus, for example, Dryden, in the person of Neander, puts in a plea based on the argument that diversity exists in nature and that a corresponding diversity is pleasing in works of dramatic art:[18]

A continued Gravity keeps the Spirit too much bent; we must refresh it sometimes, as we bait in a Journey, that we may go on with greater ease. A Scene of Mirth mix'd with Tragedy, has the same effect upon us which our Music has betwixt the Acts, which we find a Relief to us from the best Plots and Language of the Stage, if the Discourses have been long. I must therefore have stronger Arguments ere I am convinc'd, that Compassion and Mirth in the same Subject destroy each other, and in the mean time, cannot but conclude, to the Honour of our Nation, that we have invented, increas'd, and perfected a more pleasant way of writing for the Stage, than was ever known to the Ancients or Moderns of any Nation, which is Tragi-Comedy.

Approximately the same considerations later induced Dr Johnson to break away from stricter 'classical' ideas:

> I know not whether he that professes to regard no other laws than those of nature, will not be inclined to receive tragi-comedy to his protection, whom, however generally condemned, her own laurels have hitherto shaded from the fulminations of criticism. For what is there in the mingled drama which impartial reason can condemn? The connexion of important with trivial incidents, since it is not only common but perpetual in the world, may surely be allowed upon the stage, which pretends only to be the mirror of life. The impropriety of suppressing passions before we have raised them to the intended agitation, and of diverting the expectation from an event which we keep suspended only to raise it, may be speciously urged. But will not experience show this objection to be subtle rather than just? Is it not certain that the tragick and comick affections have been moved alternately with equal force, and that no plays have oftener filled the eye with tears, and the breast with palpitation, than those which are variegated with interludes of mirth?[19]

Although this debate no longer seems to have much significance save for historians of literature, it does possess some real interest. Clearly, those neo-classicists who belonged to the sterner sect were both wrong and right; and similarly their more liberal brethren were both right and wrong. The former argued erroneously in endeavouring to keep the drama strictly bound within the two forms of tragedy and comedy, and yet their instinct was correct. They saw that the drama, if it is to be true to itself, requires to follow a pattern established by the authors' conception or vision. Sidney was fully justified in condemning the amorphous mixture which characterized the early Elizabethan popular plays, although it should be noted that one phrase in his attack upon these pieces—"not because the matter so carrieth it"—by implication almost admits the possibility of a mingling of styles provided that such mingling be harmoniously conceived. Shakespeare was able to invest the Porter's speech in *Macbeth* with a temper adjusted to and intensifying the central vision of the play; the Grave-diggers' jests contribute to the whole spirit of *Hamlet*. But no breaking down of the 'kinds' can give support either to the practice of these other Elizabethan playwrights who ran two utterly unrelated themes together in the course of a single work, or to that of those who, like Fletcher, dishonestly excited the passions only to turn them into cheap theatrical tricks.

It was, of course, absurd to lay down absolute rules; Dryden's Neander and Dr Johnson were warranted in their views. At the same time, the argument based on reference to 'nature' was palpably misleading and dangerous. The drama may always use material from life, but an attempt to justify and to praise any particular play because of its truth to life has no validity; total dramatic effect determines the worth of such a play, not truthfulness interpreted as verisimilitude.

Before passing from consideration of this subject, we should perhaps pause at least for a moment to observe one further thing. While tragedy and comedy, in one sense, stand at diametrically opposite poles, both have much in common, and both join in opposition to the mood which determines much of the realistic play of ideas. Where that kind of play is formless and lacking in clear orientation, tragedy and comedy are formal, conventional, and patterned. In all countries wherein the theatre has flourished these two have taken their rise concurrently. Plato made Socrates in *The Banquet* force his companions to admit that the same dramatic genius could excel alike in the comic and the tragic, while later investigators have demonstrated how closely allied are the two *passions de l'âme*—to employ the title of that book by Descartes in which the tragic approach and the comic are discussed. Many are the individual writers who have excelled in both. In England, Shakespeare wrote his *Twelfth Night* as well as *Hamlet*; in Ireland, Synge succeeded both in *The Playboy of the Western World* and in *Riders to the Sea*. The same nations have produced both kinds contemporaneously. In France, Racine framed his incisive neo-classic tragedies while Molière was penning and acting his mellow comedies.

The final test for a work of dramatic literature in which these elements are combined must be one based not on 'nature' but on the artistic effect of the whole, and the parts of that whole, in truly great plays, are conventional, not naturalistic. Thus, for example, it may be observed that certain forms of comedy bear an intimate relationship to certain corresponding types of tragedy; although they inhabit different worlds, their patterns are alike. Shelley realized this when, in his *Defence of Poetry*, he stated that

> the modern practice of blending comedy with tragedy, though liable to great abuse in point of practice, is undoubtedly an extension of the dramatic circle; but the comedy should be as in *King Lear*, universal, ideal, and sublime.

Shelley was thinking, of course, about the Elizabethan style of tragedy; had he extended his view, no doubt he would have agreed that there could have been no satisfactory union of the kind of comedy introduced into *King Lear* and, let us say, the heroic drama of the Restoration. That heroic drama, strangely enough, finds its comic affinity in the sphere of wit and manners. Dryden has written plays, such as *Secret Love*, where something of the heroic note is struck in some scenes, something of the manners note in others; and the two seem well to harmonize. The reason may lie partly in the fact that in both the persons and the actions are deliberately polished and made artificial. The heroism of the Drawcansir serious dramas is as far removed from the ordinary realities of life as is the airy dallying of Congreve's comic nurse. Partly, too, it may be explained by the rhetorical conventionality displayed both in the one and the other.

Various types of tragic and of comic expression, then, have correspondences, and Shelley was right in emphasizing the converse truth, that the association of certain forms of comedy with inappropriate forms of tragedy can prove destructive to both. The Restoration comedy of wit undoubtedly is cynical; precisely because the heroic drama lies beyond the reach of cynicism, this comedy need not be inimical to the mood which created Almanzor and Almahide. But were we to imagine its appearance in *Othello*, we should recognize at once its fatal impact. If *Othello* is to be accepted, an atmosphere, a mood, fitted for the reception of its plot and character must prevail. Let but a single cynical thought enter in and the whole structure of the play is shattered. Thomas Rymer thus found it impossible to appreciate this tragedy, partly no doubt because of neo-classic prejudice, but chiefly because he applied to it concepts based on the prevailing comic style of his period.

"The difference between tragedy and comedy," says Christopher Fry,

> is the difference between experience and intuition. In the experience we strive against every condition of our animal life: against death, against the frustration of ambition, against the instability of human love. In the intuition we trust the arduous eccentricities we're born to, and see the oddness of a creature who has never got acclimatised to being created.... Tragedy's experience hammers against the mystery to make a breach which would admit the whole triumphant answer. Intuition has no such potential.[20]

What Fry calls the 'experience' and the 'intuition' are distinct, and yet they draw together. The 'experience,' moreover, has many variations, and the comic 'intuition' assumes many diverse forms. Both, being attitudes of mind and not merely records of observed facts, may unite when the quality of the one is in accord with the quality of the other. The admixture of comedy and tragedy can thus clearly give much to the theatre, but the critical support for such an admixture must not rest simply upon an appeal to nature; rather must it rest upon a keen awareness of the approaches made by the dramatists towards the natural world.

NOTES TO CHAPTER 5

1. H. B. Charlton, *Shakespearian Comedy* (1938), p. 10.
2. H. Ten Eyck Perry, *The Comic Spirit in Restoration Drama* (1925), pp. 10, 6–7.
3. J. Morrison, 'A Note concerning Investigation on the Constancy of Audience Laughter' (*Sociometry*, iii, 1940, 179–185).
4. *An Apologie for Poetrie*, ed. E. Arber (1868), pp. 65–66.
5. *Discours de l'utilité et des parties du poëme dramatique* (1660).
6. Sir Philip Sidney, *An Apologie for Poetrie*, ed. E. Arber (1868), p. 45.
7. H. Ten Eyck Perry, *The Comic Spirit in Restoration Drama* (1925), p. 6.
8. Northrop Frye, 'The Argument of Comedy' (*English Institute Essays* 1948 (1949), p. 61).
9. E. E. Stoll, *Shakespeare Studies* (1927).
10. W. Hazlitt, *Lectures on the English Poets and the English Comic Writers* (ed. 1916), p. 15.
11. J. Sully, *An Essay on Laughter* (1902).
12. W. Hazlitt, *op. cit.*, pp. 44, 48.
13. H. B. Charlton, *Shakespearian Comedy* (1938), p. 20.
14. George Gordon, *Shakespearian Comedy and other Studies* (1944), p. 34.
15. Christopher Fry, 'Comedy' (*The Adelphi*, November 1950, p. 28).
16. Sir Philip Sidney, *An Apologie for Poetrie*, ed. E. Arber (1868), p. 65.
17. *The Spectator*, No. 40, April 16, 1711.
18. John Dryden, *Of Dramatick Poesie* (1668).
19. *The Rambler*, No. 156.
20. Christopher Fry, 'Comedy' (*The Adelphi*, November 1950, pp. 28–29).

6

Dramatic Dialogue

ACTION is to drama what his body is to man; in its language resides the drama's soul. A playwright essentially is, or should be, an artist in words.

Despite this self-evident truth, comparatively little critical attention has been paid to dramatic dialogue, chiefly no doubt because the analysis of verbal forms presents far greater difficulties than the discussion of structural matters. Certainly the majority of theoretical writings on the nature of drama have tended to concentrate upon plot and character, catharsis and hamartia, concept and 'meaning,' leaving largely neglected examination of the dialogue by means of which these are expressed.

In approaching a consideration of this subject it is essential to bear in mind, first, that traditionally in the past the playwrights never dreamed of using anything save verse measures for their tragic characters, second, that, even when comedy turned from verse to prose, the form of prose it employed was definitely patterned and conventional, and, third, that thus both the tragic verse and the comic prose were entirely distinct from that simulation of common, everyday speech which later became the ideal of the realistic endeavour. The practice of the past, then, was completely distinct from the usual practice of the present.

This statement, in itself obvious, requires, however, some qualification. By the beginning of the twentieth century, it looked as though the earlier tradition had been completely and irrevocably overthrown; only a few lonely heretics, excommunicated by the theatres, dared to ask whether the drama, in abandoning the old, might not have impoverished itself. Then, during the thirties of our era something fresh began to stir; the tentative questions turned into asservations; instead of almost apologetic whispers, we started to hear boldly voiced pronouncements. The past few decades have thus been marked by the appearance of numerous pleas for the re-establishment of 'poetry' on the stage—and peculiarly impressive is the fact that these pleas have come not only, or even chiefly, from the poets, who might be thought to have a vested interest in the matter, or from the academic critics, whose opinions might be deemed influenced by their affection for by-gone tradition, but also from within the professional theatre itself. We might have been prepared, perhaps, to pay but little attention to the pleas had they come only from a Lascelles Abercrombie, a Gordon Bottomley, even a W. B. Yeats or a T. S. Eliot, but we are bound to stop and ponder when we hear a Somerset Maugham saying

> I cannot but state my belief that the prose drama to which I have given so much of my life will soon be dead.[1]

Still longer are we compelled to stop and ponder when we hear the same sentiment voiced by actors[2] and scene-designers. "The theatre we knew, the theatre we grew up in," declares one of the most distinguished scenic artists of our time,[3]

> is dwindling and shrinking away, and presently it will be forgotten. It is essentially a prose theatre and of late has become increasingly a theatre of journalism.

Ordinary Speech

Although these pleas are nearly always expressed in terms of 'prose' and 'poetry,' basically the contrast in the minds of those who utter them is that between dramatic dialogue which reproduces more or less faithfully the speech of ordinary life, and dramatic dialogue which makes use of a definitely conventional form of language. For this reason, instead of talking rather indefinitely of 'poetry' and 'prose,' it will be well here to think and talk of 'patterned language' and 'ordinary speech.' Only by so doing is it likely that we shall be able to explore this theme adequately or to reach any valid conclusions. Use of the word 'poetry' in connexion with drama is apt to bring to mind either Shakespeare or Stephen Phillips; use of the word 'prose' is apt to obscure the fact that much of comic dialogue in the past (and some, indeed, in the present) is almost as far removed as 'poetry' is from current speech forms.

There is, of course, no doubt that a play set in familiar, contemporary surroundings and presenting characters who are made to behave in lifelike manner must properly make these characters speak in

K

equally lifelike manner. The one thing which is anathema for plays of this sort is anything which savours of the 'literary' or 'artificial.' Where this simulation of ordinary speech is concerned with situatons which are commonplace and unemotional, it provides a perfectly satisfactory, if often unexciting, medium. The world of the drama, however, is, or should be, the world of emotions, and every one knows that our common speech has no power to express our passions intimately. In ordinary life passion tends to make us tongue-tied or incoherent; the trite phrases, 'stunned with grief,' 'spluttering with anger,' and the like, testify to a universal recognition of this fact.

Because of this, when the realistic playwright, as inevitably at times he must, introduces scenes of emotional content, he finds himself confronted by a serious problem. He is, in fact, forced to adopt one among a limited number of inadequate procedures.

He may, if he is determined to remain absolutely faithful to the naturalistic principle, make his characters maintain precisely the tongue-tied silence they would display were they living persons. "Some of the post-Chekhovian style used in plays of to-day," remarks Ivor Brown,[4]

> is so scrupulously faithful to the suppressions and mutterings of ordinary conversation that it strains the ears of the audience and misses its heart.

The actors are 'made mum.'

This method, however, is obviously unsatisfactory for performers and spectators alike, and consequently other dramatists have deliberately sought to concentrate upon the depiction of persons whose unsettled mental conditions might warrant a greater loquacity. Without doubt this explains why we have lately had such a run of plays concentrating on hysterical and mentally disturbed characters, and why so often other modern dramatists present their main persons, at climactic moments, in a state of intoxication. A woman who suffers from some delusion or obsession is likely in real life to express herself more volubly than one who is sane; and a man who is a drug-addict or mentally biased may similarly gabble more than one who is better balanced. Such characters certainly offer to actors and auditors more than those who remain mum; but the stage cannot always be peopled by hysterics and mental cases and drunks.

Faced by this problem, numerous modern playwrights take a

third path. They have their emotional scenes and they endeavour by a slight heightening to make them expressive. In attempting such a task, however, they find that they can do little else save rely on broken sentences and ejaculatory phrases, and the resultant sense of inadequacy becomes amply apparent when we note how the texts of these scenes are commonly bespattered with as many exclamation marks and underlinings as might disfigure a schoolgirl's letter.

To demonstrate this we need only glance at the climax scenes in almost any modern realistic play. When, for example, Lavinia confronts Orin in O'Neill's *Mourning Becomes Electra*, hardly a single sentence lacks its concluding mark of exclamation; hardly one is truly expressive. We move from

LAVINIA (*furiously*): Stop talking about her! You'd think, to hear you, I had no life of my own!
ORIN: You wanted Wilkins just as you'd wanted Brant!
LAVINIA: That's a lie!
ORIN: You're doing the lying!...

down to

LAVINIA (*chokingly*): Stop it! I—I warn you—I won't bear it much longer!...

and

LAVINIA: No!
ORIN: Don't lie!

It is all rather pathetic. The whole of this scene struggles vainly on in a plethora of meaningless words; "garrulousness," as Lee Simonson has noted, rules in this realistic realm, whenever it tries to express more than statements intellectually conceived.[5] Exactly similar in essence is a climax scene in Tennessee Williams' *A Streetcar Named Desire*:

That's how I'll clear the table! [*He seizes her arm*] Don't ever talk that way to me! "Pig—Polack—disgusting—vulgar—greasy!"—them kind of words have been on your tongue and your sister's too much around here! What do you two think you are? A pair of queens? Remember what Huey Long said—"Every Man is a King!" And I am the king around here, so don't forget it! [*He hurls a cup and saucer to the floor*] My place is cleared!

Exactly similar, too, another scene from Arthur Miller's *Death of a Salesman*:

> I got so mad I could've torn the walls down! How the hell did I ever get the idea I was a salesman there? I even believed myself that I'd been a salesman for him! And then he gave me one look, and—I realized what a ridiculous lie my whole life has been!

Where the speeches dramatically should be expressive, should soar high or plumb the depths, they shamble awkwardly along. And the reproduction of ordinary speech, for serious purposes apart from the communication of factual concepts, must in general inevitably shamble.

One is compelled to say 'in general' because two authors, Ibsen and Chekhov, did succeed in overcoming the obstacles. This they managed to do by the adoption of a couple of special devices. The first of these was the association of emotions with some selected objects charged with almost symbolic significance—Ibsen's wild duck and church-steeple, Chekhov's seagull and cherry-orchard. By this means emotions for which the realistic dialogue could give but slight expression were evoked in the spectator's imagination. The cherry-orchard is omnipresent; it becomes the spirit which is central to the play, and its image in our minds enriches and deepens the words actually spoken. The second device is that employed by Chekhov, wherein two characters conversing together pursue their own lines of thought or feeling; through this a kind of counterpoint effect results, and once again the auditors' imagination is stimulated into experiencing more than the actual words directly convey.

While observing the force of these two devices, however, we must admit that they strain the realistic method so far that it is carried almost into another sphere. "The paradox of Ibsen's naturalistic tragedy," it has been said, "is that it depends so much on the non-naturalistic elements for its success";[6] Chekhov's style has often been called 'poetic'—and rightly so, because of its conventional utilization of material selected from life. Still further, neither Ibsen nor Chekhov can profitably be imitated. Both have carried their characteristic styles so far that they cannot serve as effective models; imitation is bound to mean only uninspired copying.

Patterned Language

If the dramatist should be an artist in words, if the drama itself should deal mainly with emotional material, and if its limitations demand that playwrights should have the most perfect of instruments available for their use, then certainly the employment of our common familiar speech, even when carefully selected and manipulated, is not sufficient for dramatic dialogue. It is, of course, the realization of this that has led to the recent pleas for 'poetry.'

But vague pleas for 'poetry,' and especially pleas for what more than one writer has called the "ornament of verse," will not take us far. To assume that 'poetry' is merely something pretty which can be added or left out misconceives entirely the foundation upon which the older dramatic tradition was firmly based. That tradition, so long as it remained vital, depended upon a central approach to drama which made patterned language the only possible medium for its expression. The design of the plays as a whole and the design of the dialogue were in harmony, and both were calculated to permit the presentation of an inner and emotional reality instead of a merely surface reality. Where the present-day realism continually keeps the characters associated with and bound to things—the tables and chairs, the teacups and saucers, the bottles and glasses of familiar surroundings, the Greek and Elizabethan characters inhabit a world in which material things are reduced to a minimum. The convention—and the drama must always depend upon conventions—was focused upon a human reality independent of time and place.

In so far as the dialogue was concerned, these dramas of the older tradition adopted and moulded to their needs a second kind of language the potency of which from time immemorial man had recognized—the language employed in primitive times for magical and incantatory purposes and later exercised for the communication of emotional experiences. Its peculiar quality resided in its dependence upon carefully determined form. In familiar everyday speech all that matters is the intellectual content; a particular thought may be phrased in any one of half a dozen ways; so long as the idea has been made reasonably clear no more is asked for. In the other kind of language, the pattern of the words, apart from their meaning, possesses a force of its own. Therefore the magical formula and the verses penned by a poet are fashioned in exact shapes which cannot be altered without destroying the whole. The pattern, in other words, becomes necessarily an integral and significant part of the formula.[7]

Needless to say, not any kind of formula will do, and that is one reason why vague demands for 'poetry' may be dangerous. In particular, four things are demanded of the patterned language to be used for dramatic scenes—suitability for the actor's speech and the auditor's comprehension, consonance with the familiar current style of familiar speech, variety, and dynamic quality. A non-dramatic poet may pen stanzas difficult to recite and to understand; for a playwright such a formula would be fatal. Shakespeare's blank verse, in perfect accord with the everyday language of his time, lost its force when that everyday language changed. A non-dramatic poet may win success in measures which, although modulated, have no bold variations within them, but measures of this kind would be tedious for an audience; and similarly he may felicitously produce a purely static effect, whereas the theatre constantly demands movement. This final requirement involves much more than the obvious necessity in dramatic dialogue for an adjustment and correspondence between the actor's words and gestures; it means that the language itself must contain within it a sense of dynamic action. In *Macbeth*, for example, the hero stands motionless on the stage after he has heard the news of his wife's death, yet the words given to him conjure up in the mind a motion unseen. The to-morrows "creep" in their "petty pace"; the fools follow a link-boy on their "way to dusty death"; life's shadow is "walking"; the poor player "struts and frets his hour upon the stage."

In these, and indeed in other, ways the formula, if it is to possess vitality, must be modified to suit the drama's needs. Yet basically it depends upon a triad of conventional devices common to all patterned speech, from the primitive magical incantation down to the poetry of to-day—definite rhythmical movement, concord of sounds, and associative imagery. As a general rule, those who plead for patterned language in drama stress two values in the use of these devices. They point out, rightly, that by using such means language can communicate emotional experience to the listeners; and they point out, too, that the sheer beauty thus created has a decided appeal in the theatre. Somerset Maugham, for example, speaks of the "specific dramatic value" of this style—a value which, he adds, "anyone can see by observing in himself the thrilling effect of a tirade in one of Racine's plays or of any one of Shakespeare's great set pieces"—a value "independent of the sense...due to the emotional power of rhythmical speech."[8]

Without doubt, these values are centrally important, but other values, since they are commonly neglected, deserve to be stressed. Let us take the concord of sounds. In its simplest form, this device, one of the three bases of patterned speech, offers the dramatist a means of securing, without effort, effective emphasis, of fixing and riveting the auditors' attention:

Fair is foul, and foul is fair . . .
Bring with thee airs from heaven, or blasts from hell . . .
These are but wild and whirling words, my lord—

the phrases, through the very boldness of their sound, startle the mind and fix themselves in the memory.

The importance of not discussing this question in terms of 'poetry' and 'prose' becomes evident when we note that in comedy's almost equally conventional speech the same effects are frequent:

God help the noble Claudio! if he have caught the Benedick, it will cost him a thousand pound ere a' be cured.

And lest it be said that this is simply Shakespeare at work, we may listen to Congreve's Millamant:

Vanity! No—I'll fly and be followed to the last moment. Though I am upon the very verge of matrimony, I expect you should solicit me as much as if I were wavering at the grate of a monastery, with one foot over the threshold. I'll be solicited to the very last—nay, and afterwards.

Simple emphasis upon sound, however, indicates merely one value of this device. Even more significant is the way in which at times the dramatist has deliberately made sounds do the work of contrasting characters. In *Coriolanus*, for example, Shakespeare is confronted by a problem in the persons of Brutus and Sicinius. They are associated together in their functions; they both have to say fundamentally the same thing; there is no call to give them individual personalities—indeed, had that been done it might have broken the fabric of the drama. At the same time, if they are not distinguished from each other, they must certainly prove a dead drag on the scenes in which they appear. What Shakespeare does is to distinguish them by sound. In his first speech of seventeen lines Brutus splutters out words emphasizing both explosive *b* and *p* and harsh *k* and *ch*: "*b*leared . . . *p*rattling . . . ra*p*ture . . . *b*aby . . . *p*ins . . . '*b*out . . . *b*ulks . . . *p*ress . . . *p*opular . . . *p*uff . . . s*p*oil . . . *b*urning . . . *p*other . . . *p*osture . . . spea*k* . . . s*p*e*c*tacled . . . *c*ry . . . *ch*ats . . . *k*it*ch*en . . . mal*k*in . . . ri*ch*est . . . lo*ck*ram . . . ree*ch*y . . . ne*ck* . . . clam*b*'ring . . . *b*ul*k*s . . . *c*ommit . . . damas*k* . . . gawded *ch*ee*k*s . . . *k*isses . . . *c*re*p*t." That this is not merely coincidental becomes evident when, twenty-two lines later, the same concatenation of sounds once more is made to dominate: "*people* . . . *power* . . . *pleaders* . . . *dispropertied* . . . *action* . . . *capacity* . . . *camels* . . . *provand* . . . . . . *bearing burdens* . . . *blows.*" In contrast, Sicinius' words are given a constant hissing note; his first speech conveys a sound value quite distinct from that of Brutus':

> This, as you say, suggested
> At some time when his soaring insolence
> Shall touch the people—which time shall not want,
> If he be put upon't; and that's as easy
> As to set dogs on sheep—will be his fire
> To kindle their dry stubble.

Not by what they say, but by how they say it have they been granted their individual personalities.

Exactly the same effect has been secured by Goldsmith in the opening scene of *She Stoops to Conquer*. Mr and Mrs Hardcastle are revealed to us when the curtain rises. Naturally, we know nothing about them, but, since they are to be the principal opposed characters against which the love story and its adventures are set, the author has to use every means in his power to make us aware of the differences between them. Their sentiments, of course, are in contrast, but the contrast has been underlined and enriched by the very sound of their words. Mrs Hardcastle's speech is marked by hard stops and dentals, from her initial query,

> Is there a creature in the whole country but ourselves that does not take a trip to town now and then to rub off the rust a little,

down to her

> And all our entertainment, your old stories of Prince Eugene and the Duke of Marlborough. I hate such old-fashioned trumpery.

Hardcastle's utterance, on the contrary, abounds in soft labials, from his first sentence,

> Ay, and bring back vanity and affectation to last them the whole year,

down to his final speech,

> And I love it. I love everything that's old: old friends, old times, old manners, old books, old wine; and I believe, Dorothy, you'll own I have been pretty fond of on old wife.

A variant of this appears in the first scene of *The School for Scandal*, although here Sheridan has been faced by a slightly different problem. First, he has to establish the sibilant hissing of scandal in general, and, secondly, he has to differentiate the two scandal-mongers. Like Goldsmith, he achieves much of his initial effect by an adroit use of sound; the stress on *s* and *k* are made common to both Mrs Sneerwell and Snake, but in the speech of the one the hiss is the predominant note, in that of the other the hard stops are characteristic, while, in addition, the latter is given an undertone of *f* largely absent in the former. Her opening sentence,

> The paragraph*s*, you say, Mr *S*nake, were all in*s*erted?

thus contrasts with his

> They were, madam; and as I *c*opied them myself in a *f*eigned hand, there *c*an be no suspicion whence they *c*ame.

Snake concentrates upon "the *c*ommon *c*ourse of things," "the *c*ause of six matches being bro*k*en o*ff*," and "*c*lose *c*on*f*inements," Lady Sneerwell upon "*S*he *c*ertainly ha*s* talent*s*, but her manner *is* gro*ss*."

In all conventionally planned dialogue effects of this kind may be harmoniously introduced. Although Synge was inspired by actual peasant speech, the dialogue in his plays is almost as highly patterned as that in any poetic drama, and so it is entirely proper that, in *Riders to the Sea*, we should listen to the music of

> There's a great roaring in the *w*est, and it's *w*orse it'll be getting *w*hen the tide's turned to the *w*ind,

or

> Let you *g*o down now to the spring *w*ell and give him this and he passing. You'll see him then and the dar*k* *w*ord *w*ill be bro*k*en, and you *c*an say 'God speed you,' the *w*ay he'll be easy in his mind.

So, too, in the final part of *Back to Methuselah*, wherein Shaw deserts the argumentation and the familiar environment of the middle sections, Lilith's great peroration may appropriately take shape in a series of distinct movements—movements which Shaw himself said were composed under the inspiration of music and which make their advance with ever-modulated resonance:

> They have a*c*cepted the *b*urden of eternal life. They have ta*k*en the agony from *b*irth; and their life does not fail them even in the hour

of their destruction. Their *b*reasts are without mil*k*; their *b*owels are gone; the very shapes of them are only ornaments for their children to admire and *c*aress without understanding.

. . . . .

I*s* thi*s* enough: or *s*hall I labour again? *S*hall I bring *f*orth *s*omething that wi*ll s*weep them away and make an end of them a*s* they have *s*wept away the bea*s*ts of the garden, and made an end of the crawling thing*s* and the *f*lying thing*s* and o*f* a*ll* them that re*f*use to li*v*e *f*or e*v*er?

. . . . .

I had pa*t*ience with them for many ages: they *t*rie*d* me very sorely. They *d*i*d t*errible things: they embrace*d d*eath, and sai*d* tha*t* e*t*ernal life was a fable. I *s*too*d* amaze*d* at the malice and de*s*tru*ct*iveness of the things I ha*d* ma*d*e.

. . . . .

Mar*s* blu*s*hed a*s* he looked down on the *s*hame of hi*s s*ister planet.

We follow the interweaving of changing sound in these and in successive paragraphs—the sudden stress in "The *p*angs of another birth were already u*p*on me when one man re*p*ented," the movement to "I gave the woman the *g*reatest of *g*ifts," to "*Lili*th wi*ll* be on*l*y a *l*egend and a *l*ay that has *l*ost its meaning," and to the final sentence,

and though of its *m*illion starry *m*ansions *m*any are e*m*pty and *m*any still unbuilt, and though its vast *d*o*m*ain is as yet unbearably *d*esert, *m*y see*d* shall one *d*ay fill it and *m*aster its *m*atter to its utter*m*ost confines.

Needless to say, passages of this kind can effectively be introduced only when they are in unison with their context. Ordinary speech rarely employs alliterative patterns except perhaps as a joke, and accordingly these patterns are in general avoided in realistic plays. Occasionally, however, the writer of such a play, desperately trying to secure an emotional effect, feels that he must intensify his lines— and the result is nearly always fatal. Thus, for example, in Clifford Odets' *Golden Boy* we find:

What will my father say when he hears I *m*urdered a *m*an? Lorna, I see what I did. I *m*urdered *m*yself, too! I've been running around in circles. Now I'm *s*mashed! That's the truth. Ye*s*, I wa*s* a real *s*parrow, and I wanted to be a *f*ake eagle! But now I'm hung up by my *f*ingertips—I'm no good—my *f*eet are o*ff* the earth!

Here, instead of listening to music we seem to be confronted only by a blatancy akin to that of an alliterative newspaper headline.

These examples will, perhaps, be sufficient to demonstrate that what we may call conventional dialogue—which includes both poetry for serious drama and patterned prose for comedy—offers opportunities to a dramatist which he absolutely needs, but of which he is deprived if he chooses to fetter himself by the mistaken notion of verisimilitude. And the diverse ways in which sound can be made to play its potent rôle form only one of the opportunities. The freedom offered by patterned language for the introduction of imagery inappropriate to the simulation of ordinary speech is equally significant.

Numerous studies published during the past twenty or thirty years have demonstrated to the full what powerful force the images exert in Shakespeare's dramas. No doubt the exact significance of these images becomes intellectually apparent only when the plays are examined meticulously in the study, but without a doubt they impinge upon the auditors' emotions and assist in creating the total effect of tragedy and comedy. And they do so in two ways. The over-all imaginative pattern comes first—the concentration upon light and darkness in *Romeo and Juliet*, upon disease in *Hamlet*, upon reverberating echoes in *Macbeth*. In addition to this, however, Shakespeare in his maturer plays was able to make use of imagery, much as he had made use of verbal melodies, for the purpose of intensifying and contrasting his characters. In *Othello*, for example, Iago's speech is characterized by his use of simile, that of Othello by his use of metaphor; Iago's images tend to be concrete and commonplace, Othello's vast and spacious; both refer repeatedly to the sea, but Othello's allusions suggest infinity and mystery, while Iago's descend to caracks and tackle.[9] It is perfectly true to say that

> as Shakespeare grows in poetic power, he employs his images, not only for ornament, but for far higher purposes; his metaphors, transmuted in his imagination, interpret and in a sense create the life he depicts.[10]

Comedy's conventional language admits of a kindred employment of imagic material, although with a very marked difference. In the serious drama metaphor rules: the object spoken of and the object with which it is compared become so fused in the mind that the distinction between them vanishes. In comedy, on the other hand, the simile proves more characteristic and apt: in spite of the comparison the two objects are held distinct in the mind and the differences between them, as well as the likenesses, are stressed directly or by implication. Two examples, one from Shakespeare and one from Congreve, may be used to illustrate the distinction. First, there is the famous description of Cleopatra:

> The barge she sat in, like a burnished throne,
> Burn'd on the water: the poop was beaten gold;
> Purple the sails, and so perfumed that
> The winds were love-sick with them; the oars were silver,
> Which to the tune of flutes kept stroke and made
> The water which they beat to follow faster,
> As amorous of their strokes.

The rich, subtle, palpitating rhythm obviously aims at identifying Cleopatra with the barge; the two become one in our imagination. From this we turn to Congreve:

> Here she comes, i'faith, full sail, with her fan spread and streamers out, and a shoal of fools for tenders.

The whole comic effect here rests in holding Millamant distinct from the ship to which she is compared and in mentally contrasting, not identifying, the one with the other. The first is emotionally imaginative, the effect secured by an association only indirectly implied; the second is intellectual, the effect secured by direct reference and emphasis. "The ship rides the waves" might be a phrase, if somewhat trite, incorporated in a poetic framework; but "He bumped up and down on his horse as if he were a freighter on a heavy sea" could be appropriate only to a comic atmosphere. When we hear Hamlet speaking of

> Exposing what is mortal and unsure
> To all that fortune, death and danger dare,
> Even for an egg-shell,

no picture of an actual egg is in our minds; but a line in *As You Like It*—

> Truly, thou are damned, like an ill-roasted egg all on one side—

has been so phrased as to cause us to hold two things at once distinct in our consciousness. So in comedy we have, from *The Way of the World*:

> He has brought me a letter from the fool my brother, as heavy as a panegyric in a funeral sermon, or a copy of commendatory verses from one poet to another—

or from *The Full Moon*:

> I am feeling as if the five fingers of my hand to be lessening from me, the same as five farthing dips the heat of the sun would be sweating the tallow from—

or from *Patience*:

> Do you know what it is to be heart-hungry? Do you know what it is to yearn for the Indefinable, and yet to be brought face to face, daily, with the Multiplication Table? Do you know what it is to seek oceans and find puddles?—to long for whirlwinds and yet have to do the best you can with the bellows?

In modern plays wherein the comic spirit has dominated over the realistic endeavour, similies of a kindred sort certainly appear, even although often they may clash with other elements conditioned by the desire to achieve a measure of verisimilitude; but in serious dramas written in the modern manner imagery becomes in general impossible. Once more we find the playwrights inhibited and thwarted, denied the opportunity of utilizing all the tools which ought to be at their command.

Variations on Form

One further matter of intrinsic significance requires attention, and it may best be dealt with by reference to Shakespeare's work. There is, of course, no question of suggesting here that the Elizabethan forms are suitable for or can be utilized in the present age; but possibly a consideration in broad outline of the medium through which Shakespeare found dramatic expression may provide us with a few principles to serve as standards, and at the very least we may derive from the inquiry a mental picture of a great dramatist working under ideal conditions.[11]

When Shakespeare came to maturity as a playwright he found that he had four chief instruments available for his dialogue, all inherited in basic form from his immediate predecessors and all enriched by his own earlier efforts.

1. Blank verse, with its staple norm, the line of five 'rising' feet, was basic, capable of variation in a thousand different ways, of which the chief were modifications in the foot measures, expansion or contraction of the usual ten syllables and the multiform diversity possible in the linking of line to line.

2. Secondly, Shakespeare had the possibility of using prose of different kinds, such as the comic prose of the clowns and the familiar speech of gallants in easy conversational moments—both subtly modified so as to harmonise with the general pattern.

3. Thirdly, he had available several sorts of rimed ten-syllable lines. Of these, the commonest were the simple couplets; next to them came the quatrains; next to them longer stanza units, of which the sonnet was chief.

4. And finally Shakespeare could on occasion employ shorter rimed lines, generally eight- or six-syllabled, and generally, too, in couplets or quatrains.

Between most of these, particularly in longer passages, the contrast, even when we hear the words spoken rapidly in the modern theatre, is patent. We thus will readily recognize the difference in measure between:

> 1. Now, fair Hippolyta, our nuptial hour
> Draws on apace: four happy days bring in
> Another moon; but O, methinks how slow
> This old moon wanes! She lingers my desires,
> Like to a step-dame or a dowager,
> Long withering out a young man's revenue. . . .

> 2. Is all our company here? You were best to call them generally, man by man, according to the scrip. Here is the scroll of every man's name which is thought fit, through all Athens, to play in our interlude before the Duke and the Duchess on his wedding-day at night. . . .

> 3. Helen, to you our minds we will unfold;
> To-morrow night, when Phoebe doth behold
> Her silver visage in the wat'ry glass,
> Decking with liquid pearl the bladed grass,
> A time that lovers' flights doth still conceal,
> Through Athens' gates have we devis'd to steal. . . .

and

> 4. Over hill, over dale,
>   Thorough bush, thorough briar,
>   Over park, over pale,
>   Thorough flood, thorough fire,
>   I do wander everywhere,
>   Swifter than the moon's sphere;
>   And I serve the Fairy Queen
>   To dew her orbs upon the green.

Even although Shakespeare's measures, born of the Elizabethan age, are far removed from us, we all recognize the differences here; but it cannot be too heavily stressed that the ears of Shakespeare's contemporaries were far more keenly attuned than modern ears to detect variations much subtler than these. These measures, for them, were the measures of their own age; the auditors were trained in an atmosphere of formalism and convention; the printed page, particularly in the shape of the daily newspaper, had not dulled their power of alert listening—all these combined to make their aural senses acute. We must even believe that Elizabethan audiences were able in a moment's flash to detect the pattern of blank verse: a single line was sufficient for them. In *As You Like it* Orlando enters and addresses the disguised Rosalind:

> Good day, and happiness, dear Rosalind.

We certainly could not hope, in that passing moment, to identify these words as a line of verse, but Jacques' comment shows at once that the Elizabethans did:

> Nay then, God buy you, an you talk in blank verse.

The point of the joke rests in Shakespeare's assumption that his audience will be as quick as Jacques to catch the measure.

The two facts, (1) that his blank verse provided a standard, and (2) that it was immediately recognized for what it was, meant that Shakespeare could play with effects which, even if they still contribute much to our appreciation of the tragedies and comedies, have now less power than they had in his own time. At the first performance of *Macbeth*, for instance, the spectators saw three strangely clad, enigmatic figures appear before them, and heard those creatures uttering their lines:

> When shall we three meet again,
> In thunder, lightning or in rain?

Immediately the octosyllabic lines, in place of the normally-to-be-expected blank verse, must have suggested the supernatural, while the prevailingly trochaic or falling movement—

> Fair is foul, and foul is fair—

must have given the impression of inversion and, imaginatively, of the presence of evil. By the very rhythm, therefore, Shakespeare was enabled to make on his audience the initial impact he desired.

A similar effect is secured in the opening lines of *Hamlet*. In the first seven short utterances of that play there are three regular blank-verse lines:

> Nay, answer me: stand and unfold yourself. . . .
> You come most carefully upon your hour. . . .
> 'Tis now struck twelve; get thee to bed, Francisco.

This is the established norm; but the first speech-line is the brief, emphatic "Who's there?", and that is accompanied by three other broken lines, "Long live the King!", "Bernardo?", and "He." To listeners keen and able to detect and evaluate variations in the medium, therefore, the impression created in rhythmic sound would have been precisely what the dramatist aimed at—a blank-verse world broken and disturbed by tension and nervous anxiety.

The passages from *Macbeth* and *Hamlet* illustrate the association of the verse forms with the content of a scene. In addition, the forms often are employed to secure contrast. In *Romeo and Juliet*, for example, we have the balcony scene, with its rich lyrical blank-verse ecstasy:

> 'Tis almost morning. I would have thee gone;
> And yet no further than a wanton's bird,
> That lets it hop a little from her hand,
> Like a poor prisoner in his twisted gyves,
> And with a silk thread plucks it back again,
> So loving-jealous of his liberty.

The following scene introduces Friar Lawrence, and with him clearly the author requires to set a different mood. Comic prose might have been employed to provide a sharp distinction, but here nothing of the kind can be allowed: the atmosphere must be poetic, serious, and dignified. The effect he desires Shakespeare gains by boldly resorting to rimed couplets and by substituting for the light rhythms of the balcony-scene a heavy spondaic measure:

> The gray-ey'd morn smiles on the frowning night,
> Check'ring the eastern clouds with streaks of light,
> And fleckel'd darkness like a drunkard reels
> From forth day's path and Titan's fiery wheels.

Laboriously the phrases bear down upon us—"gray-ey'd morn . . . from forth day's path . . . night's dark dew . . . I must up-fill . . . in herbs, plants, stones, ... naught so vile ... aught so good ... with that part cheers each part." Once more, by rhythm's sound alone Shakespeare conveys his emotional atmosphere to the audience.

Elsewhere the contrast may be in terms of character. A good example of this appears in the person of Caliban in *The Tempest*. More than one critic has suggested that the monster's speech beginning "Be not afear'd" shows Shakespeare extra-dramatically indulging in a little bit of lyric poetry put clumsily into an inappropriate mouth. The fact is, however, that, except when he is drunk, Caliban is consistently a blank-verse speaker and thus kept distinct from Trinculo and Stephano. His very first lines set the tone:

> This island's mine, by Sycorax my mother,
> Which thou tak'st from me. When thou cam'st first,
> Thou strok'st and made much of me, wouldst give me
> Water with berries in't, and teach me how
> To name the bigger light, and how the less,
> That burn by day and night; and then I lov'd thee
> And show'd thee all the qualities o' th' isle.

The verbal music here may properly contrast with Prospero's polished utterance; but the lines are verse, and through his use of that verse Caliban is sharply differentiated from the clowns. He breathes an air richer than theirs; and consequently it is entirely in keeping with his whole presentation that the lyrical passage should finally tumble from his monster lips:

> Be not afear'd. The isle is full of noises,
> Sounds, and sweet airs, that give delight and hurt not.
> Sometimes a thousand twangling instruments
> Will hum about mine ears; and sometimes voices,
> That, if I then had wak'd after long sleep,
> Will make me sleep again; and then, in dreaming,
> The clouds methought would open and show riches
> Ready to drop upon me, that, when I wak'd,
> I cried to dream again.

Even further can this method of contrast go; instead of applying to the speaker it may apply to the object of his speech. In *Troilus and Cressida*, the heroine enters with a servant who describes the various warriors going to battle. His remarks on Hector are cast in blank verse:

> Hector, whose patience
> Is as a virtue fix'd, to-day was mov'd.

L

> He chid Andromache, and struck his armourer;
> And, like as there were husbandry in war,
> Before the sun rose he was harness'd light,
> And to the field goes he; where every flower
> Did as a prophet weep what it foresaw
> In Hector's wrath.

But when the servant comes to Ajax, his medium changes:

> This man, lady, hath robb'd many beasts of their particular additions:
> he is as valiant as the lion, churlish as the bear, slow as the elephant—
> a man into whom nature hath so crowded humours that his valour is
> crush'd into folly, his folly sauc'd with discretion.

One other aspect of this subject must be referred to. In many Shakespearian passages we encounter broken lines in the midst of the blank-verse utterance. To our audiences of to-day these broken lines do not stand out; they pass us by unperceived; but we may well believe, first, that to the keener ears of the Elizabethans they marked breaks in the music, second, that consequently they possessed a value of their own, and, third, that they were deliberately introduced by Shakespeare with a dramatic end in view.

This can be seen even in the planning of some single speeches. When, for instance, we look at Hamlet's soliloquy "O what a rogue and peasant slave am I!", we observe that five broken lines break the speech into six sections—*For Hecuba!*, *Yet I*, *Ha!*, *O vengeance!*, and *A scullion!* Even although not all of these are printed in the Folio and Quarto texts as broken lines, obviously they are all extra-metrical, and obviously, too, they are designed to play a significant part in the flow of Hamlet's speech. If we look upon the soliloquy, not as something to be read in the study, but as something to be spoken by an actor and heard by an audience, we must acknowledge that these broken lines and the sections which they mark off from each other exactly correspond with the changing emotions of the speaker. They form signals and pointers both for the actor and for the listeners.

The first eight lines, with their sibilant emphasis, from the self-contemptuous opening down to "And all for nothing!", express Hamlet's wonder at the passion displayed by the actor:

> O what a rogue and peasant slave am I!
> Is it not monstrous that this player here,
> But in a fiction, in a dream of passion,
> Could force his soul so to his own conceit,

> That from her working all his visage wann'd;
> Tears in his eyes, distraction in's aspect,
> A broken voice, and his whole function suiting
> With forms to his conceit? And all for nothing!

The sudden final melodic drop in "And all for nothing!" prepares the way for the break "For Hecuba!" As though this were the signal for a change of thought, and of sound, another eight lines follow, with an insistent hammering stress on "*weep* . . . *tears* . . . *cleave* . . . *speech* . . . *free* . . . *indeed* . . . *ears*," in which Hamlet imagines what this actor would have done had he had a real and not merely a fictional motive:

> *For Hecuba!*
> What's Hecuba to him, or he to Hecuba,
> That he should weep for her? What would he do,
> Had he the motive and the cue for passion
> That I have? He would drown the stage with tears
> And cleave the general air with horrid speech,
> Make mad the guilty and appal the free,
> Confound the ignorant and amaze indeed
> The very faculties of eyes and ears.

Once more a signal comes with "Yet I," and nine lines, with a new insistence on the sounds of *b*, *d*, and *p*, are devoted to the searching query as to whether Hamlet is not, in fact, a coward:

> *Yet I,*
> A dull and muddy-mettled rascal, peak,
> Like John-a-dreams, unpregnant of my cause,
> And can say nothing—no, not for a king,
> Upon whose property and most dear life
> A damn'd defeat was made? Am I a coward?
> Who calls me villain? breaks my pate across?
> Plucks off my beard and blows it in my face?
> Tweaks me by the nose? gives me the lie i' the throat
> As deep as to the lungs? Who does me this?
> *Ha!*

The exclamation "Ha!" clearly forms for the actor the rising broken close to this section of the speech: to print it as

> Ha, 'swounds, I should take it

destroys completely the effect that is being aimed at. The "Ha!", in its position here, becomes almost a note of defiance, contrasted with the sudden descent to the despairing " 'Swounds," which opens six lines of self-laceration and spluttering anger, ending with the broken "O vengeance!":

> *Ha!*
> 'Swounds, I should take it: for it cannot be
> But I am pigeon-liver'd and lack gall
> To make oppression bitter, or ere this
> I should have fatted all the region kites
> With this slave's offal: bloody, bawdy villain!
> Remorseless, treacherous, lecherous, kindless villain!
> *O vengeance!*

These two words in turn introduce a new movement wherein Hamlet casts scorn on himself for losing in words what should have been done in action:

> *O vengeance!*
> Why, what an ass am I! This is most brave,
> That I, the son of a dear father murder'd,
> Prompted to my revenge by heaven and hell,
> Must, like a whore, unpack my heart with words,
> And fall a-cursing, like a very drab,
> *A scullion!*

And "A scullion!" serves as a cue for the final words of the speech in which Hamlet plans the 'Mousetrap' play.[12]

It appears that the broken lines have their proper artistic place in the composition of the soliloquy and that their inclusion was inspired by Shakespeare's awareness of his audience's keen appreciation of the poetic forms of which he was making use.

The Modern Endeavour

This cursory examination of some among the advantages which Shakespeare, and his companions, possessed has value not merely for further stressing the fact that a modern playwright who strives to pen serious dramas in terms of common speech does so with one of his hands tied firmly behind his back, but also, and more importantly, for pointing to the problems to be faced and the principles to be adopted by any dramatist of to-day who seeks to escape from such fetters.

The first problem clearly is to find a form of language which may have such a connexion with our debased common speech as the standard Elizabethan blank verse measure had with the richer, less stereotyped, and more expressive familiar utterance of that time.

This problem, onerous in itself, is made the greater by its association with another. Shakespeare was in the advantageous position of being able to adapt for dramatic purposes much that already existed in the non-dramatic verse of his time. He could do so because the greater part of this non-dramatic verse was 'public' rather than 'private.' No doubt there were poets in his time who, despising the vulgar, wrote obscurely for a small circle of like-minded friends, but, in the main, Elizabethan verse addressed itself to wider circles. Some of it was confessedly 'easy'—the hundreds of ballads, for example, printed for common consumption and sung in the alehouses and market-squares; and much even of the poetry written by more ambitious authors for cultured readers, although it might be subtly invested with recondite allusions and associative values, had on the surface a direct and easily appreciated significance. We all know, however, that poetry has of late tended more and more towards the 'difficult,' often replete with private meanings unintelligible save to the initiate, and inclined towards introspection rather than towards 'public' utterance. Hence, for the most part, modern non-dramatic verse offers little to the playwright that he can satisfactorily use.

Furthermore, this non-dramatic verse of our age has veered towards formlessness. 'Free verse' instead of formal verse has become the characteristic style. Certainly there are poets to-day who put older measures to work, but the general stream of verse written during recent decades has had the effect of destroying the earlier sensitivity on the part of reader or listener to variations on established forms. It goes almost without saying, therefore, that many of the effects easily secured by Shakespeare are to-day impossible to reproduce, or at least reproducible only with the expenditure of severe effort.

Above all, the task which confronted Shakespeare and the task confronting any modern poetic dramatist are utterly at variance. Shakespeare and his early companions were faced with the problem of toning down. The rime royal and other stanzaic measures employed by the dramatists who had preceded them were too formal, too conventional for theatre use; and thus the blank verse, couplets, and occasional quatrains represented the reduction of an 'elevated' style to more ordinary levels. In contradistinction, the modern dramatist who essays to write conventionally patterned dialogue starts with virtually nothing, and consequently he has before him the immeasurably harder task of building up. He is somewhat like a man set on a sandy waste, assigned the problem of erecting a firm structure without material or means apt to prepare a solid foundation for his walls.

A fundamental question concerning objectives arises here. In view of the difficulties and of the particular conditions operative in the modern theatre, should the dramatist take a bold course or should he work, as it were, by concealed infiltration? When, in 1935, T. S. Eliot produced his trumpet call, *Murder in the Cathedral*, he left his auditors in no doubt concerning the conventional nature of his dialogue. The opening chorus—

> Here let us stand, close by the cathedral. Here let us wait.
> Are we drawn by a danger? Is it the knowledge of safety, that draws
>   our feet
> Towards the cathedral? What danger can be
> For us, the poor, the poor women of Canterbury? What tribulation
> With which we are not already familiar?

set the tone, and the later choral speech increased the poetic tension—

> There is no rest in the house. There is no rest in the street.
> I hear restless movement of feet. And the air is heavy and thick.
> Thick and heavy the sky. And the earth presses up against our feet.
> What is the sickly smell, the vapour? the dark green light from a
>   cloud on a withered tree? The earth is heaving to parturition of
>   issue of hell. What is the sticky dew that forms on the back of
>   my hand?

Fifteen years later, however, Eliot had changed his views, and in his *Poetry and Drama* firmly he laid down another method for the cultivation of the poetic drama. In brief, he there argued that, instead of boldly exciting the audience to recognize and respond to verse dialogue, every endeavour ought to be made to conceal from the auditors that what they are listening to is verse. "The verse rhythm," he declares, "should have its effect upon the hearers without their being conscious of it," and the use of prose alongside of verse ought to be avoided precisely because its introduction would make the audience aware of the rhythmic quality of the other passages. Thus, he further explained, in *The Cocktail Party*

> I laid down for myself the ascetic rule to avoid poetry which could not
> stand the test of strict dramatic utility; with such success, indeed, that
> it is perhaps an open question whether there is any poetry in the play
> at all.[13]

If, however, there is any virtue in our cursory observations concerning the indebtedness of Shakespeare to his dramatic style and in the analysis of the conventional nature of dramatic art, it must be obvious that such an endeavour as Eliot's deliberately denies what the conventional pattern can most potently offer. When 'poetic' drama is made to "enter into overt competition with prose drama," so that the hearers are, as it were, cheated into believing that no verse is present at all, the very foundations of that poetic drama are destroyed. Shakespeare's plays were given strength to endure not merely because Shakespeare was an outstanding poet, but also because the openly acknowledged verse forms which he employed were in close harmony with his dramatic objectives.

The only course likely to lead to a true revival is one concerning the orientation of which no one can be in any doubt. And there is a particular reason for this. The poetic play cannot make a profound impact in our time until the audience is given some basic form, equivalent to what blank verse was for the Elizabethans, which it can recognize and the music of which can be kept in its mind as a measure. In discussing Christopher Fry's work, J. L. Styan has asked:

What are the advantages of Shakespeare's firmer metrical line?

and he answers:

Mr Fry's rhythms are comparatively limp because he cannot fall back upon a standard of regularity from which any departure provides a rhythmic meaning to the ear.[14]

This question and answer, although specifically concerned with Fry's work, applies to all the modern attempts at the writing of plays of this kind, and they will continue to apply until some Marlowe of to-day succeeds, by his boldness and intensity, in startling his auditors into immediate acceptance of his measure.

The invention of the measure is unquestionably the most important thing, but with it, too, must come the subtly incisive metaphors and the inner sense of movement which gave strength alike to the Greeks and to the Elizabethans. In our present days, no single dramatic author has succeeded in fusing all the elements into a single integrated form of expression.

This becomes evident when we examine the work of those three men, Maxwell Anderson, T. S. Eliot, and Christopher Fry, who more than any others have won popular success in this sphere. First we listen to a passage from *Wingless Victory*:

> Why was this body gathered out of dust
> and bitten to my image? Let that day be evil
> when a lover took a lover to mould the face
> that stares up blind from my agony! Stares up
> and cries, and will not be still! Let all women born
> take a man's love with laughter, and leave it; take
> the coil of animals they give, and rise
> in mockery. And you dark peoples of the earth,
> cling to your dark, lie down and feed and sleep
> till you are earth again; but if you love,
> love only children of the dark—keep back
> from the bright hair and white hands, for they are light
> and cruel, like the gods', and the love that breeds
> between us is honeyed poison. Let no flesh
> of theirs touch flesh of yours; where they have touched
> the welt rots inward! They are unclean, unclean
> and leprous to us! To lie with them is sweet,
> but sweet with death! I bear that death in me
> in a burning tide that rises—choking—Oh, God—
> torture me no more!

One thing is vital here—the dynamic quality of the verbs. The lines drive forward with stress on "gathered ... bitten ... mould ... leave ... rise ... cling ... keep back ... touch ... rots ... bear ... rises." But that is all. The metaphors have no driving force; the language is repetitive and woolly. It has been said that "Mr Anderson's facility often betrays him into a willingness to accept emotional clichés as well as verbal ones," that in his work one has "the feeling that one has heard or seen it all before," that there is "the absence of any sense that one's thought or feeling is being anywhere enlarged."[15] And this is true: the speech quoted above has no patterning in sound; it is over-exclamatory; its imagery seems ornamental rather than organic.

The presence of a dynamic quality in Anderson's writing, however, aids in drawing attention to its lack in much of the dialogue penned by T. S. Eliot, an author far more distinguished as a stylist and gifted with a poetic imagination far beyond his. T. S. Eliot is indeed a great poet, but when we turn to, say, Thomas' climactic utterance in *Murder in the Cathedral* we must be forced to decide that his poetic style, because remaining static, has not been given true dramatic quality:

> Now is my way clear, now is the meaning plain:
> Temptation shall not come in this kind again.
> The last temptation is the greatest treason:
> To do the right deed for the wrong reason.
> The natural vigour in the venial sin
> Is the way in which our lives begin.
> Thirty years ago, I searched all the ways
> That lead to pleasure, advancement and praise
> Delight in sense, in learning and in thought,
> Music and philosophy, curiosity,
> The purple bullfinch in the lilac tree,
> The tiltyard skill, the strategy of chess,
> Love in the garden, singing to the instrument,
> Were all things equally desirable.
> Ambition comes when early force is spent
> And when we find no longer all things possible.
> Ambition comes behind and unobservable. . . .

Even those few words in this passage which suggest action have intellectual rather than physical connotations: "come in this kind" does not really imply movement; "the way in which our lives begin" is static, not active; "that lead to pleasure" has no sense of action; "Ambition comes," because of the commonplace quality of the verb, does not bring to the mind a physical, stalking figure. And this motionless quality becomes even more pronounced in the later plays. Sir Claude speaks in *The Confidential Clerk*:

> I'm not so sure of that. I've tried to believe in facts;
> And I've always acted as if I believed in them.
> I thought it was facts that my father believed in;
> I thought that what he cared for was power and wealth;
> And I came to see that what I had interpreted
> In this way, was something else to *him*—
> An idea, an inspiration. . . .

And Celia similarly expresses herself in *The Cocktail Party*:

> I know I ought to be able to accept that
> If I might still have it. Yet it leaves me cold.
> Perhaps that's just a part of my illness,
> But I feel it would be a kind of surrender—
> No, not a surrender—more like a betrayal.

> You see, I think I really had a vision of something
> Though I don't know what it is. I don't want to forget it.
> I want to live with it. . . .

Christopher Fry exhibits more theatrical vitality, and, particularly in his later verse, an inner movement is frequently suggested by his lines. Thus, for example, Henry's reflections in *Curtmantle* have a dramatic vigour that goes beyond the reflections of Eliot's Becket, Sir Claude, and Celia:

> Dear Christ, the day that any man would dread
> Is when life goes separate from the man,
> When he speaks what he doesn't say, and does
> What is not his doing, and an hour of the day
> Which was unimportant as it went by
> Comes back revealed as the satan of all hours,
> Which will never let the man go. And then
> He would see how the natural poisons in him
> Creep from everything he sees and touches
> As though saying, 'Here is the world you created
> In your own image.' But this is not the world
> He would have made. Sprung from a fraction of life,
> A hair-fine crack in the dam, the unattended
> Moment sweeps away the whole attempt,
> The heart, thoughts, belief, longing
> And intention of the man. It is infamous,
> This life is infamous, if it uses us
> Against our knowledge or will. . . .

The day "goes separate"; the hour, having passed, "comes back"; the natural poisons "creep from everything he sees and touches"; the moment has "sprung from a fraction of life"; it is a crack in the dam; it "sweeps away the whole attempt." At the same time even Fry sometimes pens dialogue that suggests the passivity of ideas rather than the dynamics of forcible and energic motion. Jennet in *The Lady's Not for Burning* thus is made to utter her thoughts:

> I am interested
> In my feelings, I seem to wish to have some importance
> In the play of time. If not,
> Then sad was my mother's pain, sad my breath,
> Sad the articulation of my bones,
> Sad, sad my alacritous web of nerves,
> Woefully, woefully sad my wondering brain,

> To be shaped and sharpened into such tendrils
> Of anticipation, only to feed the swamp of space. . . .

Fry has brought much to the drama of our time, and we may well feel that his particular form of patterned language comes closer than any other towards suggesting a measure appropriate for the modern theatre; yet this speech of Jennet demonstrates that even he has not been able to reach a complete solution of the problem.

It is true that the passage quoted above is concerned with the "wondering brain," but we have already noted with what ease Shakespeare gave dynamic movement to Macbeth's speculations, and perhaps, for purposes of contrast, even more impressive is another exhibition of the "wondering brain" in *Julius Cæsar*. Brutus, like Macbeth, stands motionless on the stage:

> It must be by his death; and for my part,
> I know no personal cause to *spurn* at him,
> But for the general: he would be crown'd.
> How that might *change* his nature, there's the question.
> It is the bright day that *brings forth* the adder,
> And that craves *wary walking*. Crown him—that!
> And then, I grant, *we put a sting* in him
> That at his will he may *do danger* with.
> Th'abuse of greatness is, when it *disjoins*
> Remorse from power; and to speak truth of Cæsar,
> I have not known when his affections *sway'd*
> More than his reason. But 'tis a common proof
> That lowliness is young ambition's *ladder*,
> Whereto the *climber-upward turns his face*;
> But when he once *attains the upmost round*,
> He then *unto the ladder turns his back*,
> *Looks in the clouds*, scorning *the base degrees*
> *By which he did ascend*. . . .

The actor on the stage is still; but in imagination we see before us a figure spurning, changing shape—an adder crawling from its shell, stinging and doing danger—remorse disjoining itself from power— a youthful aspirant climbing a ladder to its topmost rung, turning from it, and raising his countenance to the sky.

The lack of such a dynamic quality as is exemplified in Brutus' soliloquy is perhaps the most important weakness in much of the poetic dialogue written by those modern poets who have turned to the stage; but there are others as well. Some of these are due to external conditions; there are some for which the playwrights themselves must be deemed responsible. That a certain feeling of strain is perceptible in many modern poetic plays is not the dramatists' fault; they are working in the midst of an atmosphere far different from that enveloping the Elizabethans, when all writers for the theatre were familiarly referred to as 'poets' and when the audiences normally expected to listen to verse forms in the words given to the actors. The very fact that they are striving to offer to their auditors a kind of speech distinct from that of current theatrical fare means that, instead of the patterned dialogue taking shape naturally in their imagination—so that the shape itself becomes the only possible way of conceiving and expressing the themes and characters—the poets of to-day approach their writing with a sense of deliberate purpose, and thus, to a certain extent, the poetic form given to their dialogue at times may almost seem a mere ornament. For this we cannot blame the authors; they are attempting to do something which came easily and without effort to Shakespeare and his companions, but which to-day can be achieved only with extreme difficulty.

If, however, the dramatists are not responsible here, many of them are responsible for a failure to give to their works an immediately perceptible and firm outline. Among the plays which have recently been written in this style, a large proportion have proved difficult for audiences to grasp, partly because the plot-material was too subtle and intricate, partly because the dialogue itself did not possess the power of making a strong primal impact on the spectators' minds. No auditor, however unlettered he may be, can fail to understand the plot of *Hamlet*, *Lear*, *Twelfth Night*, or *Much Ado*; and modern revivals of such plays as *Œdipus Rex*, *Antigone*, and *Medea* have shown that even the Athenian dramas, dealing with legendary matter which was part of the cultural heritage of their original auditors, but which to-day is familiar to few save specialists, tell their stories in a manner readily understandable. In contrast with this, we find that the plots of many modern poetic plays are so complex, involved, and perplexing that even the most alert among the audiences find it impossible to grasp their implications.

In addition to this, numerous speeches assume forms which may not be too hard to unravel when read on the printed page, but which have not the power to convey a primal meaning when they are heard from an actor's lips. When Shakespeare makes Ulysses deliver his great orations to Agamemnon and Achilles, or when he causes Leontes to give explosive expression to his passionate jealousy, the exact significance of the words indeed becomes clear in our consciousness only after we have devoted to them a very great deal of minute scrutiny; but, even if we have never read them, when we hear an actor delivering the lines we know at once what he is talking about. Ulysses is telling Agamemnon how order ought to be maintained; he is warning Achilles how easily reputation may become tarnished; Leontes' jealousy is palpable. Even in the most distinguished of modern poetic plays we often listen to speeches, no doubt savouring their sound, but having not the slightest idea of what the actor, and the author, intend to convey to us.

The problems are many. Certainly the journalistic play of verisimilitude has little chance now of contributing vitality to the stage, both because it already has had its run and because it struggles against the true theatre's current; yet the task of establishing something to take its place remains full of hazards. Patterned language in drama means far more than just 'poetry'; at the same time, it must draw its strength from the traditions of poetic utterance, moulding these to suit the conditions operative in the theatre of our time. And audiences will not be likely to acclaim the efforts until dramatists come along who can embody in modern forms the basic principles which impelled and inspired the Greek and Elizabethan playwrights, and who can speak directly and unequivocally to the modern ear. Manifestly, such a style, if it is to come, will not result from conscious ratiocination, but from intuitional awareness of the stage's requirements; nevertheless, an analysis of some of the basic principles (of which the foregoing discussion is merely a rough sketch) can assist us in reaching standards for the appreciation of what, we trust, the creative artists may have to offer.

NOTES TO CHAPTER 6

1. W. S. Maugham, *The Summing Up* (1938), pp. 144–146.
2. Sir Cedric Hardwicke (*Theatre Arts*, February 1939, p. 107).
3. Robert Edmond Jones, 'Toward a New Stage' (*Theatre Arts*, March 1941, p. 191). See also Lee Simonson, *The Stage is Set* (1932), p. 436.
4. Ivor Brown, 'After Chekhov' (*Drama*, Spring 1960).
5. Lee Simonson, *The Stage is Set* (1932), p. 431.
6. Eric Bentley, *The Playwright as Thinker* (1946), p. 121.

7. Among the Zuñi Indians, for example, "the efficacy of the formula depends upon its absolutely correct repetition." (Ruth L. Bunzel, 'Introduction to Zuñi Ceremonialism' (*Report of the Bureau of American Ethnology*, xlvii, 1933, p. 492).

8. W. S. Maugham, *The Summing Up* (1938), p. 144.

9. W. Clemen, *Shakespeares Bilder* (1936), pp. 166–182.

10. Logan Pearsall Smith, *On Reading Shakespeare* (1933), p. 79.

11. Some paragraphs in this section are reproduced from an article, 'Shakespeare and Elizabethan Poetic Drama' (*Kwartalnik Neofilologiczny*, vi, 1959, pp. 1–15).

12. It should, of course, be observed that at various times attempts have been made to 'regularize' the blank verse of this speech and to attribute to actors some of the extra-metrical phrases. Thus, for example, Harold Jenkins (in an essay on 'Playhouse Interpolations in the Folio *Hamlet*' (*Studies in Bibliography*, xiii, 1960, pp. 31–81)) would reject "O vengeance!" on these grounds, seeking to argue that it is "condemned by its context." But it is by no means condemned by its context: the tenor of the speech demands this exclamatory conclusion to the frenzied verbal attack upon Claudius; in effect, it provides a moment of pause before the Prince turns upon himself with "Why, what an ass am I!"

13. T. S. Eliot, *Poetry and Drama* (1950).

14. J. L. Styan, *The Elements of Drama* (1960), p. 42.

15. J. W. Krutch, *The American Drama since 1918* (1939), pp. 291–293.

Conclusion

CREATIVE authors, in general, certainly do not have their styles determined for them by the precepts of critics, yet perhaps some measure of distinction may be drawn between those who apply themselves to the drama and those who are concerned with other forms of literature. Throughout its history, the drama has shown itself peculiarly sensitive to the impact of theory. Discussions regarding lyric poetry, the epic, or prose fiction tend for the most part to be only retrospectively 'theoretical'; they are concerned with critical analysis of existing works and seldom play a really significant rôle in influencing the writing of other lyrics, epics, or novels. From the very beginning, on the other hand, dramatic theory has inclined to assume a double function, engaging in retrospective analysis and also definitely influencing the shape of the drama to come. Even during periods of flourishing creative endeavour, even among dramatists most emphatic in their assertions of independence, the impress of critical thought is patent; and the realization of that impress has been amply attested by the numbers of playwrights who, in preface or in separate volume, have applied themselves to critical, theoretical speculations and pronouncements of their own about the art of the stage.

This influence of theory on drama has, in the main, had greatest force rather in broad directives than in practical, particular matters. There exist, of course, several 'manuals of craftsmanship' which essay to instruct authors how to write their plays; but it seems likely that not many dramatists have gained much profit from these volumes and few have really composed their scenes by following the instructions in detail. On the other hand we encounter again and again, during different periods, clear indications of the manner in which these authors have had their works shaped, consciously or unconsciously, by general views, critically enunciated, concerning the drama's objectives.

Naturally, this influence has for the most part been exerted by the outlining of positive programmes. For example, Ibsen openly confessed how much he owed to the reading of Hermann Hettner's *Das moderne Drama* (1850), a work in which stress was laid upon the importance of building plays upon an awareness of current strains within the social fabric. Besides such direct and positive influence, however, there is something else. At times critical thought has inclined to neglect or to minimize the significance of certain aspects of the drama, and these omissions in the theoretical writings have negatively played a part in shaping the objectives and methods of contemporary dramatists. Of this a typical instance can be found in the not inconsiderable series of twentieth-century volumes designed to offer practical advice to authors which were published during the first decade of the present century. One of the earliest of these was William Archer's *Play-making*, issued in 1912. When we examine his manual we find that it is almost wholly taken up with discussions of plot construction. Nearly three hundred pages are devoted to the mechanical framework of drama, with chapters which extend from 'Exposition,' 'The First Act,' 'Tension and Suspension,' on to 'The Obligatory Scene,' 'Logic,' 'Keeping a Secret,' 'Climax and Anticlimax.' The truly significant feature of the book is that, following these three hundred pages, a beggarly eight are considered sufficient for the treatment of 'Character and Psychology,' while barely nine are all that Archer can spare for what he calls 'Dialogue and Details.'

Almost precisely similar proportions appear in a kindred work published about a quarter of a century later, John Howard Lawson's *Theory and Technique of Playwriting* (1936). Well over a hundred and twenty pages are devoted to such subjects as 'Dynamics' and 'Mechanics of Construction'; only eight are needed for 'Characterisation' and eleven serve for 'Dialogue.'

The impression created here is obvious—that in the construction of drama, which after all is a part of literature, the 'mechanics' are all-important, and that the actual writing, the providing of the dialogue, is a matter of minor significance. That, however, is not all. The attention paid to craftsmanship in this school of critical opinion, with the corresponding neglect of other qualities, has led to a confusion concerning the nature of these qualities themselves. An instance of this may be selected from a recently published volume by J. L. Styan, especially revealing because this critic is one who elsewhere shows himself intent upon effective dialogue. "The first minute in Ibsen's *Rosmersholm*," he says, "demonstrates his meticulous use of words."[1] Ibsen was, of course, a master of drama, and Styan's statement sounds satisfactory until we proceed closely to examine the lines he quotes in support of his statement. Without doubt, the opening twelve short speeches of *Rosmersholm* are adroitly arranged for the purpose of establishing the situation, but the force of the dialogue definitely does not depend upon "a meticulous use of words"; it depends upon excellent craftsmanship in manipulating facts. The first line spoken by Mrs Helseth—

Hadn't I better begin and lay the table for supper, miss?

does not owe its effect to the words employed but to the conjunction of her question with Rebecca's answer,

Yes, do. Mr Rosmer ought to be in directly.

The words themselves are not only commonplace; in the original Norwegian or in translation they could be modified in a dozen different ways. Mrs Helseth might be made to say

Perhaps I ought to get the table ready for supper, miss,

and Rebecca might answer

Yes, I think so. I expect Mr Rosmer will be in any minute now—

and absolutely nothing would be lost. The effect is secured by an arrangement of question and reply the precise form of which does not matter.

That the craftsmanship here is excellent cannot be denied; but, equally, it cannot be denied that the critical emphasis has the effect both of misconceiving the power which a true "meticulous use of words" can mean in the theatre and of darkening our appreciation of the essence of that power.

The Break in Tradition

Considerations such as these serve to underline the necessity, particularly urgent in our time, of exploring basic principles and of determining our own attitudes. Even although it may involve a re-examination of matters already discussed above, the entire field must here be surveyed as a whole.

The pivotal facts to be observed in any such survey are the shift in orientation which came in the middle of the eighteenth century

M

and the later development, within our own century, of a further
shift which, so far from suggesting an altered view, might be regarded as a more exactly determined objective based on the
eighteenth-century sentimentalists' programme.

In general, as we have seen, this eighteenth-century movement involved the virtual overthrow of the various traditionally established
genres and the cultivation of an all-embracing concept of 'play'—or,
as the French called it, *drame*; it laid stress on the theatrical presentation before the audience of aspects of ordinary life; it thus tended
to replace audience involvement by documentary interest; it sought,
not for poetic expression, but for the simulation of common speech;
and, above all, it encouraged plays inspired by an 'idea,' intent upon
conveying a message.

All of this did not actually appear in the early manifestos issued
by Beaumarchais and Diderot, and some of the concepts summarized
above had to wait for many years for full enunciation by Hettner and
others; but within the relatively limited scope of the essays penned
by the two French dramatist-critics the germinating seeds for a new
theory had been firmly planted.

For the planting itself much can be said in defence. Without re-
servation we may admit that, when the new anti-Aristotelian poetics
was promulgated, the endeavour had full justification. At that time
the 'classical' style based on imitation of Racine's tragedies had lost
its vitality; even Voltaire's emphatic genius could not bring it to life.
These French eighteenth-century dramas suffered from precisely the
same debility as afflicted the corresponding run of English plays
constructed out of an amalgam composed of elements selected from
Shakespeare and elements taken from the love-and-honour dramas.
All these works were dully imitative—second-rate and third-rate
copies of their originals, completely out of touch with their immediate surroundings, stiff-jointed, and uttering their platitudinous
sentiments in stilted terms. During the years that they held the
boards, the majority of dramatic critics were unable to do more than
repeat what had already been repeated a hundred times before and
to niggle in pettifogging manner over unimportant, often absurd,
issues. The theory underlying the older tradition, like the plays
written according to its precepts, had clearly lost all power. Without
doubt, then, there was virtue in a fresh approach.

True, we may now discern a number of anticipatory signs before
the publication of these two essays, but all such signs had been frag-

mentary and tentative; no single critic had thought out their implications. The whole early development and extension of tragicomedy,
for example, had demonstrated the operation of a desire to move
away from that rigid adherence to the time-honoured genres which
alone were approved by the Aristotelian theorists; the selection, even
as far back as Shakespeare's time, of common domestic themes and
circumstances for tragic treatment had broken shatteringly into the
hitherto sacrosanct area of subject-matter considered proper for
tragedy; the gradual adoption of prose as the prime medium for
comedy had dissipated the concept of drama as fundamentally poetic;
and when George Lillo startled London and other capitals by his
boldness both in choosing for his tragic hero a young criminal
apprentice and in casting his play's dialogue in prose, the ground had
been well prepared for the concepts enunciated by Diderot and Beaumarchais. Not surprisingly, too, these innovations in dramatic composition had already come to influence at least some theoretical speculations: even half a century before Lillo's time, John Dryden found
himself prepared to accept tragicomedy and he was even led to
wonder whether Aristotle, if he could have had the opportunity of
seeing English seventeenth-century plays, might not "have changed
his mind" concerning some of his critical pronouncements.[2]

None of these deviations in practice and in critical thought, however, brought about any general break with already existing principles; Dryden's ideas on the drama, despite the independence of his
mind and his many deviations from the views of stricter critics,
remained founded upon the Aristotelian formula. We must, then,
fully admit the freshness of the new concept as it shaped itself in
Diderot's and Beaumarchais' essays—a concept which had the merit
of proposing, in place of an outworn approach, something basically
fresh.

We may further admit that, in presenting their views, these two
men were implicitly recognizing a truth—that the drama, if it is
to be vital, must reflect the changing cultural patterns and interests
of the society to which it is addressed. Diderot and Beaumarchais
lived before our modern scientific age, but their steps had carried
them at least to its threshold; before its gates they stood and these,
slightly ajar, offered them glimpses of what was to come. Science
depends upon material things; its realm is the realm of fact and of
physical reality; and thus the stress laid by these two critics upon
the dramatic presentation of actuality was fully justifiable. Drama

deals with human beings, and human beings exist in a society of their fellows; in this expanding scientific *milieu* it was natural that a principal preoccupation of the time should be the question of man's social life, the ordering of the social community and the relationship of that community to the individual. When, therefore, these critics suggested that the lives and surroundings of ordinary men and women were of greater significance in a play than regal splendours and the terrors of legendary or historical courts, they were engaged in applying to the theatre a prevailing trend in the thought of the world they lived in.

That this emphasis upon the actual and familiar possessed an inspiring force becomes amply apparent when we look at the stage's development during the following century and a half. We must, of course, acknowledge that the development of a new drama founded on these principles was slow and gradual. The sentimental playwrights themselves were not able to create anything of enduring worth; their hands fumbled, and in any event the theatrical conditions of their time were not yet ripe for the true cultivation of what the theory demanded. Different methods of lighting the stage, fresh scenic devices, and machinery apt to provide a fitting background for a realistic drama came only in the nineteenth century; and hence many decades had to pass by before, in a series of successive movements, a firmer foundation was laid for plays inspired by the sentimentalists' concept—and that concept itself had to be more fully elaborated before it could inspire anything of prime distinction. Eventually, however, the end was reached; by the close of the nineteenth century, Ibsen, Strindberg, Chekhov, and others had succeeded in reaching a culmination, and, in doing so, had brought to the drama a distinction such as it had not exhibited since the days of Elizabethan England and those of late seventeenth-century France. Without the faintest shadow of a doubt, a *Wild Duck*, a *Father*, and a *Cherry Orchard* possess a value, not only far beyond, but inherently distinct from, that of a *Cato* or an *Irene*. Had it not been for the enunciation of the new theory we should not now have before us a set of unquestioned dramatic masterpieces worthy of being considered alongside the masterpieces of the past. The theory, therefore, has been completely justified by what it succeeded in encouraging. About this there can be no question.

Playgoers To-day

Once we have reached this decision, however, a further question does arise.

The process of growth, as we have seen, was gradual, and equally gradual was the establishment of the new plays in the public theatres. Even at the close of the nineteenth century many of those dramatists who had reached farthest could find only a limited public within the Parisian Théâtre Libre; some had to be content with no more than occasional performances organized by such groups as the Incorporated Stage Society in London. By the 1930's, however, if not before, the achievements of the innovators had penetrated fully into the area of the ordinary stage, and the work of Ibsen, Chekhov, and their companions had become familiar.

By that time, in effect, these men had established themselves in much the same position as that occupied by Shakespeare in 1613. On his retirement from the stage, Shakespeare had completed a series of tragedies, comedies, and histories, in which almost all the stops in his particular style had been tried out in all their variety; and as a result his very mastery made it virtually impossible for his immediate successors to create any music in the same mode which might sound fresh and original. His own plays remained vital, but in so far as the dramatists were concerned the impact of these plays was too recent to permit of creative imitation, and consequently they laid a chilling hand on the tragedies and comedies immediately succeeding them. If we proceed to compare the first half of the seventeenth century with the first half of the twentieth from this point of view, we are bound to recognize that this relationship between Shakespeare and the playwrights who followed in his footsteps is very close to that between the late nineteenth-century and early twentieth-century masters of the realistic drama and the playwrights of our time.

The parallel calls for careful thought, but before its implications are explored something further requires to be noted. It is a fact that the culmination of the realistic drama and its establishment in the playhouses coincided with a rapid decline in playgoing. This fact cannot be denied: as we have already seen, audiences in the provinces are to-day only a fraction of what once they were, and all informed observers agree that the composition of metropolitan audiences has markedly altered within recent years. It is certainly true that outside forces have been partly responsible for this, but, again as has been suggested above, we need to look at the matter with care; before we hastily and superficially attribute the decline in playgoing wholly to the advent of the film, and, later, of television, we need to ask ourselves whether the erstwhile spectators, instead of having been enticed from their wonted seats by metal more attractive and cheaper, have not really been forced out of their seats from within. This might be put in a different way by inquiring whether the concurrence of audience decline and of realistic achievement may not be more than purely coincidental. Is it possible that many who, had they lived in the past, would have been regular playgoers now cease to attend the theatre precisely because they are not being given what they consciously or unconsciously look for from the stage?

Just as soon as this question is put, we are forced to acknowledge two things. First, the metropolitan success won recently by numbers of plays written in the realistic mode has depended, not upon general support, but upon the support of a limited section or limited sections, of the community. Amid the teeming millions of present-day London or New York, sufficient fans of particular players and sufficient adherents of particular political persuasions can be found to give even mediocre dramas the opportunities of runs. In many respects the run of a play in London or New York to-day may be regarded as the modern equivalent to a production half a century ago in a little specialized theatre. Often the run is not the consequence of general public appeal, but of an appeal inherently limited in scope. From this we may move to the second point. During recent years there have been numerous instances of plays, which, although they secured metropolitan runs, have bored or alienated provincial audiences. Now, it is easy to explain this by glibly assuming that provincial audiences are duller, less intelligent, and less perceptive than audiences in the metropolis; but before we accept such a diagnosis care must be taken to see that the symptoms have been properly observed. What we need to do is to ask ourselves a basic question: may the difference in reception not result from a sectionalism in the metropolitan theatres and a wider representation in the provincial? Confronted by this question, we find ourselves inclined to admit that the provincial spectators, although numerically only a fraction of what once they were, do in fact remain largely unsectionalized, embracing within their sphere a diversity of classes and interests; perhaps indeed we might almost regard them as the last remnants of the old general 'ordinary' audience. If this is so, then their tastes and attitudes, instead of being facilely dismissed, deserve serious consideration. When we find that for many of these spectators *Long Day's Journey into Night* proved, in the main, a dreary experience, that *The Wrong Side of the Park* seemed to them naïve, forced, and almost incredible, and that *Look Back in Anger* appeared both tedious and slightly absurd, we require to pause. From such plays the provincial audiences evidently failed, in general, to derive that characteristic theatrical excitement which unconsciously they craved for.

That this craving has not completely vanished is in itself encouraging, and a vivid demonstration of its enduring force is amply evidenced in the success which has attended the numerous seasonal festivals which have sprung into prominence during the very years when the ordinary theatre has rapidly declined. Of course we cannot deny that this success depends partly upon the opportunity offered by these festivals of combining a holiday with other attractions; but, in saying so, we must be careful not to imply that such a double objective deserves to be despised or condemned; after all, the theatre in the past has often flourished at its best when it was associated with the holiday spirit. Performances in ancient Athens were seasonal affairs, too; the daily work was put aside by all the inhabitants of the little city-state when they flocked into the vast Dionysian auditorium. If, however, the holiday spirit animated the Athenian citizens, their main focus was upon the tragedies and comedies displayed before them; and similarly the crowds who throng to the modern festivals have selected their centres—Salzburg, Avignon, Syracuse, any one of the three Stratfords—largely because of the dramas which they know they will have the opportunity of seeing there. This being so, it seems vitally important to note and consider the dramatic fare which the promoters of these modern festivals have found to offer most power of attraction. For the most part, the plays associated with the names of Ibsen and his companions are notably absent; in this realm Shakespeare stands supremely majestic—not only at those centres specifically dedicated to the performance of his works, but also at dozens of other places which might well have been expected to select dramas of a different kind; performances of plays by Æschylus, Sophocles, and Euripides have proved popular; many years ago Salzburg discovered the rich appeal of *Jedermann* and *Das grosse Welttheater*, and Edinburgh, somewhat to its surprise, saw *Ane Satyre of the Thrie Estaits* catch the imagination of rapt auditors. A glance at any summary list of recent festival attractions shows at once that almost everywhere dramas from the traditional past are in the preponderance; when other later plays are occasionally selected for performance, the choice tends to fall on those which have been inspired by the older tradition—Goethe's *Iphigenie auf Tauris* or Victor Hugo's *Maria Stuart*; and when new plays appear on the bills, most commonly these are poetic or historical.

This is the kind of repertoire which draws the thousands to make their long journeys of theatrical pilgrimage by aeroplane, by railway, by automobile, or by bus, and even by cycle. No doubt some of the pilgrims find most attraction in comedies such as *The Taming of the Shrew*; among these crowds there must be many spectators akin to the man who, on being asked after a visit to Stratford what play he preferred, replied that he enjoyed most the one (he had forgotten its title) where the husband beat up his wife. But, even admitting so much, we must feel considerable surprise to find that these modern holiday audiences—audiences which might have been expected to seek only for merriment and frivolity—seem to discover in tragedy qualities equally or even more attractive.

It seems clear, therefore, that the qualities inherent in the drama of the older tradition and particularly the qualities inherent in a *Hamlet*, a *Lear*, or an *Œdipus Rex* are by no means outworn in our age; it also means that the old general audience, provided it is given what it seeks for, has not disappeared. Out of festivals in ancient Athens the drama rose; it would almost appear as though the hope of calling back spectators to the theatre to-day may lie in the resuscitation of the spirit of the Dionysian stage.

Politics and the Drama

So far we have been concerned only with contrasting the older tradition with the newer tradition as it was outlined by Diderot and Beaumarchais, and as it was carried on further in the theoretical writings of Hettner and others during the nineteenth century. One further and even more significant contrast has, however, developed within our own century, and this more than anything else is creating confusion in our midst.

From the very beginning, dramatic theory has paused to ask a fundamental question: what, after all, is the use of the theatre? There have, of course, been some who were content to accept it solely for its entertainment value. Even during the period when classically inspired ideas were predominant, François Ogier could dare to assert that plays are composed merely "for pleasure and amusement";[3] and it hardly needs to be said that a vast amount of playhouse activity, from ancient days until now, has been animated by no thought beyond the putting on of a 'show' likely to attract custom. Indeed, the majority of those concerned with the practical theatre have been and still are rather contemptuous of any who try to suggest that there is need of searching for a purpose in their work beyond that of providing entertainment.

Nevertheless, most of the greater critics of the drama have declared that the stage, by the very nature of its being, possesses a 'political' or a 'social' significance, and this significance they have sought to define. We find the trend already clear and openly expressed in Aristotle's *Poetics*, a work which sets out to ask and answer the question why tragedy makes its appeal and what effect it has upon the auditor's mind. In order to appreciate Aristotle's position we need to set his critical essay against its background in thought. A few years before the *Poetics* was written Aristotle's master, Plato, had written *The Republic*, an attempt to outline what seemed to form the ideal constitution of a democratic society. In the midst of the discussion Plato had turned to consider the function in society of the poets, particularly the dramatic poets; and, since he saw that these men's efforts depended upon uncontrollable emotion, upon an imaginative force which sometimes justified the application to them of the term 'madness,' whereas his own ideal city-state was based rigidly upon the exercise of reason, he found himself forced to banish these irrational singers from his dream society. To a large extent, Aristotle's aim in the *Poetics* was to combat this harsh judgment and to offer a defence for the dramatists; this he did by developing a logical argument—first, that the drama provides legitimate pleasure, secondly that it can present an image of events more 'philosophical' than history, and thirdly that the 'terror and pity' induced by contemplation of tragic works benefits the spectators by a kind of emotional purgation—"through pity and fear effecting a purification from suchlike passions."

On the basis of Aristotle's theory, not always fully understood, succeeding critics constantly repeated their conviction that drama ought to aim at a combination of delight (which might be interpreted in one way as æsthetic pleasure and in another as sheer entertainment) and of moral teaching: Horace's *utile dulci* provides a happily epigrammatic summary of the concept. It is true that the less imaginative critics often came to interpret the moral teaching in a manner simple, artless, and unproductive, suggesting that it consisted or should consist in the presentation of directly framed moral precepts. Thus, for example, Ælius Donatus could define comedy as

> a story which deals with various habits and customs of public and private affairs, from which may be learned, on the one hand, what is useful in life, and, on the other, what is to be avoided;[4]

and even the more perceptive Sir Philip Sidney could explain that tragedy

> teacheth the uncertainty of this world, and upon how weake foundations guilden roofes are builded.[5]

Usually, however, the explanation of the drama's moral power was more delicately and more subtly framed; it was recognized that the simple presentation of a rationally conceived and expressed 'message' was not that which characteristically it had to offer. Aristotle's own penetrating analysis essentially agrees with Lessing's acute summation, centuries later, in which he emphasized that the "real general importance" of comedy "lies in the laughter itself" and that, so far as tragic drama is concerned,

> we make a mistake in looking on the final moral sentiment to be found at the close of various tragedies of the ancients as though that stood for the entirety of the piece.[6]

During more recent times, the admixture of pleasure and profit in art—which, of course, includes the drama—has been further explored and extended, with, in particular, the development of the concept of 'æsthetic distance,' which suggests that one prime social value of artistic endeavour rests in the opportunity it gives to the spectator or reader of releasing himself from the trammelling practical affairs of daily life and of entering imaginatively into a world of intense perception. When Cleanth Brooks declares that tragedy's essential worth is to be discovered in its power of "dealing with ultimates" and of enabling men to reach self-knowledge,"[7] he too is giving modern expression to what is implicit in Aristotle's speculations and to what has been a prevailing view among the theorists of the older tradition. The moral or social value inherent in drama is thus conceived in imaginative terms. According to this view, we do not, or should not, come away from a comedy or tragedy as from a sermon or political

harangue with some rationally formulated injunction or philosophical concept implanted in our minds; rather, by the stirring of
our emotions and by our involvement in the theatrical action, we
should be imaginatively stimulated to a deeper and wider perception
both of ourselves and of the world in which we live. The dramatist,
giving delight, should have enlarged our horizons; and thus the
theatrical experience, besides being entertainment, should possess a
potent value for man and society, unattainable by any other means.

What, however, must be honestly faced is the fact that in the
twentieth century another and diametrically opposed view has become widely endorsed. Diderot and Beaumarchais, Hettner and
Archer, despite their cultivation of a non-Aristotelian approach,
would in the main have agreed to accept the concept which has been
outlined above; their only amendment would have been that, since
the stress of social conflicts has become peculiarly acute in modern
times, the exposition of these conflicts must be the main business of
modern dramatists. In much modern theory, on the other hand, a
wholly different attitude towards art and the theatre is obvious, and
here, in a changed form, we return to Plato. Plato, trying to build
his ideal political community upon reason, banished the poets; the
new theory is content to keep the poets, but makes them serve ends
other than purely dramatic. The drama no longer is conceived as
possessing a value in itself; it is made subservient to a political objective—the spread of a particular social philosophy. According to this
line of thought, in those countries where communism has been
established, the drama's mission has to be rigidly conservative,
emphasizing the virtues of the communist system; in countries
where that political philosophy has not been accepted, then its
mission has to be revolutionary, partly by exposing the supposed
evils of other political systems, partly by lauding its own supposed
virtues. Whether in the one or the other, propagandist aims predomi-
nate, and a play's value is made dependent upon what it has to contribute to the political objective.

For those who have embraced this philosophy as a whole, therefore, it is entirely logical and legitimate to regard a play's 'idea' as
its chief—indeed its only significant—contribution; and it is similarly
logical and legitimate to encourage three main types of drama. The
first of these may be called the 'straight-message play,' engaged in
putting forward some political concept before the spectators. The
second is the 'demonstration play,' a sort of documentary in which

a selected aspect of social life is set on the stage as realistically as possible and from the mere contemplation of which the audience is supposed to benefit. The third, mostly associated with the work of Bertolt Brecht, may be styled the 'critical play.' This last form has special interest for us because Brecht, apart from the writing of his own pieces in that style, has seen fit to support it in theory by penning what he has specifically described as a new "non-Aristotelian poetics." The "non-Aristotelian drama," he declares,

> would not dream of handing the spectator over to an inspiring theatrical experience. Anxious to teach the spectator a quite definite practical attitude, directed towards changing the world, it must begin by making him adopt in the theatre a quite different attitude from what he is used to.[8]

The actor, he explains, must take a critical attitude towards his rôle; 'estrangement' or 'alienation' must be his objective; the spectator must be restrained from becoming submerged in the mass of the audience; his reason, not his emotions, must be stimulated; he must be summoned to action.

This, naturally, is all very well provided one believes that the ordering of social life forms the ultimate goal and that such ordering can be secured by no other means than the establishing of a particular social system; in these circumstances, then, obviously, every human activity, including the drama, has to be made instrumental towards securing the desired end. Here is a critical approach which is perfectly clear and uncompromising, and, since it is so, we can discuss its tenets rationally. By no means, however, can this be said concerning much of the current thought concerning the theatre among those who still remain primarily intent upon dramatic objectives. Recently a young playwright declared that art was beginning to have no meaning for him and that what he wanted was "bloody revolution." This is honest, and the author has every right to his social-philosophical attitude; but surely, if we are interested in the drama and not in political programmes, we are not justified in regarding the plays written from this point of view as offering real encouragement for the theatre, as some of our dramatic critics and stage enthusiasts are currently doing? In fact these critics and enthusiasts are striving to serve two masters, and the serving of two masters, as Arlecchino discovered to his cost, can result in nothing save confusion. One typical example may serve to illustrate this. Since the theatre cannot exist without an audience, and since a decline in play-going has become a patent fact, the prime question is what can be done to stimulate and encourage attendance in the auditorium. Speaking of this, a distinguished director has remarked that

> there's a whole audience that we just don't speak to at all—not only among the working class but the professional classes, among the people between 20 and 30 in industry and commerce who are earning good wages and who would sooner think of flying to the moon than coming here to see, say, a play by Shelagh Delaney.[9]

The comment, which finds reflection in scores of other similar recent comments, is revealing. Numerous persons concerned with the theatre to-day, most of them sincerely eager to further the interests of the stage, illogically muddle together the drama as an art-form to be cultivated for its own particular sake and their own pre-dilection for plays of a special kind—for the most part pieces appropriate only for those who put politics first. The plain fact, as we have already seen, is that these plays cannot give to a general audience what that general audience demands, and that consequently their appeal must remain a sectional one. The fact that one much-talked-of English theatre to-day is confessedly a "left-wing stage," while another, because of its directives, is frequently so described illustrates this well. In both of these there exists an eager desire to revitalize the drama, but what they succeed in doing is not so much discovering ways of promoting the drama as an art-form with its own character-istic social value as exploring ways of using the drama for limited political ends. And in doing so, they are apt to create confusion in several ways. By suggesting that the 'working-class' material, which forms their favourite subject-matter, is novel they are obscuring the fact that their kitchen-sink themes, so far from being new, were old-fashioned many decades ago: Gorki trenchantly explored this area, and many of the early 'repertory' playwrights built much of their work on the use of 'working-class' material. Perhaps the 'old-fashionedness' does not matter particularly; what does matter is that by the recent attempt to restrict the area of dramatic interest to material of this kind, the new school of playwrights is manifestly muddling up politics with art. Drama can deal with all things human; the kitchen-sink may as effectively inspire a great play as a royal court, a royal court as effectively as a kitchen-sink; in proposing that the proletarian is more appropriate for modern drama than the regal or the aristocratic or the 'genteel,' the same mistake is being made as that made by earlier theorists who sought to limit tragedy's realm to the courtly, or as that made by the sentimentalists when they spoke of the 'ordinary man.' For the drama, considered as an art, subject-matter of this kind is immaterial; what matters is the stimulation of emotions which may envelop an audience. Where the confused 'two-masters' trend can lead us is shown when we find in the recent assessment, written by a well-known critic, of the dramatic contributions made during the fifties, the statement that the only hopeful sign of that decade lay in the appearance of plays like *Chicken Soup with Barley*, *Roots*, and *The Kitchen*—not because these works were particularly good as drama, but because they served the interests of 'Socialist Realism.' Precisely the same preconception has led to a pronouncement that Shakespeare's *Richard II* is a dull and relatively worthless play, because, except for the two Gardeners, no "plebeians" are introduced into its scenes.

Now, all of this is fundamentally important for those who are intent upon furthering the interests of the stage conceived of as a form of artistic expression, with its own proper social value, and not merely as one among many means of promulgating sectional political ideas. If our observations of audience reactions and cravings have validity, the whole area of the 'play of ideas,' realistic in form and written in prose, once a vital theatrical force, has now become old-fashioned and outmoded, incapable of arousing genuine general appeal. Each single component word in this term is inimical to the essential nature of the drama—'prose,' because by the use of our common impoverished speech, faithfully recorded, the playwright cannot achieve more than a limited objective; 'realistic,' because Archer's lauded "art of pure imitation" is a contradiction in terms; 'play,' because the modern trend towards levelling all dramatic genres under a single unordered concept is inappropriate for the playhouse; and 'ideas,' because general audiences, unsuited through their very being for appreciating the exercise of thought and logic, are moved and stirred by emotion. A thing which is forgotten by most of those who to-day are illogically seeking to impose Brecht's concepts upon our stage is that even he, towards the close of his career, was forced by the theatre's innate power to admit that, when all had been said, the emotions could not be renounced and that the playhouse has to be regarded as "a place of entertainment."[10]

In much current dramatic criticism, therefore, there exist many elements of confusion. If our object be to draw back spectators into the playhouse, then the only hope is to consider carefully what characteristically appeals to general audiences. If we are more interested in using the stage as a platform for the promulgation of our political ideas, then we must be logical about it and acknowledge our aims. We really cannot have it both ways. And if, in fact, our main interest rests in the drama, above all we are bound to ask ourselves whether the current limitation of the word 'social' serves our ends. For many of the politically minded theorists, the ontological problems, all questions relating to the central nature of being, are put aside; but ordinary men and women, no matter how far removed they may be from areas of philosophical speculation, still remain vaguely aware that the universe is mysterious, its laws still unfathomable. Science in our days has done wonders; excitement arises from the thought of its practical achievements—the man-made satellites sent whirling round the globe and the near-approach of a time when city-states may be founded in the skies. These are testimonies of human power; and yet paradoxically they stir in the mind other, often unformed, thoughts of what man, being mortal, can never achieve—the penetration into, or even the understanding of, a universe which his instruments can pierce for thousands of light-years without any sign of reaching an end.

These matters are as social and practical as are those concerning the structure of society; and the ordinary man, however much he is immersed in his material surroundings, dimly senses that. Indeed, it might almost be suggested that the hardly conscious inquietude resultant from awareness of their force has become the cardinal "fact of contemporary life," before which all the other facts pale like tapers in the sunlight. With the advent of materialism a vast unease has grown. It has been well said that

once man's ability to respond creatively to the ontological mystery had been stunted into something that produces merely an irritated state of mystification, he was left to the spiritual destructiveness of that battle raging within himself: between the conviction of being nothing in the vastness of the universe, and the natural urge which, prompted by the un-grace of self-assertion, persuades him of his all-importance. To be nothing and yet everything—this seeming paradox is the pride and the humility of the creature before a God of infinite power and infinite love; but it is the spiritual death suffered by man in the incessant struggle between arrogance and humiliation, in his exposure to the mighty lovelessness of a chance constellation of energy.[11]

"Even when the social realist has established the need for his reform," one writer declares,[12] "the basic problems of existence remain: loneliness, the impenetrable mystery of the universe, death." And there are playwrights among us now who seek to explore this realm. Unfortunately, however, several of those who endeavour to reflect dramatically the inner perplexities of the age attempt to do so only in a kind of documentary manner. The method has been defended on the grounds that "in a world that has become absurd, it is enough to transcribe reality with meticulous care to create the impression of extravagant irrationality";[13] this means, in effect, that the inarticulateness of ordinary life is being presented by an articulateness on the stage. Signs of this approach are widespread; one dramatist declares boldly that he is "working very much towards a reduction not only of scenery, but of dialogue as well" and he describes a whole scene of a new play "in which absolutely nothing is said."[14] There are a few dramatic critics who seek to apply the term 'poetic' to methods such as these, but it seems clear that the application of such an adjective merely provides another instance of our confusion in thought.

The plain fact is that, for the drama, the presentation of perplexity and inarticulateness by means of inarticulateness is not sufficient; the inarticulateness and the perplexity have to be transformed so that they become palpable. The glory and the power of the drama resides in the spoken word. Surely, the effort to abandon the instrument of evocative language and to seek for the establishment in our time of plays based on "the elementary ingredients of pure, pre-literary theatre" must be regarded as retrogressive and offering no hope for the stage. In the same symposium on modern drama to which reference has been made above, Christopher Fry seems to express the truth effectively. "Do you think," he asks, "that when speech in the theatre gets closer to speech in the street we necessarily get closer to the nature of man?"

> Surely the business of the theatre is the exploration of that nature, so that the listener can perhaps be aware of more about himself? At the present we concentrate mainly on behaviour; but isn't it important to try to find out *purpose*, to know what we're driving for?

Even if we decide that we are driving for nothing, that drive towards nothingness can be made expressive; *King Lear* reveals much more in its tortured articulateness than the cult of the inarticulate could ever do. Here, the torment, the loneliness, and the doubt stretch our nerves almost to the snapping point, yet, by the alchemy of the language, the poet-dramatist has made his "Nothing" not merely a conundrum but an emotional experience capable of stirring the emotions.

Only by remembering that beyond the material and the physical facts exists something much vaster, that beyond the politics are metaphysical questionings, and that beyond the scientific realm of the intellect the Dionysian passions endure, can we assess rightly the social value of the theatre. All art possesses the power to explore and to make explicit the reality which lies beyond the region of the daily round and the familiar fact. And among all the arts none has shown itself so apt for this purpose as the drama, since drama addresses itself not to individuals alone but to men gathered in communion. By its stirring of the emotions, by the appeal of its beauty, and by the participation of audiences in its manifestation, it has shown itself capable at its finest of making expressive our profoundest spiritual gropings and of relieving perplexities in delight. For these things men attended playhouses in the past; and, because on our journalistic stage the tawdry and the ugly so often take the place of the beautiful, so often hysteria serves for emotion, and the only 'reality' admitted is reality conceived by minds bound within the wrappings of the political, attendance in the theatre has declined. Is it too much to say that the continued appeal of the masterpieces of the older drama, and particularly of tragedy, at the seasonal festivals rests in appreciation of that which the daily theatres so seldom have to offer?

Eclecticism and 'Modernism'

The conflict between humiliation and arrogance which has been observed in to-day's perplexed attitude towards the universe at large perhaps does not lack its reflection in the world of art. Our age seems at once strangely eclectic and strangely aggressive in its modernism. We have certainly a wider range in our appreciation of past styles: the oriental and the occidental, the medieval spirit and the spirit of the Renaissance, the classic and the romantic all come within the sphere of our interest. When eighteenth-century Augustanism ruled, the 'Gothick' was despised; when Blake discovered the vigour of early romanticism, the Augustan came to signify for him all that was most vicious. We embrace both, and more.

N

Both a reason and a result of this are that our age remains without a characteristic style of its own. Certainly the twentieth century has witnessed violently revolutionary artistic movements—the formation of a new language by James Joyce, the aberrations of Gertrude Stein, the fashioning of a fresh poetic utterance, the creation of abstract painting; nearly all the '–isms' that can be thought of, from cubism to dadaism, have flourished during our time. About all of these movements, however, there floats an atmosphere of impermanence; the very aggressiveness with which they are thrust forward suggests that they will have no more enduring power than many of the creations of our modernist architects. Never has an age given so much prominence to the word 'modern'; yet dissatisfaction rules, and we still remain without a characteristic style.

Within the realms of theatre and drama this conflict between eclecticism and 'modernism' demands close attention. In particular, two aspects call for brief discussion here. The first concerns the shape of the theatre itself. During former centuries there was a tendency on the part of each age to find and develop the kind of playhouse which best served its needs. No doubt the architectural forms adopted by the stages during different periods were not always determined by conscious thought; no doubt many changes and modifications in structure resulted from chance alterations and immediate practical necessities. Nevertheless, when we survey the historical growth of the stage, we see certain forms which belong characteristically and usually exclusively to this period or to that. Within our own century, and especially within the past four decades, two contradictory trends have become manifest. One of these exhibits itself in an extraordinary series of revolutionary designs; some of them have remained as designs on paper merely, but many have been enthusiastically carried out in actuality. In one theatre the audience is set three-quarters round a platform stage; in another it is carried the full circle, embracing the acting area; in another it is divided, one group of spectators placed so that they face a second group, separated from them by a long narrow stage; in another the audience is set in the middle, the actors performing on raised corridors running along the sides of the hall; in another the stage is made into a kind of ellipse, and in still another it becomes triangular, erected in one of the corners of the theatre structure.

Co-existent with these often extravagantly 'modern' plans we see the second trend—a desire to have all the theatre shapes that ever existed made available for immediate use. Thus in the minds of many theatre-workers to-day there hovers the dream of having a playhouse so flexible that without difficulty it may be adjusted to give us a proscenium-arch stage, an apron stage, an arena, or a complete stage-in-the-round.

Now, much may be said in support of these various endeavours. All agree in expressing a dissatisfaction with the familiar and old-fashioned nineteenth-century playhouse. All agree, likewise, in being based upon something which has hardly been fully appreciated before our time—the fact that different theatre shapes and sizes not only are aptly harmonious with different kinds of production, but also create different impressions upon their audiences. We have thus come to realize that the vast Greek open-air structures were intimately in accord with the contemporary comedies and tragedies, and that men seated in this enormous concourse were stirred, by its very structure and by its surroundings, in a way which could not be associated with either Shakespeare's Globe or Irving's Lyceum. In addition, all these trends agree in displaying a vivid awareness of the fact that stages of varying shape create divergent contacts between players and spectators; behind most of the varying experiments rests an anxious thought concerning a basic theatrical question, the nature of the actor-spectator relationship.

Despite all this, however, much remains unsatisfactory. The eclectic theatre, the theatre which can be adjusted at will to varying forms, is, of course, excellently suited to the needs of a university department of drama; and it might be considered convenient for any playhouse which aimed at being a kind of exhibition gallery for the purpose of presenting historically dramas culled from numerous periods of the past. It could simulate some of the conditions of the Greek stage for a production of *Œdipus Rex*; it could present *Hamlet* on a Globe-like platform and *The Way of the World* on the kind of apron-proscenium which Congreve knew. All these productions would assuredly prove instructive, but in the end this adjustable playhouse would be bound to remain an exhibition hall; there could be but little inspirational value in it for living dramatists; they would be able to see how Sophocles' dramas were associated with the Athenian playhouse and Shakespeare's with the Elizabethan; but they could not view these works as other than historical curiosities.

The other kind of theatre endeavour, that which applies itself fervently to some new form, is likewise unsatisfactory, precisely because almost all of the efforts in this direction are aggressively 'modern,' often stimulated merely by a desire for something novel. It is true that much may be said in favour of the experiments made in arena styles and that these are definitely based upon observation of similar stages in the past, but even here nothing has arisen which would seem to offer to our period a playhouse form completely suitable for our particular requirements. Maybe it is too much to hope for anything of the kind when we consider the enormous costs involved in the building of new theatres, the lack of incentive consequent upon audience decline and the conflicting voices to be heard everywhere around us. Yet the problem demands most careful consideration, and until we do find a characteristic playhouse of our own we may never succeed in the essential task of bringing back our errant playgoers to the play.

Unfortunately, much the same set of conditions prevails in the world of the drama. Most creative periods in dramatic history offer to us a characteristic style or styles, which, despite the appearance of hundreds of eccentric works, stand as a firm core amidst diversity. Hardly so much may be said of the drama during the twentieth century. Eclectism has ruled here too, mingled with sudden sporadic upsurgings of various 'modernisms.' All of these modernistic movements have sprung, and continue to spring, from a discontent with the realism-naturalism evolved and finally established before 1900; in so far they exhibit a forward-looking impulse; but almost every single movement of this kind has been marked rather by a desire to achieve novelty at all costs than by a deeply based assessment of the needs of the time. Typical, for example, is the work of the expressionist school which burst upon us in the twenties. Unquestionably, these expressionists succeeded in jolting the theatre of their time out of its complacency and unquestionably, too, they revealed possibilities beyond those of which the ordinary realistic drama was capable. At the same time, their strident scenes, although for the moment exciting, could last only for a moment; they were unfitted to become models for further development, and, above all, they remained sectional in their appeal. Numerous other movements within our time have displayed similar features and several of them, in this search for novelty, have palpably introduced methods and aims unsuited for the art of the stage. At the present moment we stand without any clear directive, with confused concepts of the theatre's purpose, in such parlous state that a return to old-fashioned realism, varied only by the substitution of suggestive for naturalistic scenery, is viewed by some critics as a brightly shining hope.

In these circumstances, the only true hope may be seen rather to reside in an attempt to consider afresh both the limitations of theatrical art and the opportunities which it can offer. Of course the stage of our time must, if it is to live and grow, be in close touch with the needs and desires and problems of the twentieth century, but it must be willing to search for ways of expressing these by means of devices which the drama's history indicates are immutable, and at the same time it must have thought out its orientation. As we have seen, an orientation directed towards the arousing of a critical attitude in actor and spectator, towards the presentation of a rationally conceived message, and towards stimulating audiences to practical action may all be very well for those whose gaze is set upon a political objective; but, if this objective be deliberately chosen, then we are forced to recognize that the theatre in itself has to suffer. And the attempt uncritically to seize upon methods apt enough to serve the ends of the one objective and to apply them to the other can yield no fruitful results. For what he wanted to achieve, a political result, Brecht's theory of 'alienation' possesses value; if, on the other hand, our aim be to draw spectators back to the theatre and to exploit to the full what the theatre has to offer, not only is that theory valueless, it positively defeats our ends.

This whole subject is, of course, a difficult one and divergent views will always prevail; but one thing seems certain. Never before have we had such need for a careful and dispassionate examination of basic principles; never before has there been a greater necessity for asking ourselves what, basically, we want in the theatre. Some short time ago Sir John Gielgud, writing on the subject of lost tradition and style in acting, expressed the hope that, after all, the theatre "will muddle forward and muddle through," despite the fact that "too often in the last twenty years" the stage had become dominated by "sensational modern innovations and freakish quirks of originality."[15] We certainly want to be modern; we freely may confess that the drama of the past, even in the great Elizabethan age, produced much that is now utterly worthless; but in our search for modernity it is essential that we should determine what we want to do and that we should face basic issues honestly. Perhaps, if we do so, may we not come to believe that much of the confusion surrounding us depends ultimately upon the restrictions imposed by the eighteenth-century sentimentalists, upon a consequent sense of inadequacy, and upon apparently novel but often old-fashioned, desperate, and intellectually inspired experiments in modernism? May not a frank examination of the essential elements in theatre and drama suggest that the revival of a genuinely popular stage can be secured only by pursuing a new concept which in the end will be found to be as ancient as those of Aristotle and Sophocles?

NOTES TO CONCLUSION

1. *The Elements of Drama* (1960), pp. 14–15.
2. G. Saintsbury, *Loci Critici* (1903), p. 158.
3. Preface to the *Tyr et Sidon* (1628) of Jean de Schélandre.
4. *De comoedia et tragoedia.*
5. *An Apologie for Poetrie*, ed. E. Arber (1868), p. 45.
6. *Hamburgische Dramaturgie*, No. 12.
7. *Tragic Themes in Western Literature*, ed Cleanth Brooks (1955; reissued 1960), p. 4.
8. John Willett, *The Theatre of Bertolt Brecht* (1959), pp. 176–178.
9. George Devine, 'The Right to Fail' (*The Twentieth Century*, clxix, 1961, p. 131).
10. John Willett, *op. cit.*, p. 181.
11. E. Heller, *The Disinherited Mind* (1952), pp. 13, 38.
12. Martin Esslin, 'Pinter and the Absurd' (*The Twentieth Century*, clxix, 1961, p. 184).
13. *Ibid.*, p. 177.
14. Arnold Wesker, 'Art is Not Enough' (*The Twentieth Century*, clxix, 1961, p. 192).
15. 'Tradition, Style and the Theatre Today' (*Shakespeare Survey*, 4, 1951, p. 101–108).

Notes on Dramatic Theory

THE history and analysis of literary criticism is a subject, which, during the past fifty years, has attracted a considerable amount of attention. Apart from hundreds of special studies devoted to critical writings within selected periods, to the works of individual authors and to the discussion of particular genres, we now possess comprehensive, detailed surveys of the entire area, together with anthologies containing representative texts from earliest times to the present.

Naturally, much of the material thus recorded and examined has a direct significance for those who are especially interested in dramatic theory. Many, indeed most, of the earlier essays on 'the art of poetry' concern themselves with the dramatic form, while hundreds of later literary critical studies have directed their efforts towards the exploration of the spirit of tragedy or with assessment of the creative activities of those authors—the Greek playwrights, Shakespeare, and Racine—who have excelled in this field.

Drama, however, having one foot in the theatre, is only half a literary form, and consequently a great deal of the literary criticism which bears on the dramatic form remains either negatively inadequate or else tends to be positively distracting. And unfortunately there does not exist any comprehensive and detailed survey of dramatic theory and criticism to parallel those which apply themselves to literary matters. This, in fact, need not surprise us when we consider the complexities of the subject. In order to be fully effective, the theory of drama requires to spread its net widely. It must, of course, pay close attention to literary values but, in addition, it has to consider many things which lie far outside the range of literature. Diderot's *Paradoxe sur le comédien* and other writings on the actor's art are of direct pertinence to this theme; the critical opinions expressed by such scenic artists as Gordon Craig, Lee Simonson, and Robert Edmond Jones have unquestioned significance here; and even discussions concerning theatre-planning, in so far as these are connected with audience-actor relationships, must be brought under survey. Without doubt, the complexities are numerous, and they are so varied as to render synthesis extremely difficult. Small wonder is it, therefore, that as yet we have no more than contributions towards an ultimate comprehensive survey.

These contributions, nevertheless, are many, and indeed the very assimilation of their contents, quite apart from the independent scrutiny of the original critical writings throughout the ages, presents a formidable task in itself. The library of theoretical disquisitions on drama and theatre, as a glance at any one of the available 'bibliographies' will amply demonstrate, is perplexingly vast, and for those who may wish to explore this subject perhaps a few notes may prove useful—even if these notes must necessarily be restricted to some cursory comments concerning trends in critical thought which especially relate to the theme of the present volume.[1]

ARISTOTLE. Within this extensive library of works concerned with dramatic theory one volume, Aristotle's *Poetics*, stands out preeminent both because it comes first in time and because of its intrinsic worth. Although the precise date of the *Poetics* is uncertain, in all probability it reached completion about the year 330 B.C., at a time when its author, born in 384 B.C., was in his fifties.[2] The influence of this short but incisively penetrating study has been enormous, and even to-day it remains a potent force. Not only are all the modern investigations into the nature of tragedy dependent upon its judgments, its influence may also be clearly traced within the field of practical theatre activity: the great dramatic critic A. B. Walkley confessedly took the *Poetics* as his text-book; such a study as Alexander Dean's *Fundamentals of Play Directing* (1941) was formulated in accordance with Aristotle's analysis; and even a revolutionary dramatist like Bertolt Brecht, in devising his own critical views, negatively acknowledged its significance by presenting his own views as an "anti-Aristotelian," or "non-Aristotelian," poetics.

The power thus possessed by Aristotle is the more remarkable because of his limitations. In the first place, we can be certain that the manuscripts in which the *Poetics* has been preserved neither include the whole of his philosophical analysis nor present his thoughts without errors and contradictions; still further, we may well suspect that some portions of the text are, in fact, spurious interpolations. It is entirely possible that what we know as the *Poetics* is only part of a very much larger whole; and indeed it may perhaps be merely the lecture notes taken by some pupil who had listened to the master as he discoursed in the περίπατοι, 'the shady walks' of the Lyceum. We may thus be able to explain to ourselves why such considerable parts of this work deal with apparently trivial details—details which might well fit into a more spacious volume but which here loom up disproportionately large—and why certain parts do not seem logically to cohere with the main arguments.

Other limitations of a different kind are, of course, obvious. The *Poetics* deals almost entirely with tragedy, and even although Aristotle had before him all the masterpieces of Æschylus (525–456 B.C.), Sophocles (495–406 B.C.), and Euripides (480–406 B.C.), clearly his vision of the theatre was restricted to a single dramatic style, the Athenian. Furthermore, the stress upon tragedy reminds us that in Greece comedy was of later development than the tragic play, that Aristotle was acquainted only with the one special form called 'Old Comedy' (known to us through the works of Aristophanes), and that the 'New Comedy,' associated with the writings of Menander (342–293 B.C.) and basically the foundation of all later comedy, came after his time. It may be, as some scholars have thought, that Aristotle did originally include a discussion of the comic style within a *Poetics* more extensive than what we now possess, but this after all is no more than a speculation and a guess.

The consideration of these and other limitations serves, by contrast, to underline the prime positive values of Aristotle's achievement. It is truly amazing that, thus early in the history of the drama, he should have had the power of penetrating so deeply into the secrets of dramatic art and of laying so firm a foundation for his successors. So far as dramatic theory is concerned, several sections of his study demand special attention. The opening chapters are devoted in the main to the discussion of poetry in general, with emphasis upon its basis in 'imitation'—a term widely and variously interpreted: these chapters are important for general æsthetic and critical speculations, but they have less significance for us than those which essay to examine tragedy in particular. Here, the discussion of the various elements which contribute in producing an impression upon spectators, of the distinction between 'history' (actual events) and the imaginative creations of the poets, of plot structure, of the dominant tragic emotions, 'terror' and 'pity,' of the 'katharsis' or purgation effected by the tragic spectacle, and of the tragic hero—all of this has cardinal significance both because of its influence upon succeeding critical thought and creative endeavour, and because of its delving down to essentials.

Unfortunately, within the field of Greek criticism Aristotle stands in majestic isolation. Plato's views—sometimes rather contradictory —about the poet's function are, naturally, of very great philosophical value, and Longinus' essay on the sublime is the first great study of poetic style; but very little from this period has come down to us which bears particularly upon the drama. The only major exception is to be found in those scenes in Aristophanes' *Frogs* which institute a comparison between the statuesque splendour of Æschylus' early tragedies and the 'realistic' trends evident in Euripides' writings.[3] Euripides, introduced in person, is made to rate at Æschylus for his magniloquence and ominous grandeur—a style and method alien to the later dramatist's purposes. Whereas Æschylus, says Euripides, reserved most of his poetic utterances for the nobler characters in his plays, he himself allowed no single person to "idle": "all had to work";

> The men, the slaves, the women, all made speeches,
> The kings, the little girls, the hags—

and, when Æschylus inquires whether he should not be condemned for this, "No, by the lord Apollo!" he cries, "it's democratic!" Thus early in the theory of the drama was the issue raised between 'realism' and 'convention.'

HORACE AND THE ROMANS. During the period following the decline of Athens numerous grammarians sought to codify, often in summary form, standard opinions concerning comedy and tragedy: but their works, although of considerable historical importance, have little to offer us. Indeed, the only essay in this sphere which calls for attention is the well-known verse 'Epistle to the Pisos,' written by Horace (Quintus Horatius Flaccus, 65–8 B.C.),[4] The 'epistle,' concerned with 'the art of poetry,' contains no startlingly original thoughts, but it does provide a skilfully written epigrammatic summary of classical opinion which made a mighty impress upon critical thought during succeeding centuries. His main stress Horace placed on propriety and clearly defined form. In general, he believed, comedy and tragedy must be kept distinct; characters must be drawn according to type: violent actions should not be shown to the spectators: plays ought to be written in formal five acts; the mission of drama was to combine profit with delight. These and numerous kindred critical comments all tend to emphasize the application of an ordered set of rules upon dramatic writing. Aristotle's method had been analytic—an attempt to discern the main characteristics of the plays he placed under review rather than to lay down any laws for the control of later authors. In Horace's verse-essay everything is cut and dried; the 'rules' had taken the place of deductive speculation.[5]

THE RENAISSANCE. During the last years of the Roman Empire the drama declined, and through the Dark Ages it virtually vanished, and, when the medieval religious plays took their independent rise after the tenth century, few men, if any, related the new drama with the old. These centuries, therefore, produced no theatrical criticism other than uninformed repetitions of what could be found in the writings of the earlier grammarians. Often, indeed, at this time such terms as 'tragedy' and 'comedy' lost entirely their stage significance: Dante thus called his great poem 'The Divine Comedy,' and Chaucer defined tragedy as a 'story.'

In the midst of the Renaissance reawakening of interest in art and the classics, however, scholars, architects, and poets eagerly applied themselves to studying—and more importantly, imitating—the ancient Greek and Roman stage. The comedies of Terence and Seneca's tragedies had never been completely lost during the Dark and Middle Ages; but they had been regarded almost entirely as texts for reading: indeed, many students followed Isidore of Seville (seventh century) in believing that these plays had merely been recited, by their authors or by friends, from a kind of pulpit. Now came the realization that the Greek and Roman dramas were plays, intended to be performed by actors before assembled groups of spectators; and, as a result, attempts were made to carry them from the library to the stage—and these early attempts soon led, first, to the preparing of vernacular adaptations of the classical dramas, and, later, to the composing of original works more or less inspired by the ancient models.

Naturally this induced men to look more carefully at Horace's 'Epistle' and similar essays; and, when knowledge of Aristotle's *Poetics* came from the discovery of hitherto unknown manuscripts, many men were inspired to pen critical studies in which classical precepts were invigorated by practical experience of the new drama.[6]

By 1498 Giorgio Valla had published a rough Latin version of the *Poetics*; the Greek text was printed some ten years later; and by the middle of the sixteenth century several Italian scholar-critics were engaging themselves in independent studies. These led to the issuing of a series of works destined to wield considerable power over many generations—the *De poeta* (1559) and *Arte poetica* (1564) of Minturno, J. C. Scaliger's *Poetices libri septem* (1561) and Lodovico Castelvetro's *Poetica d'Aristotele vulgarizzata e esposta* (1570; reissued with additions, 1576).[7] All of these contain some original speculations, and the prevailing 'moral' emphasis, a medieval inheritance strengthened by the religious development of the age, sometimes carries us far from the classical models; but on the whole these writings unite in preaching on the texts of Aristotle and Horace, and, furthermore, in attempting to codify immutable 'laws' for dramatic composition. Tragedy tended to be defined simply as a play which dealt with kings and ended in disaster, comedy as one which introduced 'ordinary' characters and ended in happiness; these characters, it was stressed, were to be presented according to type; and the 'unities' had to be preserved.[8] A few authors succeeded in modifying the set pattern, but the tone established in Vida's early *De arte poetica* (1527) remained dominant: "Follow the ancients," he had commanded, "Don't try any novelties," "Keep to your five acts," "Imitate Seneca," "Keep to the unities."

The same trend is equally apparent in other countries. France was as hag-ridden by the ghosts of Aristotle and Horace and the grammarians as Italy was, and in England even Sir Philip Sidney's *An Apologie for Poetrie* (written about 1581, printed 1595), despite its freshness of utterance and occasional originality of thought, bowed its acknowledgment throughout to standard opinion. Although Ben Jonson was a practising playwright, most of the critical pronouncements in *Timber, or Discoveries* (printed 1641), were similarly dependent on 'correct' Renaissance ideas.[9]

Nevertheless, despite this prevailing uniformity, some signs of unfettered judgment in certain quarters can be discerned. Obviously the development of a new romantic drama was bound to influence contemporary critical opinion. Lope de Vega could thus come forward with his *New Art of Composing Plays in this Time* (*Arte nuevo de hacer comedias en este tiempo*, 1609), in which he questioned several of the 'laws' propounded by the stricter sixteenth-century theorists;[10] Giraldi Cinthio, in his *Letter or Discourse concerning the Writing* of *Satyr-plays* (*Lettera ovvero discorso sopra il comporre le satire atte alle scene*, 1554) could turn to the third Greek dramatic form, the satyr-drama, and plead on its basis for a modern equivalent; another practising playwright, Thomas Dekker, similarly could turn in a prologue (that introducing his *If It Be Not Good*) to stress what often the theorists neglected—the mighty impact made by poetic speech which, he pointed out, could make an impress upon the auditors by the very sound of the words. One thing in particular is noteworthy among these efforts, the gradual spread of support for tragicomedy. While many critics remained assured in their opinion that this was a 'mongrel' form, and although that opinion endured until well into the eighteenth century, there can be no doubt but that the romantic dramas being currently penned in this style wrought a change in the severer application of the 'rules' supposedly derived from the ancients. There were many men who echoed the views expressed by Tirso de Molina:

> Does it matter how much the Drama may modify the laws of its ancestors, ingeniously mixing tragedy with comedy and producing a pleasant type of play of the two—and partaking of the character of each—introducing serious characters from the one, and waggish and absurd characters from the other? I claim that if the preeminence in Greece of Æschylus and Euripides (as among the Latins of Seneca and Terence) suffice to establish the laws of these Masters who are now so vigorously upheld, the excellence of our Spanish Lope de Vega makes his improvements in both styles so conspicuous that the authority he brings to this improvement is sufficient to reform the old laws.[11]

And Lope de Vega himself, in critically defending this mixture, had adumbrated the later appeal from art to nature: "Nature," he said, "gives us good example, for through such variety it is beautiful."[12]

THE NEOCLASSIC PERIOD. Quite clearly, where the stricter critics went wrong at this time was in their attempt to establish immutable 'rules' or 'laws' for dramatic writing; and this trend became even stronger during the seventeenth and early eighteenth centuries, when the Italian critics, hitherto dominant in this field, ceded their authority to the French. In this country a series of stern law-givers arose, and particular note should be made of the fact that some of their writings, such as the *Theatre Practice* (*La pratique du théâtre*, 1657) by François Hédelin, abbé d'Aubignac, were penned, not

simply as learned treatises intended in the main for scholarly reading
but as works designed to guide and control the dramatists of the
time. As a culmination to all their work stands that *Art poétique*
(1674) by Boileau (Nicolas Boileau-Despréaux, 1636–1711), which
exerted such a universal influence during the 'Augustan' period.[13]

These French writings soon became known in England: Hédelin's
volume appeared in 1684 as *The Whole Art of the Stage* and
Boileau's in 1683 as *The Art of Poetry*. Not surprisingly, in view of
the esteem in which Parisian intellectuals were held, many of their
ideas took root in London. Under their influence, for example,
Thomas Rymer could produce his *The Tragedies of the Last Age
Considered* (1678) and *A Short View of Tragedy* (1592–93), wherein
Shakespeare's plays were tested and found wanting. Shakespeare,
however, was still a popular dramatist and Englishmen were inclined, even in the midst of late seventeenth-century polish, to look
back in wonder at the glories of the Elizabethan age. True, a very
few French critics (François Ogier, for example) and dramatists (for
example, Molière) had dared to stem the imposing tide controlled
by the omnipotent Académie Française; but the corresponding English critical trend, largely supported by Shakespeare's acknowledged
genius, was far firmer and more potent. The mighty figure of John
Dryden here stands as a prime symbol. Despite his acceptance of the
neoclassic doctrines, he constantly was prepared, honestly, to recognize excellencies which could not be fully vindicated by reference to
the 'rules,' and, even more significantly, he avoided in his own critical writings enunciation of any 'laws,' preferring to discuss certain
selected literary works rather than dwell in a world of generaliza-
tions.[14] In similar wise George Farquhar, in his *Discourse upon
Comedy* (1702) could let his wit play destructively on the concept of
the unities, as these had been ridiculously narrowed and formalized
by academic writers, while Dr Johnson, although bred in the atmosphere of neoclassic opinion, was able to reach the conclusion that

> it ought to be the first endeavour of a writer to distinguish nature
> from custom; or that which is established because it is right, from
> that which is right only because it is established; that he may neither
> violate essential principles by a desire of novelty, nor debar himself
> from the attainment of beauties within his view, by a needless fear of
> breaking rules which no literary dictator had authority to enact—[15]

an admirably balanced judgment which might well be taken as a
golden rule in itself.

THE SENTIMENTALISTS. Johnson had laid much stress upon 'nature,' indeed basing his deviations from stricter neoclassical theory almost entirely upon an appeal, over the head of academic judgments, to life and experience. But for the critical cult of nature in a wider sense we have to turn to the writings of the mid-eighteenth-century sentimentalists. Theirs was, in effect, an international movement. From one point of view, we may see sentimentalism stoutly based upon a series of English novels and plays—Richardson's *Pamela* (1740), Lillo's *George Barnwell* (1731), Moore's *The Gamester* (1753). From another, we might deem that its final strength derives from the weighty authority given to it by the Italian, Goldoni. From still another, we may see its dramatic inception in a number of early eighteenth-century French plays and its theoretical elaboration by a group of theorists which centred in the great *Encyclopédie*.[16] So far as criticism is concerned, the third is the most significant.

In his discourse *De la poésie dramatique* (1758), Denis Diderot first formulated the new concept of drama, a concept to which he had already sought to give practical form in *Le Père de famille* (1758). In his essay he concentrated upon advocating a kind of "serious comedy" which should deal with "the duties of man," a sort of moral and philosophical play. A few years later, in 1767, Beaumarchais (Pierre-Augustin Caron) carried the idea yet further in his *Essai sur le genre dramatique sérieux*, in which he pleaded, by an appeal to nature, for a non-comic drama which should deal with 'ordinary' characters and aim at a semblance of the real. Fundamentally, these men, in opposition to previously held opinion, sought for plays (1) of a 'serious' (*i.e.*, neither tragic nor comic) genre, (2) with persons drawn immediately from actual life and set in a realistic *milieu*, (3) written in prose, and (4) directed towards a definite social 'idea' or 'moral.'

THE ROMANTIC PERIOD. Although sentimentalism for a time engulfed the stage, and although it was destined to have a lengthy career, its immediate exponents were not able to produce much of value, and towards the end of the eighteenth century its realistic endeavours became lost in the storm and stress of flamboyant romanticism.

During this period of romanticism we may observe two particularly significant facts. The first is a new and deeper consideration of Shakespeare's genius, and an accompanying reconsideration of the achievements of the Greek stage—a complete overthrowing of the old 'laws' through a penetrating analysis of these dramatic works. This does not mean that Aristotle was rejected; only his neoclassic interpreters came under romantic contempt, and an endeavour was made to see in Shakespeare's works plays which in spirit agreed with the *Poetics*. G. E. Lessing, for example, in his *Hamburgische Dramaturgie* (1767–69) constantly combines rich admiration for Shakespeare with profound belief in Aristotle's profound wisdom.[17] Similarly, S. T. Coleridge in England, in his interpretation of the god of his idolatry, fully acknowledges the power of the Greek philosopher-critic. The second fact is that, although periodical criticism devoted to current theatrical offerings was firmly establishing itself, although a man such as Lessing was concerned directly with the stage, although William Hazlitt, Charles Lamb, and others were keenly interested in the playhouse, much of the romantic theoretical writing tended to become divorced from the theatre. Thus a great deal of Coleridge's penetrating lectures on Shakespeare deals, not with the analysis of distinctly dramatic values, but with purely 'literary' considerations. It might almost be said that, for the only development of romantic theory which is intimately related to practical theatre affairs, we must turn to the controversy which was excited in Paris by the production of Victor Hugo's *Cromwell* in 1827. It was at this time that the romantic concept of the dramatic 'grotesque' was evolved. In England and in Italy the public theatres pursued their own melodramatic course, the poets turned out their dull bookish verse-plays, and criticism more and more remained 'literary.'[18]

As the nineteenth century advanced, the flood of books and serious articles on dramatic and theatrical subjects increased—to such an extent, indeed, that there can be no hope, within this limited space, of presenting more than a cursory summary of some main currents. If we leave aside those numerous, and important, critical-historical studies—of individual authors such as Shakespeare, Corneille, and Racine, of hitherto neglected areas such as the medieval drama, of national theatrical activities, and, most significantly, of the stage as a whole—we may discern among these currents a few of special force. The first might be called the literary-critical, following the course already taken by Coleridge. This led to the accumulation of volumes devoted to the analysis and interpretation of the works of the major dramatists, for the most part considered as poetic texts and not as plays designed for the stage. Although the effect of such writings was to a certain extent offset by the development of periodical criticism concerned with actual stage performances, it inevitably strengthened the already established disassociation between the play as a written or printed text and the play as a vehicle for actors.

A second current of a similar kind, particularly powerful during the last years of the nineteenth century and the first decades of the twentieth, tended towards the study of the tragic and the comic spirits. Discussion of the former, of course, had been continuous ever since the first Renaissance 'arts of poetry,' but discussion of comedy was virtually new. George Meredith now came forward with his *Essay on the Idea of Comedy* (1877) and Henri Bergson with *Le rire* (1900); Herbert Spencer wrote on the psychology of laughter; and these essays were later succeeded by diverse similar writings, which sought to define the qualities of wit and humour. Sigmund Freud himself issued his *Der Witz und seine Beziehung zum Unbewussten* (1905); much use was made of technical psychological investigations in such works as J. Y. T. Greig's *The Psychology of Laughter and Comedy* (1923) and Max Eastman's *The Sense of Humour* (1921).

When we turn from the literary and psychological essays to those of a more practical kind, we observe another thing—a steady emphasis upon technique. In Germany the words *Dramaturgie* and *Technik* appear frequently in titles of books issued during these years, books which were often extensive compilations running into several volumes: H. Bulthaupt's four-volume *Dramaturgie des Schauspiels* (1901), for instance, ran into numerous editions, and Gustav Freytag's *Die Technik des Dramas* (1863) was widely read. In France Ferdinand Brunetière's *La loi du théâtre* (1894) was similarly inspired, as was Francisque Sarcey's *Essai d'une esthétique de théâtre* (1876). This later led to the appearance of practical guides to playwriting, some of them at least giving the impression that good dramas could be produced simply by a strict adherence to a mechanical formula.

Above all, however, the current of realism ran mightiest during this period. Despite Victor Hugo, despite Alfred de Vigny and Théophile Gautier, despite the numerous mid-century romanticists in many lands, realism, taken up from where the sentimentalists left off, became the prime objective. Within this development of critical thought, however, we must observe that confusion reigned—as it has continued to reign down to the present—and that what one

o

theorist meant by realism was not what was meant by another. In its earliest form, realism generally meant simply the choosing of 'ordinary' characters for serious dramatic treatment. This was what the term chiefly conveyed to the sentimentalists; but generally to such a concept was allied the desire to present an 'idea' or a 'moral' of a social kind. During the nineteenth century, especially after the introduction of new and more effective methods of illuminating the stage, the word 'realism' changed course and became invested with a purely theatrical significance; during the earlier decades it signified no more than the introduction of a few 'real' objects on the boards, in the middle decades it was extended to apply to the introduction of such things as 'real' doorknobs on scenic doors, and finally it reached that 'Belasco realism' which aimed at as complete a theatrical simulation of a 'real-life' scene as was possible. Meanwhile, within the field of drama the term developed two further senses during the second half of the nineteenth century. In one, stress was laid upon the treatment of social problems, faithfully observed, and providing the main themes of plays serious and plays comic. In the other, 'realism,' or 'naturalism,' came to be interpreted as an attempt to exhibit on the stage an exactly recorded slice of life. Emile Zola, in the preface to his dramatic version of *Thérèse Raquin* (1873), thus specifically sought to plead for a performance wherein the characters would give the impression not of playing before an audience but of actual living.[19] Beyond all this, there is the sense of 'realism' as it is applied to the works of Ibsen, wherein social problems play a prominent part, but where at the same time the presentation of the 'real' is modified both by an adaptation of the technique of the 'well-made' drama and by overt or half-concealed symbolism; there is the sense in which it is attached to the writings of Chekhov; and there is the sense in which it is used when we speak of the 'realism' of the characters of Shakespeare and Sophocles. All these meanings are apparent in nineteenth-century and early twentieth-century theoretical essays; often they battled with each other; but they combined in elaborating and extending the concepts of the eighteenth-century sentimentalists, and in assuming that the prose drama which deals with contemporary matters in an exhibition of the seemingly actual represents the highest development of theatrical art.

THE MODERN PERIOD. During the second decade of the present century, an 'anti-realistic' campaign developed, and for a time it seemed as though realism had run its course. In 1923 William Archer, when he published *The Old Drama and the New*, was forced, in spite of his own firm convictions and of his devastating attack on the Elizabethan drama, to adopt an almost apologetic tone in defending the then modern stage. In the area of stage design Adolphe Appia and Gordon Craig introduced fresh ideas, and these ideas, in transmuted forms, caused a complete shifting in the orientation of scenic artists—with the result that even now, when a new realism in drama is being aimed at, the characteristic settings of plays are animated by a completely different principle. The series of more or less 'literary' critical studies which followed those of the nineteenth century may perhaps be ignored in this brief survey, since, like their predecessors, they were largely divorced from the stage, but recent decades have witnessed a vigorous development in other theoretical writings—essays on 'poetic drama' extending from Lascelles Abercrombie's *The Function of Poetry in Drama* (1912) and the works of T. S. Eliot and Christopher Fry, to such surveys as Francis Fergusson's *The Idea of a Theater* (1949), Moody Prior's *The Language of Tragedy* (1947), and Ronald Peacock's *The Art of Drama* (1957); volumes written by practising playwrights such as J. B. Priestley's *The Art of the Dramatist* (1957) and Somerset Maugham's *The Summing Up* (1938); studies of the older drama, like Willard Farnham's *Shakespeare's Tragic Frontier* (1950) and H. D. F. Kitto's *Form and Meaning in Drama* (1956); explorations of particular dramatic devices such as R. J. Nelson's *Play within a Play* (1958); as well as philosophical analyses of the kind represented in André Villiers' *La psychologie de l'art dramatique* (1951). All of these have drawn attention to qualities in the drama of the past which the current prose drama could not exhibit. At the same time various theatrical groups eagerly applied themselves to experimental efforts, sometimes absurdly bizarre, issuing critical manifestos, and programmes in favour of a 'new romanticism,' or 'expressionism,' or what not. As a result, the term 'modern drama' completely changed its significance; in 1900 that phrase had meant the realistic-naturalist play, twenty years later it meant the play of anti-realistic trends.

In all this endeavour, however, there was no real concentrating theoretical force; no single cult really established itself on the stage; the new romanticism lasted only a few years, the symbolistic style clearly could give little to the theatre, expressionism came and van-

ished with a discordant shriek. Then, within the past few decades the
sentimentalists once more have come to dominate, even although in
the interim they have changed and elaborated their views, producing
the German *Neue Sachlichkeit* and the 'Socialist Realism' of Marxist
philosophy. Here complete rupture is made with the past. Socialist
Realism has been authoritatively defined in the large Soviet
Encyclopaedia as

> an artistic method. Its basic principle is the representation of reality,
> in a faithful and historically concrete manner, in its revolutionary de-
> velopment, and its most important task is the communist education of
> the masses.

Obviously, the significant phrase in this definition is the last: the
drama here is completely subordinated to a political objective. In
looking at current theoretical writings, moreover, we have to observe
that this definition of theatrical and dramatic endeavour is by no
means restricted to the area of Marxist thought. Naturally and under-
standably it provides the foundation for the concepts promulgated by
Bertolt Brecht, himself a Communist; but it also appears in dozens
of other critical essays whose authors do not belong to the 'party.'
Within this *milieu* 'realism' has come to mean little more than
'committed'—to use the latest fashionable trite critical term—and,
as the Soviet definition states, it applies, not to style but to an attitude towards social life in the past and in the present.[20]

At the same time, the didactic belief—that drama has no object save
to serve a political end—has not completely won the day, and there
are signs in modern critical thought that perhaps the term 'modern
drama,' which, as we have seen, meant naturalism in 1900 and which
in 1960 is being applied to Socialist realism, may yet assume a fresh
meaning within a few years. In any event, it is interesting to note
that Jean Jacquot, in penning his essay designed to close and to sum
up to the valuable conference volume *Réalisme et poésie au théâtre*
(1960), chose for its title, 'Réflexions sur un débat qui reste ouvert,'
and that Jean Vilar, who, more than any man, has given vitality to
the modern French stage, in speaking of the current talk about
realism, remarks that he is

> astonished at the longevity of this word. Art is a certain way of order-
> ing or reordering nature. What then can the word 'realism' signify
> in this connection? Is Rimbaud a realist? And Corneille? And Kleist?
> And Léger? I don't see any realism in Molière's *Don Juan*, in the

apparition of the Commander, in the irrational wisdom of Sganarelle, in Harpagon's monologue, in the magnificent stanzas of the *Cid*, in Rodrigue's love-combat, in Auguste's soliloquy.

For him the only true 'realism' rests in "cadences and words"— "for realism in the theatre is achieved by language and the movements of the human body."[21]

NOTES

1. Attention may be drawn to a very useful anthology, prepared by Barrett H. Clark: *European Theories of the Drama* (1919).

2. S. H. Butcher, in *Aristotle's Theory of Poetry and the Fine Arts* (1895, fourth edition, revised 1911), and I. Bywater, in *Aristotle on the Art of Poetry* (1909, second edition 1911), present the original text, a translation, and a detailed commentary. Various other versions—notably those by W. H. Fyfe (1927, second edition 1940), C. S. Baldwin (1930), and P. H. Epps (1942)—have appeared during recent years, and interpretative studies, many in article form, are numerous. L. Cooper has a study of *The Poetics of Aristotle, its Meaning and Influence* (1923), and the same author essays, in *An Aristotelian Theory of Comedy* (1924), to reconstruct what Aristotle might have written on the comic genre.

3. J. D. Denniston has a convenient little anthology of *Greek Literary Criticism* (1924). Extracts from the *Frogs* are given there on pp. 1–36.

4. See J. F. d'Alton, *Roman Literary Theory and Criticism* (1921) and A. Campbell, *Horace: A New Interpretation* (1924).

5. The 'Epistle to the Pisos' is well rendered in G. Saintsbury's *Loci Critici* (1903,) which contains a useful series of related critical texts. It is also presented alongside some Renaissance texts in A. J. Cook, *The Art of Poetry: Poetical Treatises of Horace, Vida and Boileau* (1892).

6. The development of Renaissance criticism is well outlined by J. E. Spingarn in his *History of Literary Criticism in the Renaissance* (1908). Anthologies containing English texts are Gregory Smith's *Elizabethan Critical Essays* (2 vols., 1904) and Spingarn's *Critical Essays of the Seventeenth Century* (3 vols., 1908–1909).

7. H. B. Charlton has an excellent study of Castelvetro's *Theory of Poetry* (1913).

8. There is a serviceable summary by H. Breitinger of *Les Unités d'Aristote avant le Cid de Corneille* (1895).

9. Jonson's critical ideas have received a considerable amount of attention. There is a full commentary in the standard collected edition of his *Works* (1925–52), edited by H. C. Herford and Percy Simpson; other particularly useful volumes are E. Woodbridge's *Studies in Jonson's Comedy* (1911), F. Townsend's *Apologie for Bartholomew Fayre* (1947), and H. W. Baum's *The Satiric and the Didactic in Ben Jonson's Comedy* (1947).

10. H. J. Chaytor surveys and gives specimens of *Dramatic Theory in Spain* (1925).

11. *The Orchards of Toledo (Cigarrales de Toledo*, 1624) in Barrett H. Clark's *European Theories of the Drama* (1919).

12. Marvin T. Herrick, in *Tragicomedy: its influence and development in Italy, France, and England* (1955), traces the course of critical theory relating to the mixed form, and E. M. Waith discusses some general problems in *The Pattern of Tragicomedy in Beaumont and Fletcher* (1952); the French contributions are more fully examined by H. C. Lancaster in *French Tragi-comedy: its origins and development from 1552 to 1628* (1907). The related history-play cultivated by Shakespeare and others is dealt with in Irving Ribner's *The English History Play in the Age of Shakespeare* (1957). Elizabethan critical judgments are examined in Madeleine Doran's *Endeavors of Art: A Study of Form in Elizabethan Drama* (1954) and Mary C. Hyde's *Playwriting for Elizabethans* (1949).

13. The importance of French critical theory at this time is shown by the way in which it was associated with contemporary dramatic literature: debates concerning the qualities of Corneille, Molière, and Racine give it a practical instead of an academic importance. General trends are outlined by Charles Arnaud (*Les théories dramatiques au xviie siècle*, 1888), F. Vial and L. Denise (*Idées et doctrines du xviie siècle*, 1906), and Eleanor Jourdain, *Dramatic Theory and Practice in France, 1690–1808* (1921).

14. A. Beljame has an excellent study of the early 'Augustan' intellectual climate, with special reference to the theatre, in his *Le publique et les hommes de lettres en Angleterre au dix-huitième siècle* (1897); Dryden's criticism has been much discussed (see particularly C. V. Deane, *Dramatic Theory and the Rhymed Heroic Play* (1931) and L. I. Bredvold, *The Intellectual Milieu of John Dryden* (1934)). W. H. Durham has a valuable collection of *Critical Essays of the Eighteenth Century, 1700–1725* (1915). The *Neo-classic Theory of Tragedy in England during the Eighteenth Century* (1934) is well discussed by C. C. Green.

15. *The Rambler* (1751), No. 156.

16. Sentimentalism in England has been surveyed by Ernest Bernbaum in *The Drama of Sensibility* (1915); the corresponding movement across the Channel is analysed by F. Gaiffe in *Le drame en France au xviiie siècle* (1910).

17. See J. G. Robertson, *Lessing's Dramatic Theory* (1939).

18. A. C. Ward has an anthology, *Specimens of English Dramatic Criticism, XVII–XX Centuries* (1945).

19. C. Benchat has a *Histoire du naturalisme français* (1949), and the subject has been examined in a number of studies—notably P. Martino's *Le naturalisme français* (1923), and R. Dumesnil's *Le réalisme et le naturalisme* (1936) and *L'époque réaliste et naturaliste* (1945). The corresponding theoretical movement in Germany is dealt with by G. Litzmann in *Das naturalistische Drama: von seiner Entstehen und Technik* (1907), by R. F. Arnold in *Das moderne Drama* (1912).

20. The recent concentration on 'realism' among certain modern circles may be seen in the appearance of several weighty studies such as Erich Auerbach's *Mimesis* (translated by W. R. Trask, 1953), Georg Lukács' *Probleme des Realismus* (1955), and the same author's *Wider der missvertandenen Realismus* (1958).

21. *De la tradition théâtrale* (1955), pp. 170–171.

Index